Still Living with Questions

David E. Jenkins
Bishop of Durham

Still Living with Questions

SCM Press · London

Trinity Press International · Philadelphia

First published 1990
incorporating material from
Living with Questions, SCM Press 1969

SCM Press
26–30 Tottenham Road
London N1 4BZ

Trinity Press International
3725 Chestnut Street
Philadelphia, Pa. 19104

British Library Cataloguing in Publication Data

Jenkins, David Edward, 1925–
    Still living with questions.
    1. Christian Doctrine
    I. Title
    230

    ISBN 0–334–02439–0

Library of Congress Cataloguing-in-Publication Data

Jenkins. David E.
    Still living with questions / David E. Jenkins.
        p.   cm.
    ISBN 0–334–02439–0
    1. Theology. I. Title.
BR50.J35 1990
230'.3--dc20   89-49769

Typeset at The Spartan Press Ltd, Lymington, Hants
and printed in Great Britain by
The Camelot Press Ltd, Southampton

CONTENTS

Contents

INTRODUCTION

I have always found it very interesting that we can think. It is odd, when you come to reflect on it, that we who have evolved out of the units of energy, and then of matter, which constitute the universe, have reached a stage of organization and energy where we can think about what we are part of, about the processes which have produced us and about ourselves. The more our thinking and exploring enables us to know of our infinitesimal part and place in the processes and energies of the universe in terms of space–time, the more odd and interesting it becomes that we can think about it all. It makes it very plausible that we should accept the biblical suggestion that we are 'in the image of God'. That is to say that we should face the claim and the possibility that we are, in fact, not a chance but a creation. This would mean that we have an opportunity to respond to, and be part of, *more than* chance. But our chances of finding out what more there is to thinking than the oddness and interest of it would depend on our being ready to think, explore and respond as far as we could possibly go – and that 'as far as we could possibly go' would itself depend, for the definition and fulfilment of its 'possibly', on what or who met us and took us on our possibly infinite but certainly extending way.

So, thinking – through us as thinking and self-conscious beings – hints at Transcendence and raises questions as itself, for itself, and about itself, which is why I cannot get away from *living with questions*. Living with questions seems to me to be at the heart of being human and to be central to the practice of any living and realistic faithfulness. How do you discover, respond, explore and grow if you do not question whatever comes your way and if you are not questioned by whatever you encounter? It could, of course, be argued that to welcome living with questions is itself to express faith and live by faith. For being ready to question and to be questioned presupposes that one is somehow expectant and hopeful about the possibilities of reality. There are worthwhile things to be found out and there is Worth at work to find you. It may be therefore that seeing questioning and being questioned as the heart of being human is a direct, simple and practical expression of faith in God. I am not sure, however, that everyone who sees thinking and questioning as central to being human will also at once see this as faith in God.

I do not want to pursue this point now. I simply want to put these reflections and possibilities forward as indicative of the flavour of the presuppositions that are behind, and the hope and expectations that are involved in, the various pieces which are published or reissued in this book. Of the nineteen pieces which appear, thirteen have already been published in 1969, in *Living with Questions*. I have dropped some of the pieces from that publication which are obviously dated and put in six new pieces, one from 1974, and five from the last two years, and entitled the 1990 publication *Still Living with Questions*. My reason for making another attempt to get both the material and the approach of these pieces considered more widely is precisely that the questions do still go on facing us, challenging us, and pointing us to ways forward. I also wish to challenge any suggestion that we have somehow arrived somewhere, politically, economically, socially and, it may be, religiously, so that our human future now requires mainly the application of answers worked out and the use of methods already discovered. In fact, we need urgently to live with the questions which will force us, entice us, and excite us into new, sustainable and shareable ways for our future together. Finally, I wish to make it as clear as possible that any lively faith in the God who is pointed to in the Bible must express itself and develop itself through living with questions. These questions are the pressures of God upon us and indicators of the ways in which we must go if we are to serve him, our neighbours and his and our world in creative and hopeful ways.

I am glad that this further publication, *Still Living with Questions*, is a joint publication in the United Kingdom and the United States. Only one of the pieces in this collection was prepared for delivery in the USA. This is the lecture given at Tulane University entitled 'The Reality of God and the Future of the Human Project'. I regard this title as focussing the concerns of this Introduction and of all the pieces collected here. Is the God in whom believers claim to believe so really and truly God that he can make a living difference to us in our world which is both so clearly one, at the ecological and sustainably shareable level, and so very diverse and pluralistic at the local, regional and social level?

It increasingly seems to me that the highly pluralistic cities of the United States (and such neighbouring cities as Toronto in Canada) provide particular crucibles and testing grounds in which a faith for the future has to be developed. Will religious faith survive only as the highly sectarian and individualistic 'spiritual' back-up for groups like those which coalesce into the 'Moral Majority' or be the spiritual glue for the lives of ethnic and cultural minorities who need this faith to preserve their own ghettoes and identities? Or is there a continuing possibility of faith in God which is truly faith in a true God? That would have to be a faith which can realistically live with plurality and the necessities of particular identities and traditions, and yet have resources enough to break through to possibilities of transcendence in worship, understanding and practice which are potentially universal and shareable.

The United States, we are told, continues statistically to be more religiously observant than anywhere else. I beg leave to doubt, however, whether this means that people dwelling in the United States are more godly than anywhere else. Sectarian religion, by its very behaviour in its various forms, denies its own major premise – namely that it is the true worship of the true God. So I believe that living with questions is urgently necessary in North America as elsewhere and that the condition of many cities in North America means that they are particularly severe and therefore particularly enhopeful places to live with questions for the sake of humanity and in the hope of receiving revelation of the one true and universal God. Hence my own personal satisfaction that *Still Living with Questions* should have a Philadelphia imprint as well as a London one. Somehow ways have to be found of responding from the particularities of our own peculiar circumstances to the questions which are universally posed to our civilization and to our world. And if there truly is a truly real and universal God then we must be able to pick up a recognizably resonant and congruent echo of those questions which will serve to point us towards the ways for the future which God is offering us wherever we are.

These following pieces, therefore, are offered as working papers towards future forms of faith which will both be faithful to what we so far know of God and will take us (in ever-widening and more embracing senses of 'us') towards that future which, if there is a God who is truly God, will be both God's future and God's fulfilment.

Part One

Concerning God

1 · *There is no God*

(1956)

'There is no God.' Is it only the fool who says there is no God? Surely the declaration of atheism has been made by some of the most sensitive, the most passionate and the most serious of human beings. Sometimes they have made it as a cry nearly of despair, sometimes as an exultant cry of freedom, sometimes as a sober statement of fact. 'There is no God.' How can there be – for consider the meaning of 'God'. God, St Anselm tells us, is *that than which nothing more perfect can be conceived*. God is the summit of all possible perfections and then a perfection beyond them. God is more than we can utter, more than we can conceive; the fulfilment, infinitely beyond our hopes, of our deepest longings; the reality, infinitely beyond our conceptions, towards which our highest thoughts are striving. God is the only being who alone is worthy of worship. God is not to be reverenced *because* God is the worthy embodiment of a quality or qualities which are recognizably supremely good. If God is to be worshipped *because* God is supremely good, this would make the supremely good transcend God; God would depend for being God on being supremely good. But God is not transcended, nor does God depend. Therefore God must be supremely good – *and more*. What more? That more which makes God God, i.e. 'that than which nothing more perfect can be conceived'. God is not to be reverenced for being the supreme end of all things. If God is to be worshipped *because* all things are supremely and finally fulfilled in God, this would make the

3

fulfilment of all things transcend God and God would *depend* for God being God on the fulfilment of all things. But God is not transcended, nor does God depend. Therefore God must be the supreme end of all things – *and more*. What more? That more which makes God alone the sole being worthy of worship, the only truly worthy object of our worship.

But here is the stumbling block, that 'more' which God must be to be God. For the point about all beings known to us, about all objects of which we have experience or of which we can form a conception, is that they are not in themselves or because of themselves worthy of worship. To exist as an object, or to have any being, *means* to have limiting qualities by which the object is recognized, the being is perceived as existing. Or to put it more crudely and simply, you do not know that any object is there unless it is pointed out as being there by its qualities and properties. And when you say an object or a being exists you mean it is 'there'. 'Being there' means that it is there as 'an example of . . .', it exists 'because of'. But we have seen that God, to be God, cannot be 'an example of . . .' or exist 'because of . . .'. God, in fact, to be God must be more than an object, more than a being. But if God is more than a being, then God is not a being. You do not get yourself anywhere by saying 'a being and more' – for what sort of a being is that? But if God is not a being, then God does not exist. That is to say, 'There is no God.'

I fear that you will long ago have decided that this is merely a philosopher's discussion and not only have lost the thread but have decided that it is not worth following. Moreover, as you know, or think you know, that I believe in God, you are probably complacently sitting back and treating all this as conjuror's patter while you wait for me to produce the expected rabbit out of the hat – to wit, my explanation of how, after all, of course we may comfortably and assuredly believe in God.

Be clear about this, then. If you have not at least sensed the strength of the arguments for atheism, it is more than probable that you have not really sensed what we mean when we say we believe in God. For God must be whatever we like to say – and more, or even, whatever we like to say – but God is not (which is the same thing, logically speaking). No description of God is sufficient. But if no description is sufficient, then it would seem that no description can be given. And if no description can be given of God, how can we say God exists? To put the matter more philosophically, if God has to be defined, as we have seen, as whatever you like to say *and more*, then the notion of God's existence is logically self-contradictory. But this is not a mere philosopher's point. For this logical notion of self-contradiction in the idea of God's existence transcends and embraces all sorts of practical and theoretical difficulties which count against believing that God exists.

'There is no God.' A despairing cry: how can perfection exist when perfection means that which is beyond anything now known to exist, that which is beyond our strivings, that which our very strivings testify does *not* exist? 'There *is* no God.'

'There is no God.' An exultant cry: we are not shut in by any conception, any scheme or any pattern already existing. The world is wide open to infinite and undetermined possibilities. Patterns are to be made and ends built up. We are not shut up in that which already exists. We are free. 'There is no *God*.'

'There is no God.' A sober statement of fact: we must be content with what we can observe, measure and see. It is true that human beings strive and seek aims 'beyond' themselves. But we cannot extrapolate ourselves out of the theoretically observable universe or project ourselves beyond the theoretically comprehensible psychosomatic organisms that we are. There can be no evidence for that which goes beyond the evidence. 'There is *no* God.'

In short, worship is a mistake and perfection is a logical construction which never has existed and never will exist save as something in the minds of human beings. All that I have said in the first part of this sermon about the notion of 'more than' which is implicit in the idea of God, all the notion of transcendence, of a perfection of perfection which cannot ultimately be spoken of but which alone is worshipful – all this is a mere construction in the minds of human beings who have misinterpreted their experience on the basis of their ignorance and their undeveloped mental faculties. It may be that reverence is an innate human capacity, but it does not, properly understood, point human beings beyond themselves *to* any supreme object of worship. Neither logic nor

5

fact support such a conclusion as often as it has been drawn. 'God' is a mental construction.

It may be so – I think it is very important to see that there are plausible grounds for holding that it may be so. There is no logical step, no proof, from the fact that we *conceive* of God to the fact that God *exists*. The only thing that the observable fact that a very large number of human beings worship God goes to prove is that a very large number of human beings indulge in a practice called worship.

But there are two questions which we can ask *ourselves*; *not* as outside observers of the phenomena ('those other than ourselves believing in God' and 'those other than ourselves worshipping') but as people who are ourselves part of the evidence which we observe.

The first is this. Can we really do without that to which such notions as perfection, transcendence and worshipfulness point?

Not merely, 'Can we do without as pieces of mental furniture?' Very likely we can. Certainly we can for good stretches of time. But can we rigorously and absolutely exclude from every element of our being, activity and thought all suggestion that there is 'more than' the sum total of other selves like us, the sum total of natural phenomena like those known to us, the sum total of the dialectic of history as it is described to us by the secular historian and so on? Will it '*do*' to say that transcendence and perfection are mere extrapolations, a sort of $n+1$ of things ordinarily known to us where the '1' stands for something precisely like the 'n's' or for a mental operation on our part? Or is there in worship an activity of response as well as, or even rather than, an activity of creation and self-projection? Can we *believe* that perfection, that the dimension of transcendence wherein lies the worshipful, *is* a mere notion?

Another way to put this point would be this. In the first part of my sermon I tried to describe what the intellect means by 'God' and to go on to show that this notion is probably *logically* self-contradictory. Some people would therefore say that this notion of God is *unthinkable*, i.e. ought not to be thought of, but rejected. How many people would want to say that even if this notion is *logically* contradictory, what is '*unthinkable*' is that they should give it up? What leads them to this? An experience of God or an ignorance of logic?

I have time to refer only to my second question – which is, perhaps, the reverse of the first. It is: Why does atheism have to be justified, and why does doubt about God's existence have such penetrating and anguished quality? Is it because God is not a being like other beings, *not* in the sense that God does not exist, but rather in the sense that God is the one being whose existence cannot be a matter of indifference? That is, is it because God is the one being upon whom all beings depend? It might be, therefore, that one of the signs of God in human intellect is precisely the peculiarly intensive quality of the doubt that arises about God's existence and the need rather to assert atheism than to treat the whole issue of God's existence as 'not a proper question'.

These signs, however, real as I believe them to be, are not proofs but pointers, not substantiations but signs whose true significance can be evoked only by the witness of the Christian church and the proclaiming of the word of God. None the less, they remain as constantly fretting signs that we are made by the transcendent God for the transcendent God and that our folly is to say 'There is no God', while our joy and peace comes as in worship we confess God as 'the one who is' and as 'God of gods and Lord of lords'.

2 · *God Today*

(1966)

If one is asked to talk about God today in the context of a series on the general topic of why we should believe and what the roads to belief are, then one must clearly face up to the current tendency to maintain that all God-talk is finished. This being so, perhaps the approach to the subject should be to tackle first the question 'How can I find a use for God-talk?' and then go on to ask, 'Why should I in fact use such language?'. It will be necessary to go back to more or less these questions, but it is first necessary to be quite clear about one thing. That is, that there is only one decisive reason for believing in God, namely because *God is*. I am aware of the difficulties of the existential use of the verb 'to be', but I remain unrepentant about my formulation of this reason. The only satisfactory reason for believing in God must be because in the last analysis, the attitude, commitment and content of believing is the proper response to what is there, to what is given. We must not be turned aside by the difficulties of using object-like language about God. The basic question remains whether in believing in God we are responding to the One who is, to Truth as it is given, to Reality as it is *there*. It is very necessary in this whole area to strive after simplicity which enables us to see with singleness of eye into what the whole debate is really about.

To use God-language for any other reason than that it is held to describe or at least to point to the truth as it really is and reality as it truly is, is both blasphemous and pathological. It is blasphemous

8

because it is simply the practice of idolatry to use God-language because one is conscious of the need for a cosmic anodyne or because one must have a prop and basis for morality or a sop for one's soul in its loneliness. Such a use of language is simply making use of the idea of God to fill an alleged human gap. If God truly exists as God, then to make use of God for human ends is clearly blasphemous. But such usage is also pathological. For its object is to escape from reality, to erect a fantasy which conceals from us the way things really are. The refusal to come to terms with reality is at best immaturity and at worst madness. If, therefore, we are all atheists now, then for God's sake we must be atheists, or at any rate if there is no God then we must be atheists for the sake of humanity. I am clear, therefore, that there is only one valid answer to the question 'Why believe?' Because God *is* and God lets be known that God is.

On the other hand, such a reason clearly does not get us very far. We have also to consider the questions which in practice will often be much more pressing: 'How believe?' and 'What does it mean to believe?' Let us therefore turn to the question of how we may believe. There are many ways of coming to believe, many pointers to the possibility of believing, many ways of evoking and sustaining belief. The few examples which I am about to give are not arranged in any order of weight. I am quite clear that different pointers, experiences, arguments are 'weighty' for different people. That is to say, there are many different ways which get differing people on to God, and it is not possible to say that one argument or experience is necessarily more decisive or satisfactory than another. But the following four ways or areas do seem to me to be of particular significance and, often, helpfulness.

The first I would call the open study of human beings, both the study of humankind and of individual persons. There is a very strong case for maintaining that, in whatever way we are studying human beings, we will always find that in the end we need what might be called one more dimension than is contained in the normal structure of our method of study for doing full justice to all that is involved in the human situation. Biology might look as if it should find its firm and only basis in the reduction of its concepts to that which can be finally measurable in terms, say, of physicochemical reactions. But it is clear that ecology is as important as analysis and that human ecology raises acute problems of the possibility of exhaustive analysis. Similarly, we know that psychology is liable to be divided between those who see their aim as producing results of research which can be tabulated and turned into graphs and those who are aware that such analysis is only one side of the observational study of the dynamics of personality and human relationships. Many people may feel that graphs are far more scientifically respectable, but science is based on observation, and it is not scientific, i.e. not in accordance with the total range of observations possible and necessary, to suppose that the effects of the human psyche can be exhaustively reduced to the type of tables which record the reaction time of rats. Likewise, in the field of sociology, when one proceeds to matters such as criminology and actual prescriptions for dealing with social ills and maladjustments, it rapidly becomes clear that value judgments cannot be left out of account, and that however important proper scientific and impersonal analysis is, total reductionism is just a mistake.

This feature of the situation with regard to what might be called the human sciences is reflected also in logic. Here we are up against what may reasonably be called the mystery of the 'I'. Hume himself was not really satisfied with his reductionist version of the self. Current philosophical writing is once again tending to lend support to the view that logical analysis does not remove all mysteries from the understanding of the human situation. And there is much else which makes it clear enough that we cannot say that philosophy has done away with the dimension of mystery in human existence in such areas as 'self' and questions like the problem of free will and determinism. In philosophy in the still broader sense, it is quite clear that there is a rediscovery of the need for facing up to what I have described as the additional dimension which confronts us when we try to take into account all that is involved in human existence. I believe that an excellent example of this is to be found in the work of Heidegger, who, for all his anti-metaphysical endeavours, clearly finds it necessary to have a special way of talking about the essence of humanness which lands him in exactly the same logical problems in his own terms, as more old-fashioned ways of thinking find in their terms, over the notion of transcendence. The open study of human beings gives plenty of evidence of the need for facing up to a 'breaking out' from what we might call our normal dimensions, a necessity to go beyond our ordinary descriptive categories, in fact a possibility of transcendence.

The second significant area for the possibility of believing is that which I would call the 'exploration of commitment'. Here it is a question of exposing oneself to what is truly involved in being in relationship to other human beings and to what it is to be oneself. In such an exploration one finds that one seems to be faced occasionally with great heights and with immense possibilities and worthwhileness. At other times there is the facing of the depths and the threats of nothingness and destruction. Here the very depth of the threat seems to reflect the high significance of that which is threatened. Moreover, in such an exploration and in such a facing of heights and depths we may find resources on which we had never bargained or of which we had never thought. Possibilities are discovered of powers beyond our own powers, in fact what religious men and women call grace. This may arise as we see the need for resources that are beyond our own and glimpse the possibilities of such resources. Here again, in this whole exploration of commitment we are confronted with the possible existence of mystery and we are led to hope that the world is not 'flat'. That is to say, that measurable and predictable things do not rule over human affairs or at any rate need not rule or, perhaps, must not rule. We are therefore encouraged to ask in a meaningful way the question, Who then does rule? Might it be true, as Augustine said, that God made us for himself and that our hearts are restless until we find our rest in him? Might it make sense to learn that the one who rules is the Lord God?

The two areas we have considered so far which may lead, provoke or persuade us to believe lie in the mystery of the world and the heights and depths of commitment and are of a general nature. We turn now to something more particular, namely the way in which it is possible to be led to, and sustained in, believing through the community and practice of believers. Here we have the possibility of sharing in the response of worship and knowing, however dimly and fleetingly, that it is indeed a response. Here, too, we have the opportunity of learning for ourselves and with the help of the experience of others the response of prayer. Although this is often a difficult affair and never a guaranteed affair, there are none the less many experimental data and many ways of practice through which we may discover our particular way of entering that practice of the presence of God which has been the strength of so many different situations. Then, and in connection with the community of believers, we may also investigate the response of doctrine and discover that once the doctrinal propositions of past ages are set free from a fossilizing respect which treats them as unquestionable oracles, their content can once again become living. We may learn that they are the formulation and crystallization of what human beings have been led to discover about God and that when they are broken open by the questions which our experiences oblige us to put, then they once more become the source of discoveries about the same God. A further way of coming to and entering more deeply into belief, in sharing the life of the community of believers, is to be found as we seek to work out and to express the practice which is demanded by the understanding of God which it is alleged has been given to believers. In fact, we may well come to believe, and we shall certainly only continue to believe, as we share, however tentatively, in the enquiry of faith which is the experimental living out of the experience of the community of the people of God.

Finally, I must pass from the community of believers to one more source for the evocation of belief in, and knowledge of, God. This source is very particular indeed – it is Jesus Christ. This is the man of Nazareth who unquestionably lived and unquestionably lived as the man for God. The pattern of this living has led many to see him as also the man for others. His disciples believed that he was also discovered to be God for man, but this last point is already a doctrinal formulation, so we will leave it. At least we must agree that Jesus Christ is part of the givenness of history and that the pattern of his living is part of the data we have to consider when we are looking for the possibilities of believing. The relevance of Jesus Christ to the other areas possibly evocative of belief which I have mentioned would seem to be this. We may agree that human beings do not look as if they fit into any frame produced by any science or system of thinking, but we may well feel that this does not help us to believe in God, for there is one frame in which we exist, to wit, the universe as it is known to science, and, to put it crudely, the size of this both on the macrocosmic and on the microcosmic scale surely crushes out all grounds for believing in God. But is this so? The knowledge of this vast scale of existence has been discovered by us and we have also the opportunity of considering the givenness of Jesus Christ; we have the claimed knowledge of God that led up to him; we have the community and practice that follows from him. Why should size count more than all this, especially when we consider what we come up against when we explore commitment? Does it not still remain a proper and possible question to ask 'Who rules?'? Is it Jesus who is Lord, who rules for God, perhaps as God? Or is it the nuclear physicist or the astronomer who without question determines for us our understanding of reality? For the life of me I cannot see why we should automatically attribute the lordship to the measurers of size. Anyway, we are able to make an investigation. We can throw in our lot with the community which is seeking to live out and to live into faith in God through Jesus Christ. Certainly there is no decisive reason to conclude that God is dead. There are many pointers to how we may believe in God, many ways which may lead us to discover that God is.

But in closing I must say something about the question – what does it mean to believe in God? The first answer is that we do not know. To believe in God is to be committed to an ever-open exploration, to be open to the possibility of being able to meet a never-ending demand. In fact to believe in God is to know that we are called to enter into everlasting life, infinite possibilities. But we must ask, in practice, what does it mean? And still we must say, 'You will have to search and see.' But, perhaps this much may be said, to believe in God means to be learning that we are not surrounded by, or heading for, indifference. We are surrounded by, set in, and destined for responsive and responsible love. Therefore, to believe in God means, among other things, hope-fully learning the practice of prayer in always new ways. It means hoping always for creative possibilities that may break out of and transcend every situation. It means getting together with other believers in God in a common loyalty with them to explore what this means in understanding and practice. It means also getting together with any human being who is your neighbour to explore without weariness the infinite possibilities which lie in being human. God is, and therefore indifference does not rule. God is for us, as Jesus Christ makes clear, therefore there is always hope.

Belief in God today is what it always has been. A commitment to a way of living based on response to a way of giving – to the way in which God gives himself to us in Jesus Christ, through our fellow believers, through that of God in every human being and in the possibilities of the universe. Moreover, belief in God is experimental living and it is experiencing living. It is not being sure of a set of sentences or of a set of facts which tell us that God exists. For if God is God then God must establish the fact. If God is not God then there is nothing whatever to be done about it. But I am bound to bear witness to you that God is God – the living God who is active today to smash all the idols of religion in which we seek to shut God up, and active today to meet and fulfil all the needs and possibilities of truly human living, in this world and beyond it.

3 · *The Suffering of God*

(1966)

This is not an easy subject. I find that I need to go slowly and to meditate, think through, something which is relevant to this immense and terrifying subject of which we may scarcely dare to speak, the suffering of God. I fear I cannot make it any easier because I myself have not got far enough. I am quite clear that, in the end, all subjects to do with God are profoundly simple, and I have no doubt that there are many who know far more about this subject than I do. But while I feel I may well be confused, I see no need to be worried. God in the end is not confusing, nor are we called upon to understand things which are in one sense beyond our intellectual capabilities. We are called upon to enter into the depths of the mysteries of God, and this God gives us grace to do.

Our subject, then, is the suffering of God. Nowadays one cannot enter upon any subject to do with God by taking anything for granted. Therefore, the first question to ask is, Who are we talking about? Here we have a paradox. I am quite clear whom we are talking about, but I am not clear about him. Further, I am clear that he goes far beyond any understanding I can have at the moment. None the less, I am quite clear *whom* I am talking about. This is why I find I have to regard all attempts to talk about God as prayerful undertakings. I cannot possibly talk about the One about whom I am called to talk unless he assists me.

I am talking, then, about the God and Father of our Lord Jesus Christ. I am talking about the God of Abraham, of Isaac and of

Jacob. I am talking about the God of Moses, of Jeremiah, of Peter, of Paul and of John, and of countless others, known and unknown through the ages. In fact, I am talking about the Lord God who is involved with his people. People believe in God because people believe in God. And no amount of propaganda, complaint or commendation will cause people to believe in God unless God is there, keeping a people who believe in him. And therefore it is the case that people believe in God, because people believe in God. And there always will be a people who believe in God, because God has made it quite clear that he will keep a people for himself, and he will keep such a people despite all that we can do to run away from him.

It is quite clear that the church is used by God in his making himself known to us, and yet that the church is the greatest obstacle to believing in God. For people look at us of the church and cannot conclude that we believe in God, because of our way of living. Yet God keeps a people who believe in him and who seek to follow him. Therefore we are talking about the Lord God who is involved with his people. We are talking about the Lord, the Almighty One, the One who dwells on high, who inhabits eternity, who is profounder than the deepest depths, who is met with in the human heart, in the situations, the catastrophes and the joys of human living, in the history of the people of Israel, in the life of the church and, I do not doubt, who is met with in the lives of many people outside the church, outside the people of Israel, who do not yet know who it is with whom they are meeting.

We are therefore talking about the One who is met, the One who is known as Jeremiah knew him when he went down to Egypt in despair, but none the less knew God. We speak of the One whom the Psalmist knew, both in the heights of his hopes and in the depths of his fears. We are talking about the One who was looked for when Abraham went out not knowing whither he went, the One who was sought after when on the cross Jesus said, 'My God, my God, why hast thou forsaken me?' We are talking, therefore, about the Holy and Righteous One who has made himself known as the One who cares: the One who cares, who is the Lord God who is involved with his people. And we know that he is in one way wholly other than us, wholly different from us. This is made quite clear above all in worship. Worship is a recognition that the holiness of God, the Godness of God, the very way in which God cares, is so much beyond us that all we can do is to fall down, whether metaphorically or literally if it helps us, and have nothing to say and have nothing to do but simply to be in his presence as the Holy, the Worshipful, the Righteous One, who is other than us.

God is known also as the Holy and Righteous and Transcendent One who is trustworthy. This is a thing which has been borne in upon the followers of God, those who have been called to know that they are his people through all the ups and downs of their lives, through all the muddle and chaos and frustration, as well as through all the joy and excitement and hope. If we would only let the Bible speak for itself and just read it in simplicity, we would see that men and women do not believe in God because this gives them the answer to the problem of evil or because this shows what pattern things fit into. They believe in God because they discover God in their hopes and in their fears, constantly being renewed when they thought they were crushed; constantly being taken to higher hopes when they thought they had achieved all there was to be achieved; and what they have discovered about the Holy One who is involved with his people is that he is wholly steadfast, trustworthy, the God who has a steadfast purpose which is expressed through the demand which he makes upon his people to follow him. Moreover, in discovering the holiness and the righteousness and the otherness of God, and in discovering his trustworthiness, men and women have discovered that God is a caring God, whose steadfastness is expressed above all in love. We are talking, therefore, about the Lord who is steadfast, purposeful, demanding, promising love. We are talking of the Lord who is our God, the Lord who is my God, just as he was the God of Abraham and the God of Isaac and the God of Jacob; the God of David, the God of Peter, the God of Paul, the God of Jesus.

As we can see from the Bible, a certainty of faith was built up. It was a certainty and yet it was faith. It was a certainty because it was knowledge and experience and encounter, but it was faith because things never worked out in the way in which you might have expected if there was this God. As you see the whole knowledge of God developing in the Bible, you find that this very *certainty* of faith created the *problem* of faith. People were clear that there is the Lord who is God, and the Lord who is holy, righteous, loving. God is indeed Lord, so much the Lord that he is to be thought of as the Creator. There would be nothing if God were not there to see that there is something. God is Lord of everything in the sense that everything depends for its very existence upon him. God is also the ruler of history, so men and women believe. God is so much the Lord God that he controls for his purpose everything that could come out of, and was coming out of, the processes of history, and the processes of the universe. This was a faith which may have been built up at a time when people did not know that the universe is as vast as it is now, but the universe was quite as frightening, quite as mysterious, quite as uncertain, and had so many immeasurable quantities in it, that it must have seemed to those people quite as vast as the universe now seems to us, and they had no doubt that the Lord God was the Creator and Ruler of this whole universe and of all history in it, and was indeed righteous, holy, loving.

But this, of course, caused the very problem of faith. For God is unquestionably Lord; he is undoubtedly holy, and therefore determined to have only that which is in accordance with his holiness and righteousness. God is also unquestionably loving, caring for his people and determined to bring his purposes out of history, out of the universe for his people. How *could* such a Lord who was indeed Lord have a world as it then was, as it now is? Consider the cry of 'O Lord, how long?' 'If you are indeed Lord, why do all these ungodly things happen? If you are indeed Lord, holy, righteous and loving, what is all this unholiness, all this unrighteousness, all this frustration and fear and trembling and disappointment and death and nothingness? O Lord, how long before you make it clear, that you are indeed Lord and God?' 'Where is now thy God?'

Out of this clash between the certainty of faith and the problem of faith, there arose the expectation of the coming of the kingdom of God, and the expectation of the coming of the Messiah, who will bring in the kingdom of God. The pattern of this is very simple. God is God and does reign and therefore will reign. As God is God, he is bound to do something which will take away all those things in his world and in his history and in his people which contradict his holiness and his righteousness and his love and reign as Lord God in his kingdom. But when is the kingdom coming? Where is the Messiah? When is God going to do something that makes it clear that he is God? We cannot avoid this certainty and this problem of faith. We are committed to this expectancy which arises out of the fact that God is God, and yet is an agonized expectancy, because the things in the world are not in accordance, so often and so many times, with the Godness of God. Surely we can have no illusions nowadays. There are innumerable things in the lives of each of us and certainly in the world at large which count against the existence of a God who is Lord and Love, who is almighty and holy, who is undefeatable and righteous. And so in the midst of this sort of world, this certainty of faith and this problem of faith arises.

As you come to the end of the Old Testament period and beyond it, into the period that lies between the Old Testament and the New, there crystallizes the hope of the coming of the kingdom, when God will make it clear that he is indeed God, and the hope also of the coming of the Messiah, the One whom God has sent to make it clear that he is God. And who is it that came? Jesus. That is what has caused the Christian religion, that is why the church exists. There were a few people who were looking for the coming of the kingdom of God, who were expecting the Lord's Anointed, and they were persuaded, in a way which transformed them, that Jesus of Nazareth is the Lord's Anointed. It was this Jesus who lived a life for the very God about whom Jesus spoke and for whom Jesus lived. It was this Jesus who believed it was his mission to announce the coming of the kingdom of God. 'The kingdom of heaven is at hand. Repent, and believe the gospel.' The Christ was this Jesus who lived an impressive pattern of life which we now interpret as a life for others, but which was first a life for God and a life for others *because* it was a life for this God. This Jesus believed himself to be called to announce: to inaugurate and bring in the kingdom of *this* God. In living his life for *this* God and in living his life for others he set himself to death, even the death of the cross. I am not now talking about stories that have been coloured up by years and years of piety – which might have been interpreted rightly and which might have been interpreted wrongly. I am simply talking about the bare outlines which make it clear that we have to do with a man who so lived for God that that impression has never been forgotten. Also he so lived for men and women that *that* impression has never been forgotten. And he lived out this life for mankind and this life for God as he went on his way and died on the cross in a way which has never been forgotten, although it has often been sentimentalized.

So this man Jesus, serving this God, announcing this kingdom, died this death, even the death of the cross, and therefore once again it looked as though God was going to make it clear that he was God. But he did not. 'We thought it should have been he that would have redeemed Israel' – but now we go a-fishing: getting back to the routine and making the best of life and carrying on with the odds and ends. But – there wasn't a '*but*'. It wasn't 'We thought it should have been *but*.' There was a *yes*, for there was what we call the resurrection. There was the undoubted conviction, the undoubted knowledge, the undoubted certainty, that God has raised him up. 'This Jesus whom you crucified, God has made both Lord and Christ.' This Jesus is the God's Lord and Christ, and therefore in the midst of the frustrations and uncertainties of this world, in the very light of the doing to death of this Jesus, we are clear that the kingdom of God is declared and defined by Jesus Christ. Such was the message of the first apostles and such is the apostolic message today. Jesus *is* what God does to make it clear that he is God. Jesus *is* the shape of the kingdom of God. This Jesus Christ is how God gets things done. This is how God establishes his purposes of holiness and righteousness and love. This Jesus indeed is how God establishes himself.

'O Lord, how long?' When is the certainty of faith going to get an answer to the problem of faith? When the Lord sends the Messiah and the Messiah is Jesus. This is how God establishes himself. And it is not until we get to this point that we even dare speak of the suffering of God. For it becomes clear that the pattern of Jesus is the pattern of God. For it is in and through Jesus that God establishes himself and his kingdom, and when we seek to follow in the steps of the doubting Thomas and say 'My Lord and My God', then we are beginning to enter into the significance of the pattern of the living and dying and perpetual resurrection living of Jesus. This is the Lord. This is the way God establishes his Lordship. This is God, God involved for the sake of his people, this is God indeed, the very truth of the pattern of the life and the character of God, the Almighty. And so we are called to acknowledge Jesus Christ the Son of God, who is the 'perfect image of the Father'. Here we come up against all the complicated things which appear in the creed, complications like the doctrine of the Trinity, which is much too difficult for us to believe today because we do not have the patience or courage to think like people used to think. We have, for instance, the phrase 'of one substance with the Father'. Most unfortunate metaphysical language! We must cut it out. It cannot be understood. So cut it out! Yet it speaks of the Son who is of one substance with the Father, the very presentation of the very reality of God himself. If you want reality, if you want to know what is behind it all and in it all and through it all, look at Jesus and you will come up against the very substance of it. 'Of one substance with the Father, God Almighty.' When you see the life of Jesus, you see the pattern of the life of God.

At this point I would like to lapse into Greek if I have not spoken Greek already! You can see what are called God's 'energies', the way in which God expresses himself and comes to us. You cannot, of course, see what is called God's very Being, because God is far too great a mystery for us to penetrate to the very heart of his Being and there is always something hidden. But we can see the reality of God towards us in Jesus, the very pattern of his essential activity, even if we cannot penetrate to the inmost essence, to the very last depth. But what we can know is that God is through and through consistent and therefore what we are able to see of God in Jesus is wholly consistent with the whole pattern of God's Being. The very pattern who is Jesus is the pattern of the Father, God Almighty. Jesus is the very Son of God, of one substance with the Father. That is to say, he is the pattern of the life and the being and the consistency of God. This is why we both may speak and must speak of the suffering of God. For in the pattern of Jesus we have the pattern of the life of God, and the pattern of Jesus is the pattern of suffering.

Now here it is very necessary to stress that the pattern of God must be seen in the *humanity* of Jesus. Let us have no nonsense about the suffering of Jesus on the cross which suggests that he knew that he was God and therefore he knew that it would come all right and therefore that there was something unreal about the desolation and about the suffering. There is a much greater mystery than that. In trying to discuss this mystery it is impossible to be anything but tentative. But we can at least try to consider what is involved. It is the human Jesus who is the pattern of God and we must put on one side any sentimental talk which somehow suggests that we have God masquerading in human suffering.

A way theologians tried for approaching this mystery is known as 'the emptying'. The Greek term is 'kenosis'. *Kenosis* – emptying? In approaching any mysteries it is useful to have words the meaning of which is not obvious. We hear many words about suffering and so on, and we think we know. We hear the word love, and we think we know. Surely we do not. It would be much better, it sometimes seems to me, if half the words we used about Christianity were words the meaning of which we could not suppose we knew, so that we had to think every time until we had given them meaning in the light of Jesus. So there is this mystery of the 'emptying'. It is the pattern of the human Jesus who is the pattern of God. Nothing must detract from Jesus' humanness. Nothing must detract from the ordinary realism of the life and of the passion and of the cross. Many people, alas, suffer deeply, suffer sordidly, suffer in a way in which there is nothing ennobled to be seen. I do not believe that there would be anything visibly ennobling in the suffering and in the dying of Jesus. He died all right – right up to the reality of 'My God, my God, why hast thou forsaken me?'

This is the pattern of God. So we have to believe if we follow out the shape of the understanding of Jesus which lies against the background of the Old Testament and is proclaimed in the New. This is the pattern of the God who is involved with his people, who is involved, so great is the mystery, *as* one of his people. Here is identification. Here is God, the God who cares and is therefore involved with his people. Identification to the point of being *one* of his people, and therefore God on both sides.

God on God's side. This does not stop God's being God. I have stressed the humanness at the moment, but we must not lose the Godness. We will come back to that. God on both sides of what, because of our sin, is the division between God and humankind. God on God's side and God also on our side. God on the separated sinner's side. I cannot explain this any more here, but I think this is what is behind 'My God, my God, why hast thou forsaken me?'. I believe that God so identifies himself with us because God is love that he is enabled in the expression of his power and purpose and personality, which is love, to undergo for our sakes what we must call, I think, almost a split personality. That is to say, we have God who is God in his holiness and God who is One with humankind in his sinfulness. This is something of what lies behind the mystery of 'My God, my God, why hast thou forsaken me?'

Here we are on the edge of some very baffling mysteries which seem to me to be none the less close to the heart of the Gospel. In the man Jesus, we see God, the way in which, towards us, God has his way of being God. That is to say, this is the way God brings about his pattern and his purposes, and so in the man Jesus we see the involvement of God, and therefore it is literally true to speak of the suffering of God. This is the great and mighty wonder. This is how transcendent love, infinite love, almighty love, unchanging and unchangeable love, brings about his purposes. This is the power of God – this suffering and involvement and dying of Jesus.

And here we have something which requires facing personally, although I do not see anyone facing it except by the help of the grace of this same God and even then, by his graciousness, only being led gradually into it, because only gradually can we bear it. We have to face a very great judgment – the suffering of God. The way in which God has made it clear how he expresses the power which lies in his being God is a very great judgment upon us. 'The kings of the Gentiles lord it over them.' They have authority, they know what power is. They know how to put people in their place and show them what counts and what is authority, 'but it shall not be so among you'. For how does God get things done? The man Jesus. And therefore I believe that we must stand under the judgment of the suffering God on all our ways of doing things, whether it be outside the church or inside the church. You could equally well do research on the power structure in the Church of England as you could on the power structure in the government and so on. You could equally well, no doubt, analyse out the activities of a cathedral council, or of a local church council, and find how people manoeuvre, and how they seek to put themselves in such a position that they can put their views over on other people. But the way in which God gets things done is through the man Jesus, and we are therefore under the judgment of the suffering God – under the judgment of the suffering God to learn gradually to walk his way and to do things in the way in which he gets things done, because it is the way of suffering and self-giving love, which cannot be defeated because it never sets up new obstacles.

We may have to use negative power, which is a power that is not the power of love, for in this life we are trapped in our 'fallen' situation up to a point. Yet if we do have to use negative power, while we may get what we want done, we also set up all sorts of other obstacles all round which are carrying on their little bits of frustration and negativity and fighting. It is only as we begin to walk in the way of the cross, the way of self-giving love, that all the negative powers, all the anti-things, all the against things, all the un-loving and unlovely things are gradually absorbed. There is no doubt in my mind that to walk the way of the cross is the only practical way of getting things done in accordance with love. We are therefore under the judgment of the suffering God in all that we do, and above all in the way in which we seek to 'run' the church.

But there is an even greater judgment than this and, as I know I cannot face it, I hesitate to speak of it. I believe that it surely must be true that we are shown, in the pattern of Jesus, that God suffers with all his children. This is the fundamental answer to the problem of evil. There is no answer, but there is a way to live in it and through it. It must be the case that God suffers with all his children. For if Jesus is the pattern of God, if Jesus is consistent with the whole pattern of God which is consistent through and through, then it is surely true that God has made it clear to us that his divine sympathy is truly a godly, a God-like suffering with all who suffer. We are therefore under the judgment that every hurt we do to any creature in this world is shared by God. We are therefore under the judgment that every hurt we permit, when we might have stood in the way of it, we permit to happen also to God. 'Inasmuch as you do it *not* to the least of these my little ones, you do it *not* unto me.' The conclusion seems inescapable that this is literally true. This is a terrifying judgment, and we could not even say 'God forgive me' unless we already knew, because of the very pattern of God in Jesus Christ, that he does forgive us. We may face up to this because God forgives us through and in his very suffering, and therefore we must dare to speak of the suffering of God. The suffering of God in the dreadful pictures from Vietnam; the suffering of God in famine relief posters; the suffering of God to be seen in hospitals, to be seen in neglected homes, to be seen all round. This we may dare to speak of. Here is God involved for his people in this terrible but saving judgment.

This judgment is in fact the hope of the world, the light of the world, the salvation of the world, the very Gospel. For although it is right to insist that we see the suffering of God in the humanity of Jesus, this must also be balanced by the point that it is *God* who is involved for his people. It is God's transcendent power which is united with the suffering and with the threatened fragility of actual living. It is God, and this is so, because God is Love. Love is the very stuff of God and it is the infinite resource, the limitless power, the inexhaustible purpose, the ineffable holiness, the undefeatable righteousness of God who is Love, who is involved in this way. We must never lose our grip upon the transcendence of God, upon the otherness of God, however much we are led to see into the very humanity and the very suffering of God. And therefore we know that in this world belief in God is possible. How could we believe in a God who had not been crucified? What is God doing letting these things happen? I think the answer is that God is suffering. God is involved and this is how we face, this is how we endure, this is how we are transformed in and through the problem of evil and of suffering and of the monstrosity of so much of it. This is how we know that out of this very world and in this very world, God brings his purposes. For God is, and God is involved, and God is Love and above all this is God.

To talk of the suffering of God is not to deny the *impassibility* of God. At least, it is not to deny what the doctrine of the impassibility of God has always stood for. Impassibility literally means un-sufferingness – not being able to suffer. But we must be careful about being bound by literal meanings. It stands for the fact that you cannot in any way take away the Godness of God. A right translation for the impassibility of God might be: 'God cannot be put off being God.' Nothing that can be done or can happen can put God off being God. God is God, God is God the changeless; God is God the unchangeable; God is God the wholly perfect and the wholly infinite and the wholly independent of everything else. Nothing makes any difference to God's being God. But God is Love, and therefore God can and God does enter into the suffering of the world. This does not put God off being God.

We, of course, cannot be open to the sufferings of the world, as the cross shows that God is open to the sufferings of the world. We could not bear it for one moment, but God can bear it, because God is God, and God is Love, and it has not put God off being God. It is the very expression of God's being God. God can give himself away in being God, in the expression and pursuit of his purposes and this is how, in relation to his creatures, God is himself. God enters into the suffering of the world. Therefore I believe it to be literally true that Jesus is God and that we may and we must rightly speak of the suffering of God, but I believe also that we must be quite clear that it is God who suffers – the one true, almighty, transcendent, holy and righteous God.

As we see God in the suffering and dying of his Son, in the humanity and the true humanness and the realistic human being, Jesus, so we must believe in the self-same God who is the Almighty Father, not just immanent in suffering, by no means exhausted in suffering. We are concerned with the suffering of the transcendent God. The whole of God, if I may put it so, is in Jesus, but we must not suppose that Jesus alone is a sufficient symbol for all that God is. We must also have the understanding of God the Almighty, God the Transcendent, God the Father. God is Love. God therefore is God in and through his suffering, but it is God who suffers, and this involved and suffering love is the expression of transcendent and triumphant power. This surely is the decisive and the transforming good news. This is the Gospel, the Gospel of Good Friday and the Gospel of Easter Day; the Gospel of the cross and the resurrection. God is, God is Almighty and God is Love and God is to be seen in Jesus. And the Almighty God, who is transcendent love, is for *you*, he suffers with you, he suffers in you and he suffers for you.

God was in Christ, reconciling the word to himself, and the way of the cross is the practical and undefeatable way of purposeful and redeeming love. Therefore we know, as Paul also knew, that there is nothing, nothing in death or in life, in the realm of spirits or superhuman powers, in the world as it is, or in the world as it shall be, when science has discovered more and more things – in the forces of the universe, however they are measured, however they are plumbed, in heights or in depths, nothing in all creation that can 'separate us from the love of God in Christ Jesus our Lord'.

4 · *Christian Faith in God*

(1968)

Why believe in God? Until surprisingly recently the instinctive answer of believers in God to this question would have tended to be – 'Because everyone does, it's *natural* to believe in God.' When a little reflection on this answer threw a bit of doubt on it, then the next move would have been to agree that there are atheists, but that they are the odd men out, the eccentrics and unbalanced radicals of civilized and cultural thinking. But if one wasn't quite convinced by this it was always possible to shore up this taken-for-granted belief in God as the natural attitude of all truly reasonable and normal men and women by moving on to the assertion: 'And, in any case, come to think of it, it's reasonable to believe in God. There must be some cause for the existence of things, some basis for goodness, some purpose to which everything tends.' So – if the question came up 'Why believe in God?', the answer was 'Because it is natural and reasonable and, surely, inevitable when you come to think about it.'

In 1963, owing to a series of accidents which included illness and some nearly fortuitous publicity, the Bishop of Woolwich finally made it public knowledge that this sort of answer to questions about God is quite unrealistic and unacceptable as a beginning and end to the matter. Belief in God is not natural in the sense that the vast majority of men and women obviously display it, enjoy it and admit it. The way men and women reason about the world for the purposes of science and technology does not require any talk about

28

God at all, indeed rigorously excludes such talk, so that 'reasonable men and women' seem to be much more likely to be atheists than believers in God. And far from belief in God being inevitable, a large number of people, including many of the most sensitive and humane, seem to find it impossible. Belief in God has clearly ceased to be an automatic or obviously necessary part of our culture, our civilized approach to life, our human understanding. 'Why believe in God?' 'Why, indeed, unless you cannot outgrow a nostalgia for inherited religion or an immaturity which refuses to face the fact that stories about the heavenly Father are nothing but stories and that we are on our own?'

John Robinson was, as a matter of fact, simply discussing a situation which had been developing for well over two hundred years and which had long been commonplace to every educated person who has not been ecclesiastically drugged, but he had the courage and humility to reflect this situation in a peculiarly personal and, indeed, ordinary way. This allowed, or even compelled, people to admit that this too was their situation. To many this seemed peculiarly wicked, not least because it was so peculiarly threatening. How dare the Bishop publicly face what they could not bring themselves privately to admit, viz. that the world no longer believed in God, and while the church continued officially to speak of him this talk carried very little conviction even in the hearts and minds and lives of many of her members? A real ferment of faith has been reflected, and to some extent caused, by and in this debate about God.

There must be no doubt that this is a splendid thing. For by this debate and through this ferment we Christians are being challenged to faith in God and recalled to faith in God. We are being deprived of any opportunity to rest in a culturally inherited belief about the world, or a traditional conformity with what we have supposed the church can guarantee to us. That is to say that we cannot convincingly answer the question 'Why believe in God?' either by replying 'Because it is the natural/reasonable/civilized thing to do' or by the reply 'Because the church tells us to.' Further, the failure of 'the church' to operate as an authority for God, or *the* authority for God, is tied up with the inadequacy of the first answer. The church no longer works as a taken-for-granted

29

authority for God because the church, as an institution, is tied up with just that type of society which took it for granted that belief in God is natural/reasonable/civilized. And *that* type of society belongs to the past. Its sorts of authority are no longer authoritative. The church was one of those authorities, consequently its authority, as an institution of society, is just as *passé* as all the rest. This is a very important point which people seem to find extremely difficult to comprehend. It is not, however, difficult to *understand*; it is simply difficult, for church people at any rate, to *accept*. It must therefore be pondered on at great length until it can be faced, for until it is faced we shall not be set free for Christian faith in God today.

Perhaps we may become clearer about the actualities and the opportunities of our present situation if we consider the description not infrequently offered of our present plight, that we live in a 'post-Christian age'. This is to suggest that some period of the past was an age, era and society which, as an age, era and society, accepted Jesus Christ as the Word and Son of God and was identified through and through with this acceptance. The age took it for granted that God was God. Society assumed and acted on the assumption that Christianity was the basis and guide of behaviour, the era was based on the presupposition that the worship of the church indicated the true goal and end of humankind. But an assumption of this sort is historical nonsense and biblical blasphemy, lent some plausibility by the historical fact that for a considerable period, in what might be called Christendom, the church was one of 'the powers that be'. (A faint reflection of this lingers on with us in such facts as that the Archbishop of Canterbury has a precedence well up in the 'top ten' of the Realm!)

In fact there never has been a Christian age. The Christian era and the Christian society will not arrive until the kingdom of God has fully and finally come and everything is at its end, its fulfilment, in the God and Father of our Lord Jesus Christ. The only place where the kingdom of God can be unambiguously identified on earth and in history is in the person of Jesus himself. To identify even implicitly some stage in history, culture and civilization as a 'Christian age' (which can be measured and therefore be past) is to treat Jesus Christ as nothing but a historical accident, to accept Christianity as nothing but a cultural phenomenon, to identify the God and Father of Jesus and of Christianity as the mythological focus-figure of a particular way of looking at the world. Hence talk of a 'post-Christian age' is symptomatic of the absence of Christian faith in God. It shows that men and women have not been exercising or enjoying faith in God but have been conforming to a cultural habit and a historical fashion which is now very nearly over – thank God! – as we are surely required to say.

For the God and Father of our Lord Jesus Christ is not and never has been identified with any age, era, civilization or culture whatever. He identified himself with Jesus and identified himself through Jesus. But Jesus is 'the despised and rejected of men'. He 'came unto his own' and 'his own received him not' because 'his own' had *identified* their particular pattern of society and religion with God. And this despite the fact that they, the Jews, owed their very existence to the discovery that God was not identified with the civilization of the tribe of Judah or the Temple of the people of Judah. The glory of the Lord had departed from the Temple with the fall of Jerusalem, but this did not mean that the glorious and living God was dead. He was rediscovered or rather he revealed himself again by 'the waters of Babylon', and he was known to and through his suffering remnant. Again and again the people of God have had to go through the experience of thinking and feeling that their God was dead because they have insisted on identifying him with the means by which he once came to them and locating him in the institutions through which, at one particular stage in history and culture, they tried to respond to him. But God is the Lord and God does not change. God remains absolutely freely himself and does not dwell in temples made with hands, nor does God have a favourite age or era. All times are equally God's and God is as much to be discovered and responded to in an age that is avowedly godless as in an age that is avowedly godly. Neither godlessness, so-called, nor godliness, so-claimed, have the last word on God. God keeps that last word for himself. God has uttered it in Jesus and will utter it when all things are summed up in Jesus. Meanwhile we are called to Christian faith in God, not to the defence of so-called Christian institutions or Christian formulae.

It is the nature, being and activity of God which makes the present debate about God and the present ferment of faith so truly radical. So-called radicals rarely get to the root of the matter, just as so-called conservatives rarely penetrate to the fundamentals which cannot be shaken. 'Radicals' attack, 'conservatives' defend, but God lives and challenges us through and beyond the self-centredness of attacking or the self-cowardice of defending. The question with which God is facing us, individually and collectively, takes the form: 'Do you believe in what human beings believe or do you believe in God?'; 'Do you believe in the church or do you believe in God?'; 'Do you believe in the capacity to give answers to questions or do you believe in God?'; 'Do you believe in belief in the creeds or do you believe in God?'. But how can we face this question posed by God himself as to whether we know God, whether we are committed to him? What can we say positively and constructively about Christian faith in God?

We can say this. God has always gathered a people for himself and will continue to do so. People believe in God because people believe in God and God sees to it that a sufficiency of believing people are maintained for his purposes in the world and for the world. This is a basic picture of the Bible and a repeated message in the Bible. God is the Living and Holy One who gathers people for himself and who makes himself known to his people in and through their very vicissitudes. The knowledge of himself which God gave to his people was, when hammered out on the anvil of their history, so sure a knowledge of so reliable and active a God that his people were sure that he would act among them and for them in accordance with his abiding reality and his everlasting concern. They believed that God would send his Messiah to bring in his kingdom, to establish the affairs of his people consistently with his own love and being. Christianity exists because a Jew called Jesus believed himself to be called to announce this kingdom of God. He lived out his conviction to the very death, even to death on a cross, and then, in the unexpected eyes and reluctant hearts of a handful of his followers, he was vindicated. To them, in them and for them he was raised from the dead. They knew that the God whom Jesus served and the God for whom Jesus died had raised him up. They knew, therefore, that it was in Jesus that they had encountered the very power of God, the very kingdom of God. He was Jesus the Christ, and, as the very embodiment of God's power and reality, he was Jesus Christ their Lord. Henceforth he was the focus of God's people.

And so he proved to be. For the original handful of disciples, turned apostles, were able to share their faith in God and their experience of Jesus with an increasing number of men and women of an increasing number of races, classes and conditions. This, to them, was evidently the work of the Spirit of God who was the Holy Spirit of Jesus. God who was at work in Jesus, God who raised up Jesus, continued to be God at work gathering in his people as God the Holy Spirit. And this activity of God, Father, Son and Holy Spirit, continues to this day bringing about Christian faith in God and working through Christian faith in God.

We must realize that this is the living activity of a personal God with, in and through persons. There is no other basic and guaranteed continuity of Christian faith in God, no other source for it and no other foundation to it, than the living faith maintained by the Spirit of God through a living people in a living God. Thus we as individuals, as a congregation of Christian people, and as members together of the Christian church, can neither enjoy faith in God nor be a means of the kindling of faith in others unless we are ready to receive the grace to live faith as an experiment and an experience. Nothing can establish God. We can hope only to be established by God in God.

We are not in a post-Christian era but we are in a post-Christendom era. Civilization and culture do not take God or Christianity for granted. This puts us back into the situation of the people of God for most of their history, certainly into the position of the New Testament church and of the church of the first creative centuries. The world does not help us to believe in God nor do we strengthen our faith through conformity. Rather we have to find out whether God will build up our faith within his people and often against the stream of current fashion of what is taken for granted. This does not, however, mean that we are to withdraw into the church and seek somehow to cultivate our faith with our backs to the world. Such church-centredness can only be the death of faith. God is to be found in what he makes of the world for his people and in what he makes of his people for the world. It is abundantly clear from the Bible that God's people always lost their living faith in the living God when they supposed that they themselves were the focus both of God's activity and of God's reality.

I believe that the practical way to Christian faith in God in our present ferment of faith lies in this understanding that 'God is to be found in what he makes of the world for his people and in what he makes of his people for the world.' This means again, as I have already said, that we must 'live faith as an experiment and an experience'. Our possibility of faith in God has come to us through our association with the people who call themselves Christians, even if now we find that many manifestations of the church's life seem to count against faith in God. We must start, therefore, from what has been given to us and expose this through ourselves to the world and thus learn by experience what it is good for.

We have been given membership of the people of God through baptism. Do we find that we experience a Christian community as an open and a sustaining group which on the one hand helps us to come to terms with ourselves and to know that there is a God who forgives and accepts, and on the other gives us strength to face the problems and perplexities of our lives and to know that God the Father Almighty is at work through his Holy Spirit to give purpose and pattern to creation and human living? If our baptism means nothing about belonging and being sustained then we must set about realizing our baptism openly and find others with us to move towards this sort of open and sustaining community. For clearly unless baptism is, so to speak, practised we shall find nothing in it to rely on, and it will become a meaningless and magical formula. God is not known through labels. He is known through obedient, risky and lively action.

Similarly we receive the reality of the presence of Christ in the celebration of the holy communion. What does the reality of our worship then have to say about the realizing of worthwhileness in all that we are involved with in our daily lives and responsibilities? How can we bring thankfulness from our weekdays to Sunday eucharist, and what power of thankful receiving expectant openness does the gift of Christ to us enable us to have on each and every day? If we find no connection, can we face the nothingness at the eucharist and have the courage to face our lack of faith there, and see if the sacrament is indeed a real gift through which God makes himself real to us? How do we offer our weekly failures for the forgiveness and re-creation of Jesus Christ who gave himself and gives himself 'for us men and our salvation'? We must risk finding that our Sunday worship means nothing to our daily lives so that the Spirit of God is free to re-create both our faith and our worship and so, also, our daily lives.

We have been given the Bible as the record of the creative experience of the people of God. Are we prepared to admit that we find it absolute nonsense and then wrestle with it until we find that it makes sense of our nonsense and nonsense of much of our sense? Are we ready to risk getting our views of God and ourselves changed by putting the Bible furiously to question because of our experience, and exposing our questionings and our experiences to judgment and radical re-evaluation? Such a readiness presupposes very long perseverance, a never-ending experimentation and willingness really to find out what way of life seems to be required if we are to begin to understand the biblical experiences for ourselves.

We are presented with the faith of the Christian people symbolized in the creeds. Are we prepared to try and get at what is behind them? To ask how descending into hell can be related to actual depths of human suffering and bewilderment and to probe into the relationship between the allegation that Christ is seated at the right hand of God the Father Almighty and the hope that we can discover a possibility of love that can never be defeated? In other words, are we prepared to risk the sort of experiment that would be required if we really believed that love reigns?

If the Bible is anything to go by, such experimental approaches to the reality and the realizing of faith will not guarantee any one of us necessarily comforting and reassuring experiences. We may be taken out of the half-light of a pseudo-faith or semi-faith into the darkness of doubt which is the ante-chamber to the reality of God. But if the experience of the people of God is anything to go by, if the life of Jesus Christ is anything to follow and to gain hope from, then we may be sure that anyone who will throw in his or her lot with the people of God and who will join with them in going out into the world's uncertainties and into the depths of their own perplexities will find, in God's time and not their own, that they are not alone in this journeying. Rather they will learn that they are on the way to a city whose builder and founder is God and that on this way they are given enough knowledge of God or, at least, sufficient hope that God will be known, to continue hopefully. Together we shall find growing in us a Christian faith in God which is not shaken by ferment nor defeated by frustration but rather strengthened and deepened because its source and its end lies in God alone.

5 · *Where are we now and where does God want us to go?*

(1989)

I want to draw attention to certain features of where we are now which, I believe, point to God's pressure upon us to discern direction, programme and possibility for the future. What is it that God requires of us, and offers to us, *now*? To discern this we need to consider where we are now *as human beings*, where we are now *as faithful Christians* – and those who have been so called need also to consider where they are now as clergy of the Church of England.

Each of these so to speak interacting and interpenetrating layers of being and doing are essential to any discernment of what the Spirit is saying. God speaks in and through the interactions between the actualities of what is happening to us and the tradition so far of his revealing, communicating, saving and guiding acts and encounters. Revelation is now or never. But it could not occur *now* unless it had occurred *then*. The God who gets in touch, empowers us and directs us now had already got in touch in his chosen way with his chosen people who, despite their disobedience, inadequacies and betrayals, were enabled by God so to respond to God then that the tradition of revelation and the people of revelation were built up. It is this people and this tradition who keep the possibilities of revealing encounter and saving dependence alive through every 'now' and into the future which is God's. Revelation, therefore, is always in practice now or never, in order that we may be related in hopeful and saving ways to that end which God has intended from the beginning.

First, therefore, where are we now as human beings? Consider where we do now stand as human beings. With regard to the physical realities of the universe we human beings are scaled down. With regard to the future of ourselves and of life on earth we are scaled up. As to the latter, i.e. life on earth, we now have the upper hand – at least as far as the possibilities of destruction go. Natural calamities such as volcanoes or earthquakes or even AIDS (if that is properly to be described as a 'natural' calamity) can cause great havoc and many personal and individual tragedies. But they do not threaten life itself or the human species as a whole. It is we who do this with our activities, inventions and exploitations through which we pierce the ozone layer, pollute or empty the food-bearing oceans and threaten the very possibilities of rain by destroying forests and creating dust-bowls. These effects may be looked on as by-products of fantastic inventiveness, organization and effort by which we have harnessed energy, organized information and communication and manipulated our environments with their many threats and possibilities, so that we can survive, flourish, explore and enjoy as never before and in totally un-dreamed-of ways. And there is no telling what more we shall be able to do, if we survive. But we now threaten ourselves.

Nonetheless, in this threatening posture we now dominate the earth. The survival of ourselves and of the eco-system on which we depend depends on us. We do have the upper hand, even if it turns out to be the sinister hand of destruction. Where does God come in?

Scaled up as we are with regard to the future of our sort of life on our planet the earth, we are on a very small scale with regard to the time of that planet, while the planet itself is immensely scaled down in the dimensions of the observable universe. The sort of considerations, observations and systematic speculations which lead me to talk as I do are clearly indicated in one of the most recent and most enthusiastically received efforts by a leading physicist to explain as simply as possible what is currently the most widely accepted account of or theory about the universe. This is Stephen J. Hawking's *A Brief History of Time*.[1]

His book includes statements like the following:

The general theory of relativity describes the force of gravity

38

and the large-scale structure of the universe, that is, the structure on scales from only a few miles to as large as a million million million million (1 with 24 zeros after it) miles, the size of the observable universe (p.11).

We now know that our galaxy is only one of some hundred thousand million that can be seen by using modern telescopes, each galaxy itself containing some hundred thousand million stars . . . We live in a galaxy that is about one hundred thousand light years across and is slowly rotating . . . Our sun is just an ordinary, average-sized, yellow star, near the inner edge of one of the spiral arms (p.37).

The present evidence therefore suggests that the universe will probably expand for ever but all we can really be sure of is that even if the universe is going to re-collapse, it will not do so for at least another ten thousand million years, since it has already been expanding for at least that long. This should not unduly worry us; by that time, unless we have colonized beyond the solar system, mankind will long since have died out, extinguished along with our sun (p.46).

On this scale, therefore, we are diminished in a way with which our imaginations cannot cope and yet with which our mathematics apparently can. But the aspects of our reality to which I am trying to point by the use of the notion of 'scales' is, of course, even more complex than I have so far indicated. There is the whole matter of quantum mechanics – scarcely something to be taken up by a lay person, but nonetheless something to be reckoned with. It is, perhaps, sufficient at this stage to add one more very brief quotation from Stephen Hawking.

Quantum mechanics, on the other hand, deals with phenomena on extremely small scales, such as a millionth of a millionth of an inch (p.11).

We cannot now plunge ourselves into the issues raised by the famous uncertainty theory of Heisenberg, but merely to refer to it only underlines the vastness, complexity and depth with which we all, and faith and theology in particular, have to live as we take seriously where we are as human beings. In fact we stand somewhere in the midst of a universe which ranges, according to our present limits of observation and analysis, from ten to the power of twenty-four to ten to the power of minus sixteen.

Just as we are forced to ask of our 'scaled-up' position as possible destroyers of life on this planet 'Where does God come in on this?' so we have to ask of our 'scaled-down' position in the observable universe 'Where can God be located in relation to all this?' Our best and most urgent way forward, surely, is to reflect with all the intensity of intellectual, spiritual and moral energy that is available to us, 'Where are *we* to be located in relation to all this?' This question, I believe, if lived with persistently, gazed at intensively and wrestled with responsibly, will confront us with an awe-inspiring, strangely terrible yet dawningly wonderful mystery which will turn out to be the fringes of the awe-inspiring, strangely terrible and gloriously wonderful mystery of God.

Clearly we have to do with matters which are exceedingly difficult to talk about, except in ways which are loosely fitting, analogously to be alluded to and appropriately responded to by commitment, exploration, discipline of mind and of behaviour, and by wonder and worship. But *we* do have to do with all these matters. The convergence of all the scales of reality – moral, biological, macrocosmic and microcosmic – occurs in *us*. It is we who are aware of the scales. We have even, in some sense, invented them, although in a sense which reverberates also with the sense that we have discovered them (an issue or sensitivity which is crudely and roughly pointed to by all the arguments and anguishes about objective/subjective). It may very well be, therefore, that in some basically true and real sense, and therefore in a way which is truly alarming and potentially destructive because it is so real and responsible, we actually are in the image of God – but in the image of the God who is to be wondered at and worshipped in, through and beyond all the scales and dimensions now known to us.

If this is so, or possibly so (and of course I believe that it is so, for I am a biblical believer in the God who is known in Jesus Christ through the Spirit), then the intimate connection of the theological task and, indeed, of the very mystery of God, with risk, exploration and development, is surely clear. Just as dogmatic science has developed itself out of appropriate existence, so must dogmatic theology. Einstein could apparently never bring himself to accept the apparent implications of the scientific theories to which he had made so crucial a contribution. 'God,' he said, 'does not play dice.' Similarly, it is clear that theology, faith and worship have a daunting task ahead of them in being brought through the realization that the comparatively small-scale omnipotent God who has everything buttoned up in an imperialistic fashion with guaranteed rewards for his chosen is not on. But the mystery of the universe and the mystery of love and the abuse of the selves who can love are all very much on, and *we* are in the midst of them – and in some very real, exciting, pressing and decisive way at the heart of them.

So that, or somewhere very like it, is where we are now as human beings. Where are we now as faithful Christians? For me the starting point is the revelation of God as Holy Trinity. That is, I take as revelation about the reality of God the symbol, icon or holy diagram which indicates that the one, true, living, universal and mysterious God is to be worshipped by us Christians as Father, Son and Holy Spirit. These three terms or names ('Father', 'Son', 'Holy Spirit') designate or label three foci or personal symbols around which the corporate Christian experience of dealing with God, and being dealt with by God, has crystallized out. God has made himself known to us, and has shaped our responsive knowing of him, in and as the Father, in and as the Son, and in and as the Holy Spirit. The context, the set of activities and experiences which start giving meaning to these names ('Father', 'Son' and 'Holy Spirit') is first the activities, experiences and traditions reflected and reported in the Bible. This is taken up into and shaped by the worshipping, living, questioning, formulating and continuing exploration of the whole body of Christians as they live 'in the name of God, Father, Son and Holy Spirit'. This living in the name of the Holy Trinity involves openness to what is going on in the world. The questions and experiences of history and the world are part of the shaping of what the Holy Trinity means for us because we believe that the world is created by God the Father, redeemed by God the Son and sanctified by God the Holy Spirit – with a view to that transforming of all things which is promised in the end. This is the end which God will bring out of all creation so

41

that, in the end, he is all in all and the kingdom of holiness, glory and love is established and fulfilled.

The Holy Trinity, therefore, symbolizes, focusses and points to that glorious, saving and promising mystery of God which is the sole source of our faith, the whole promise of our hope and the full enticement of our love. God as Holy Trinity is God the universal Father and source of all being and all blessing who is greater than great – transcendent over all. Yet this same God as Son and Saviour is one with us in the particularity of our flesh and blood to overcome that which separates us from his glory and love. The God who is greater than great is, in a down-to-earth way, more loving than love. And it is this same transcendent and down-to-earth God who is available at all times and in all places as the Holy Spirit who is both freely transcendent and yet closer than close – available at the very heart of each one of us and as the bonds of sharing and empowering between us. Each one of the terms, symbols and names of the Holy Trinity points to equally essential truths, possibilities and promises stemming from and offered by the one, true and only God. The meaning, bearing and scope of these names can be followed up in authentic and appropriate practice only if we are constantly and worshipfully careful to let what we are seeing in and through each of the names and activities interact with, and be modified by, what we are pointed to by the other two names and activities. It is a spiritual axiom which has somehow or other to be coped with that when we attempt to think about God we must be ready to think about more than one thing at once. For example, we must be very careful about the way we understand (or misunderstand) the *power* of God. Are we to see 'the Father' as some sort of divine emperor of the universe who rules with an instantly effective and irresistible power when the Son, Jesus, who is, for us Christians, Christ our Lord, has done his work through the life and passion of a crucified slave? (It is important here to remember the inappropriateness of thinking in terms of 'the comparatively small-scale omnipotent God who has everything buttoned up in imperialistic fashion with guaranteed rewards for his chosen'.)

The Trinity requires us to be very careful and humble and reverent about what we claim to know about God and about the practical effects of this knowing. The mystery is very great. But one thing is simply clear, alarmingly clear and has unending implications, the end of which we shall not know until we come, if by grace we do, to God's end. (Then, but only then, shall we, as Paul puts it in I Corinthians 13.11, 'see face to face. Now [we] know in part, then [we] shall know fully, even as [we] are fully known.') The one thing that is clearly indicated by our Christian revealed understanding of God as Holy Trinity is that in having to do with God we are engaged with, and being engaged by, he who and that which is the dynamic, the essence, the substance and the fulfilment of all that is, can be or will be. That is to say that in the simplest possible sense, and the most basic possible sense, God is ultimate reality, and the power, possibility and promise of this ultimate reality has the pattern, the engagement and future pointed towards by God as Father, Son and Holy Spirit.

So, the God who is worshipped as Father, Son and Holy Spirit is God who is the whole truth, the glory of truth and the truth which is love. To be given faith in, and to be called to the worship of, this God is to glimpse the tremendous possibility and promise that everything that exists has a chance and an opportunity of being transformed into its best possible being or self and so caught up into a fulfilling and enjoyable worth which is worthy to be part of the worship of God. This is so because God expresses his whole worth as love: in the creating of mutual worth, the sharing of mutual worth, the redeeming of mutual worth and the fulfilling of mutual worth. Everything that is, will be or can be is capable of being redeemed, offered and shared. Of course, there could be no realistic, sustaining and promising authenticity in such a faith about God and reality in the world as we know it, and with beings such as we are, without the cross. Truth must go with judgment, cost, endurance and pain; hope about the fundamental praiseworthiness and worthwhileness of all things must go with passion. But, at the heart of the life of the Trinity (such is our faith), there is the one who has been crucified. What we know of God is as much pointed to and patterned by what we know of Jesus as by what we know of the Father or by what we know through the Holy Spirit. Thus in the very life of God and in the very midst of the world there is the cross, making real the link between reality, worship and hope. So it simply is the case that to struggle nearer to

43

the truth and reality of things is to be brought closer to their praiseworthiness and promise. Hence one is given the opportunity and grace to offer, use and celebrate these things so that praise, enjoyment and glory are built up towards the final glory, praise and worship of the kingdom. At least this is how we Christians believe, know in faith, and express it in New Testament terms.

Which brings me to a very important, sensitive and crucial point with regard to the exploration to which, I believe, we Christians are now being invited, or even compelled. New Testament faith in God is kindled by, focussed through and concentrated in Jesus. And this is not, if I may so put it, simply an instrumental or even doctrinal matter. It is a matter of devotion and personal commitment. To put this point as briefly and clearly as possible, I will put it autobiographically. My way in to a faith in God the Holy Trinity which I have been trying to outline to you as the given starting point of a necessary contemporary Christian response to where we are now was 'through Jesus Christ' or 'in the name of Jesus'. Some simple evangelical preaching, related to exciting Bible study, persuaded me that Jesus showed that God was 'for me'. This was (and is) in a two-fold sense. God was '*for* me' – that is, on my side in offering me repentance, newness and abundance of life. God was also 'for *me*' – that is, this was an offer directed to me personally, which caught me up, and about which I could and should do something, the doing of which was related to much greater doings by God. So it was by a response to *Jesus* as the way, the truth and the life that I was set on the way which has lead me to share in the churches' faith in God, the Holy Trinity. There is no time to explore this further, save to say that the movement of faith was through the discovery that the God who was 'for me' in Jesus Christ was so because he was the God who was 'for all' in Jesus Christ and, indeed, God the Creator of all, who in and as Jesus Christ was committed to being the Redeemer of all and, in and as the Spirit, at work to transform all. The particularity of the encounter and call lead to the discovery and vision of the universality of the God and Father of our Lord Jesus Christ and therefore to the universal implications of faith in God in the name of Jesus Christ through the power of the Spirit. What is linked together here is strong and specific particularity, experienced with a deep intimacy and yet caught up into an all-embracing universality. Universality does not imply vagueness, particularity does not imply narrowness and intimacy does not imply self-centred turned inwardness. This dynamic combination of intimacy, urgency and universality is something which our faithful understanding of where we are now as Christians obliges us to bring to bear on our understanding of where we are now as human beings.

As Christians, we are now in matters of faith where Christians always were: that is to say, knowing that we are called to worship the one, true, living and only God as Father, Son and Holy Spirit, the Father who is to be served in the name of Jesus through the power of the Spirit. What has changed is where we are as human beings. We can no longer plausibly or credibly believe that the universe is anthropocentric, created by a sky-dwelling God so that out of it there should emerge some human souls who could be saved to occupy a limited number of seats in a limited heaven (front seats being reserved for angels). Given what we know about space, time and processes of evolution can we really believe that God went in for all this just to save *me*? Surely a steady look in a mirror is a sufficient refutation of this.

What we can, perhaps, believe – in the name of God: Father, Son and Holy Spirit – given grace and faith, given worship, practice and hope – is that the vast, mysterious and strangely wonderful universe is theocentric and God-informed. Therefore we who have strangely, mysteriously and briefly emerged in his image have the opportunity of responding to him and so of sharing with him in whatever it is he is pursuing in this vast, unimaginably great work of creation, of risk, of threat and of love.

It is in this context of where we are as human beings and of where, therefore, we are located as Christians who have our faith based in, and directed by, God the Holy Trinity, that some of us have to consider where we are as clergy in the Church of England.

First, there can be no doubt about our call. The intimacy and urgency of our personal calling as priests and deacons are in no way diluted or confused by the bewildering immensity of our physical context or the mystery and awe-inspiring glory of God the Holy Trinity. Quite the contrary. This is *the* insight of the biblical and Christian faith. At the heart of everything is the God of personal concern – God who is love, God who can cope no matter what (this is declared and demonstrated particularly and precisely in the cross and resurrection of Jesus Christ), God who is always getting in touch. So persons have the amazing opportunity of responding intimately, urgently and individually. The same point is declared in baptism. To put it as simply as possible, God intends me to have my name and to respond as myself to him. And this, of course, is in potential relation to all other selves and to God's purposes of love in creation, redemption and the completion of the future. So, our personal ministerial call is at the heart of our opportunity to join in with the purposes, possibilities and promises of God. The mystery of this is both personally cogent and yet infinitely great. For God does not do what he does 'for me'; he does it as himself and so for love and for all. But what he does, he does in such a way that it includes 'for me' and gives me my call – gives us our call.

On this given and promising basis we can go on to face the in some ways threatening realities of where clergy in the Church of England are. They serve in a church which is a remarkably ramshackle historical accident, left by the vagaries of its history with apparently rich resources, widespread national and local presence, and a surviving toe-hold among the 'powers that be'. But, in fact, the resources are pretty widely stretched and distributed and tied up in ways which often hinder rather than facilitate lively responses to present conditions and opportunities. Moreover, they are heavily subsidized by the past. My diocese, for example, despite a very considerable growth in regular giving over the past decade or more, does not produce fifty per cent of its budget from current local giving. Congregations alone could not possibly pay for clergy as they are. And something like this applies to the whole Church of England.

Thus our resource base is oddly ambiguous and insecure, even while (taken as a consolidated whole) it is very considerable indeed and makes us appear, in the eyes of many, to be a survival from the past which retains a place among the privileged, the rich and the powerful. In practice and on the ground, as we all know only too well, we tend to be in some ways greatly over-extended. The cry goes up from clergy and regular members of the congregations alike that far too much time has to be spent on endless tasks of money-raising and maintenance. The demands of basic pastoralia seem to have many clergy following an exhausting schedule which leaves them far too little time (or none!) for reading and development, consistent and consolidating teaching, careful planning or being with their families. And so on.

Further, all this is not unrelated to the smallness of the percentage of the whole population which attends our churches in any regular way and the even smaller number of people who are ready to invest time and money in sustaining and developing a lively church and neighbourhood life. If one wants to feel really depressed one can add to all this the way in which our attempts to introduce synodical structures into our life together as a church seem, so far, to have misfired. At the local and diocesan level they seem, largely, to promote boredom and be an excuse to multiply bureaucracy, while at the national level General Synod seems to provide the media with pictures of clergy being nasty to one another about matters of faith, morals or church order. Synods, it seems to me, bring out the worst in us – and that in public too. It may be that a careful study of the early councils would show that it was ever thus. But at least they did not have television. In any case, all this does not seem very helpful in enabling the church to set before our largely paganized or pluralistic society the possibilities of help, wholeness and hope which are offered by God: Father, Son and Holy Spirit. So is the title 'Church of England' simply a historical survival, preserved by an unusual amount of historic endowment, but actually labelling a struggling Christian sect which is one among the varieties of Christianity on offer in a market which includes other groupings of variations of religion (Jewish, Islamic, Hindu, Buddhist, Sikh, etc.), a market, moreover, in which a large number of people prefer not to deal at all?

It is the possibility or indeed the necessity of facing *this* question if we realistically consider where we are as human beings, as faithful Christians, and as clergy in the Church of England, that points us, I believe, to the direction in which we should look for our answers to the really pressing and practical question 'Where does God want us to go?' Seeing God has indeed called us in Jesus Christ through the Spirit to know him as the holy and glorious Trinity, God of all, God of love and God of suffering grace, and seeing he has given us our call and our ministry in and through the Church of England, it is certain God has a way forward for us in facing up to and living with the realities which at present call us in question, bewilder us and seem too much for us. If we are brought to a place where we are judged, bewildered and cut down to size, then it is certain that God offers us this place as the fresh starting point for opportunities of repentance, renewal and enlargement.

Let me close, therefore, with some headings which I believe we are asked to explore as we work together to find out where God wants us to go. This working together will be on the basis of shared faith, shared hope and shared conversation which will often spill over into shared controversy. For while relying on God is a simple matter, responding to God is a complicated one, because of the complexities of the world, the limitations of our own understandings and misunderstandings and the contributions of our own sinfulness and blindness.

First, then, we have to recover – and support one another in recovering – Abrahamic faith. As Hebrews 11.8 says of Abraham: 'By faith . . . when called to go to a place he would later receive as his inheritance, (he) obeyed and went, even though he did not know where he was going.' You will note how this reflects the shape of faith. Abraham showed his faith in God by his readiness to go out. He showed the assurance of this faith by knowing that he would later receive an inheritance. However, he did not know where he was going and therefore he did not know the nature of his inheritance. Faith is faith in God and does not necessarily guarantee particular sorts of knowledge, or church ordering, or patterns of church life, or ways of doing things as we have hitherto done them. We do not know what we have to give up in order to go out and to get on until we discover that *this* is what we have to give up because we must go on in *this*.

Which leads to my second heading. It is God's future that we are called to serve, not God's past that we are called to preserve. This must be so for at least three pretty practical and compelling reasons. First, the whole thrust of the Bible is *eschatological*. This is especially so with the discovery of Jesus as the Christ through his resurrection from the dead and the gift of the Spirit. All this, as the New Testament makes clear, is a series of signs of the last times.

God is about to make an end and we are called to repent and receive our share in that end. For us – and until the end – the end lies in the future. So we must be concerned to move towards and to contribute to the future. Secondly, we now know that our time, not only on the earth as individuals, but also as species, is both limited and linear. 'Redeeming the time' therefore means being picked up by the purposes of God and given the opportunity to share in, and contribute to, his future. Thirdly, an understanding of God as Holy Trinity has, and must have, *universal* implications. However sect-like Christians may have to risk becoming for their own survival, pastoral and identity needs, the worship of Christians is potentially universal. We cannot possibly begin to cope with this unless we see the necessity and opportunity of moving on towards an all-embracing and all-fulfilling future wherein God picks up, sorts out and puts together all the riches of human history, culture, religion and inventiveness *universally*. So – we have to work out practically what it means to receive the Christian tradition from the past in the present for the sake of God's future.

Which leads me to a third, slogan-like, heading which might serve as a provocation for working at all this on the ground. We need to escape from the danger of settling down as God's bureaucracy into being a lively, flexible and expanding agency for God's future. This, I think, is probably both the most threatening and the most promising thing with which we are faced. It must mean, for instance, being more and more ready drastically to reorganize and renew our practical structures and programmes so that we move towards putting into actual practice dreams like the following which I find myself seriously considering as indicating ways forward.

I dream of a laity which steadily becomes more liberated in their exploration of faith and more enlarged in their grasp of the scope of faith in, and praise of, God. This liberation and enlargement would make us more and more a community of communities of pilgrims who enjoy discipleship, rejoice in challenge and celebrate our fellowship in the praise and truth of God. Such a laity would both challenge the clergy by insisting on playing a much fuller part in running and directing all the activities of the church and its finances and would also relieve the clergy by putting them in their

49

place and insisting that they be kept free for their representative priestly and ministerial duties. Such a body of celebrating and exploring pilgrims could also become more and more effective in witnessing to, and working with, all those who seek and care and long for, but are, at present, very much 'out there' and 'outside' as far as the church is concerned.

I also dream of a clergy which is set free from false guilt and trying to do the impossible, both about pastoralia and about buildings, so that they are free to be priests and deacons indeed and to enjoy this (by and large, in the midst of inevitable stresses and strains – and occasional sufferings).

I further dream of a collection of plant (that is to say churches, halls and buildings for joint use) which is constructed in a planned way with regard to availability, is planned and constructed or reconstructed so that it is maintainable with an effort which is, although inevitable, also possible and within the likely scope of funds which can be raised or earned locally without incessant strain, and is fit to serve as a series of outgoing bases: that is to say that all the plant will have uses which are rooted in the community as well as in the congregation.

Finally, I dream of appropriate ecumenicity which contributes to, and stems from, the preceding dreams. Such ecumenicity, I believe, would for the immediately foreseeable future not be concerned with time-wasting schemes about amalgamations or complicated doctrinal agreements but with the practical, close and trusting collaboration in localities between congregations and churches which find ways both of keeping their ecclesiastical identities and of presenting a common front and working for common efforts, not infrequently from common buildings.

Finally, along lines such as these, I believe we could find – or rather be given – worthwhile ways, for the immediately foreseeable future at any rate, of living up to our title of 'Church of England' by being that church in England which uses its historical accidents and opportunities to be at the disposal of Christianity as a whole in England for England as a social and national whole.

I have found in my own dealings with other churches in the North-East of England as we try to work out common ways of doing things together for mission and service in particular areas that for all our Church of England failings, small-mindedness and turned-inwardness we do still retain a feeling that the church should be a sign and a practice of God's universal concern for all in any neighbourhood of society or institution. So while we may be a ramshackle historical accident, God has given us, in and through the accidents which constitute us, a practical sense of the *universality* of his intimate and urgent offer of love – in both judgment and salvation. Therefore I believe that we must get rid of all false triumphalism, security bolstered by financial endowment or superiority claimed because of doctrinal or ordering orthodoxy, but that we must do so in order to be at the service of Christianity at large in this society of ours at large.

We are obviously a minority and we need to get reorganized as a viable, continuing and open minority. But we do not worship, serve or represent a minor, an optional or a sectarian God. We are called to know him intimately, to love him urgently, and to serve him for his universality.

I therefore believe that it is right to dream, hope, imagine, work and plan for a Church of England that becomes more and more ready and organized to go forward in the service of Christianity as a whole in this society as a whole in the name and the power of the God of the whole – whom we know and worship as Father, Son and Holy Spirit.

Note

1. Stephen J. Hawking, *A Brief History of Time*, Bantam Doubleday Dell Inc. 1988 (one and a half million copies of the book are in print!).

Part Two

Concerning Men and Women and Concerning Jesus

1 · *Personality and Freedom*

(1965)

Can you study personality in a scientific manner and a scientific way? Clearly this partly depends on what you mean by 'person' and what you mean by 'scientific'. But whatever it is decided to mean by those terms, there is a problem to which I wish to draw attention. To do so I cannot do better than begin my discussion with a quotation from Lady Wootton's *Social Science and Social Pathology*. I do so as she so well raises the problem and dilemma in question. In the course of her discussion of 'Mental Disorder and Criminal Responsibility', she writes:

> In this and some others matters the only ultimate proof of the pudding must be in the eating; and that proof is essentially a statistical one. Subject only to the over-riding social and moral limitations mentioned below, the role of medical or psychiatric, as against educational, or what are now regarded as penal, methods in the treatment of backsliders will depend upon the actual success which each can show in dealing with different types of case. Dr Glueck's concept of the 'anti-social individual as a sick person' must stand or fall, not by the compelling logic of psychiatric theories, but by a simple demonstration of the degree to which doctors are more successful than other people in inducing favourable modifications of deplorable behaviour; and that is a matter that can only be demonstrated in statistical terms. No matter who has the first word, the last is always with

the statistician. The task of the social sciences is to mobilize indifferently the results of *every* form of expertise and the evidence of *all* available methods of handling cases of anti-social behaviour; and it is not by deductive argument but only by willingness to submit to the test of experience and by a temper at once 'critical, distrustful of elaborate speculation, sceptical, candid, and tough' that psychiatry or any other science can hope to justify whatever claims it ventures to make.[1]

The problem which is pin-pointed by the language of this paragraph, although it is not clear to me that Lady Wootton is aware of it, is that which is concealed or revealed by the phrase 'social sciences', and which would be posed even more sharply if we were allowed to call the social sciences 'human sciences', in the sense that they are the sciences which deal with human beings in the various aspects of their operations which express and exercise their humanness. The problem is this. To be essentially scientific is to be essentially concerned with that which is measurable. As Lady Wootton says, in the scientific field the ultimate proof 'is essentially a statistical one'. 'No matter who has the first word, the last is always with the statistician.' That this is the view adopted by many psychologists and psychiatrists is made evident enough by the way in which they take great pains to lace their articles and books with stiff doses of diagrams, statistical tables and, above all, graphs. As Lady Wootton makes clear enough elsewhere,[2] the object of this procedure is to remain clearly in the field of science by arriving at and operating with value-free definitions and judgments. The point I wish to make is that this is a logical, theoretical and practical impossibility. It may therefore be that the phrase 'social sciences' or 'human sciences' is a logical contradiction. (I myself think that it is more likely that we should make the decision to allow the use of the word 'science' in a rather broader sense than that which is tied to measurement and statistics. But this is a wider theoretical question than can be pursued here.) The point is this. Anything that can justifiably be given the description 'social', where the reference is to human society, automatically includes the notion of value and must operate at all times with the complication that the notion of value introduces. In the paragraph which I have quoted, Lady Wootton is unable to exclude the two adjectives 'favourable' and 'deplorable'. Although, no doubt, an attempt would be made to assert that these two adjectives are to be taken as strictly descriptive in the sense that their meaning can be defined by determining what the particular society involved in fact favours and deplores, we do well to remain sceptical about the possibility of a total value-free description being produced. Procedures for determining what groups of human beings in fact do always require initial choices about what constitutes a significant grouping and about the significant features which are to be statistically organized. If the scientific conscience rebels against the arrogance and ignorance of these philosophical statements, then it is to be pointed out that we can never demonstrate that the value-free procedure is in fact a possibility. It is simply a presupposition and a faith that it is so. My presupposition, which I hold to be more in accordance with the evidence of the actual procedures involved, although it cannot be decisively established, is that belief in value-free procedures is mistaken. Value-free observations of human beings operating as human beings are not possible for a human being. Science does not provide an escape route from our humanity, as scientists must be human, for scientific activity is an activity of human beings.

This truism is not rhetoric, but logic. And obvious as it is, it is the sort of truism which has constantly to be reiterated in view of its practical importance and of the way in which it is constantly neglected. The particular area on which I wish to bring these considerations to bear is that of personality and freedom. And here let me stress that the arguments which I have just used and also those which I am going on to develop are not based on religion but on logic and practice. The basic considerations with regard to personality and freedom are philosophical and theoretical ones long before we get to religious considerations. The basic consideration is this. The real possibility of freedom is a necessary part of what it is to be human, not least of what it is to be a human being engaged in scientific activity. This is so regardless of any facts of any sort which may be validly established about human beings by the scientific method. The basis for this statement is two-fold, having one of its foundations firmly rooted in logic and the other equally firmly rooted in experience. The logical point is that the 'distinct perceptions' (as Hume called them) which are the subject-matter and constitute the facts of science presuppose a 'perceiver' (i.e. observer) who, as far as this particular set of observations goes, stands over against or transcends (logically) the observed facts. Logically speaking, objects presuppose a subject who is opposed to them. And the fact that any given person who is a subject in respect of a given set of observations can himself or herself (and so throughout this illustration), together with his or her observations, become an object for another observing subject, does not alter the logical point that there must always be a subject who is not determined by the observed facts, but free enough to observe them.

This logical point of the necessary independence of some observer passes over into the experimental point of what it is like to be an observer or a subject. Here one must insist on the uniqueness of self-awareness, and one must be clear that the self-awareness in question is not what I make of your self-awareness or what you make of anyone else's self-awareness, for that is a question of what an observer makes of that which is to him an *object* characterized by self-awareness, i.e. by the fact that he is aware of himself as a person. The unique self-awareness which is decisive for the argument which we are at present pursuing is the self-awareness which each man has of himself as he has it to himself. This true self-awareness (a subject's awareness of himself as a subject) is the 'experiential inside', so to speak, of the logical necessity of the transcendent observer. Anyone who sets out to give an exhaustive account of human behaviour and experience and who does so simply on the basis of his observations of other humans (who to him are objects) plus an attempt to treat himself purely as an object to himself, is leaving out of the account both the logical and experiential fact which makes his observations possible. He is failing to take into account the unique fact and experience of what it is to be a subject, i.e. a person. However mistaken may be the factual information about oneself which self-awareness may give, this does not alter the significance of the uniqueness of subjective self-awareness (of what it is like to me to be me), nor reduce its necessity for the possibility of there being any objective knowledge at all.

The above line of argument is one which cannot be refuted by facts of any kind, for it is about the process by which the observation of facts is made possible. I would maintain that to reduce human personality to the sum total of the facts which are actually or theoretically discoverable by scientific methods is in the first place always to make a decision which does not fall within the scope of the scientific method. So the weight of science cannot be put behind such a choice. And in the second place, it is a wrong decision because it precludes the possibility of that which is a presupposition of any knowledge or scientific activity at all. Therefore, however uncomfortable and complicating it may be for a proper scientific study of human beings, we have unavoidably built into our field of study what I would call the irreducibility of 'I'. Indeed I would be so bold as to insist that one should call it the *mystery* of the 'I'. We are back here to our initial problem, which I suggested was pin-pointed by the possible contradiction in the term 'social sciences'. Science implies in essence the clarity and definition achieved by measurements. The possibility of measurement implies the 'mystery' of the subject who measures. How, then, can the scientific study as objects of persons who for the possibility of science must exist uniquely as subjects, be carried on?

It may be thought that whatever the superficial plausibility of the above treated as a self-contained philosophical argument, it remains manifestly untrue in practice. It suffers, in fact, from being self-contained and philosophical and therefore cut off from the practical world. For the fact is that human beings in groups are susceptible to observations which can be reduced to statistics, and their behaviour can be the subject of statistically probable prediction. Moreover, there are manifest and notorious cases in which the individual person suffers from defects, whether physiological or psychological or a complex combination of both, which render any notion of personal freedom in these cases quite nugatory. The scientific observation of persons as objects in the most objective manner possible has already increased our capacity to deal with personality disorders in remarkable ways, and to introduce the notion of mystery is to threaten a return to the dark ages (scarcely yet fully passed), in which madness was attributed to evil spirits and in which flogging and hanging were thought to be righteously appropriate to a terrifyingly wide range of human deviant behaviour. It is certainly clear that to go back on the discoveries and procedures of psychology and psychiatry would be scientifically outrageous and morally disastrous. It is from this very fact that the urgent need arises of a confrontation and consultation between psychology and psychiatry, philosophy and religion. For I would maintain that it is as a matter of fact in theory and practice true, on the one hand, that there is the mystery of the 'I' which we could reasonably call the mystery of personality. But, on the other hand, it is equally true that human beings, whether as individuals or in groups, are affected by and even determined by, forces and factors which are open to discovery, measurement and manipulation by scientific methods. It would seem, therefore, that we have to consider how we may best pursue our knowledge of the structure and dynamics of personality, whether in the case of the individual or in the case of groups or even of 'humanity at large', with the proper awareness of the fact that the actual or theoretical sum-total of this knowledge is not exhaustive of the total understanding of what it is to be a human being (the mystery of personality).

But even supposing it is granted that the concept of the mystery of personality is allowable, indeed required, by the logic and facts of the case, it is quite clear that this mystery is pretty strictly interconnected with the dynamic structure which is exhaustively observable by the methods of science. This is clearly and acutely brought out by what I would call *limiting cases*. These are cases in which, in my terms, the mystery of the personality or the 'I' does seem to have been reduced to the sum total of the structure. The sort of things I have in mind here are, for example, cases of acute physical lack which prevent the development of personality and cases of intense psychopathic determinism which lock personality in a seemingly incurable distortion. It seems to me that cases of this nature do count for the idea that the mystery of personality should ultimately be reduced to scientific observables and count against taking the decision that it is a mystery which is the defining thing about being human. But while the fact that some human beings seem to have to be regarded as objects alone without the capacity to be free subjects is certainly a difficulty for believers in any sort of good and omnipotent deity, I do not think that these limiting cases decisively alter the logical and practical position for which I have been arguing. The fact that the mystery of the 'I' is so interrelated with the structure and dynamics of physical and psychological relations that, in some cases, the former is reduced to the latter does not alter the prior fact that even to know of and to be capable of describing these limiting cases requires observers within these limits who are free from the reduction which the limiting cases exemplify. Moreover, this problem is perhaps eased by the very fact that our increasing knowledge and understanding of the structural and dynamic features which produce these limiting cases is continually enhancing our capacity to push back these limits and to increase the number of cases in which human beings are given the opportunity to develop into free personalities. In all this very difficult field it is of the utmost importance to remember that knowledge of determinants facilitates freedom. Hence on all grounds we find reinforcements of the need for a full and open interplay between an awareness of the mystery of human personality and a scientific knowledge of the structure which is the basis of such personality. It is here, surely, that religion and the human sciences must enter, and must be able to enter, into dialogue if both are validly concerned with the humanity of man.

The following considerations, among others, would seem to support the view that the development of such a dialogue is urgently necessary. First, all who have any concern for the humanness of men and women must find one practical focus of that concern to be an urgent desire to do all that is possible in all possible cases to free as many human beings as possible for greater human freedom. Hence the possibilities already referred to which arise, in the advance of psychological and psychiatric understanding, for removing some of the defects and disorders which inhibit or limit the development of personality are of the utmost practical interest to all who have a religious or ethical concern for their fellows. The increase and dissemination of such liberating knowledge cannot but increase the opportunities for a practical, responsible caring for one's fellows which is both the aim and the heart of love. Secondly, and this point develops out of the first, knowledge of this sort is a great and therefore potentially dangerous responsibility. Knowledge which gives the possibility of liberating or enhancing the development of personality in any individual or group at the same time creates the possibility, indeed involves the responsibility, of shaping and directing the personality thus liberated, at any rate to some extent. Hence it is of supreme importance that the very difficult line be drawn between liberating a personality and manipulating it. This is a matter which demands the utmost human sensitivity, the most critical self-awareness and constant reassessment. No one must ever be allowed to settle down into the complacent belief that he or she is really quite certain precisely how any human being is to be directed in becoming himself or herself. The practical procedures of psychiatry and psychotherapy need to have their explicit, and still more their implicit, assumptions constantly challenged by the posing of questions from the ethical and religious point of view.

But, and this leads on to a third point, such challenging must not be done in any offensive or superior way. It must take the form of questions sincerely and humbly posed as between human disciplines and activities which are all equally concerned with the furthering of humanness. And while ethics and religion have questions to put to psychology and psychiatry, they have also questions which they need to have answered by these disciplines. These questions extend further than those about the removing of limitations to personality development already referred to. Even if we insist, as I believe we must, on the impossibility of reducing the mystery of the 'I' to the observables of its dynamics and structure, it is surely also clear, if I may put it this way, that the mystery cannot be moved towards its true goal against the grain of its structure. The sort of thing I have in mind here is probably illustrated as well as anywhere in the field of punishment. Here it becomes increasingly clear that the motives of punishers and the effects of punishment are by no means as simple or as productive of desired and desirable effects as much ethical and religious practice or exhortation supposes. The understanding of the 'grain of the structure' of personality which psychological research can supply here is clearly vital in assisting religion and morality to move practically towards their self-confessed aims for men and women. But (and once again the pendulum swings in the opposite direction) we may, fourthly, point out that all programming of experimentation in the sciences of human behaviour almost certainly involves both prior and continuing evaluation, whether explicit or implicit. Nowhere will this be more true than in investigations concerned with concepts like 'guilt', 'blame', and 'ideals'. Hence, once again, it is not only proper but necessary that religion and ethics should have their say in a dialogue. Finally, just to touch on perhaps the biggest and the most controversial issue of all, it is generally agreed that the continuing happiness of a human being is related to his or her capacity for adjustment to reality. And what a problem is concealed by that last word! Here dialogue is more than ever necessary, for while I would not suppose that we dare leave the definition of reality to any scientist to be settled in terms of science alone, I am quite clear that religious people who do not care to correlate their approach to life with the realities discovered and organized by the scientists are only escapists who are betraying their religious faith.

I would wish to close with a few comments arising out of my last point, but now made from a specifically Christian point of view, whereas the argument hitherto has been of a more generally philosophical nature.

As I see it, developments in the social and biological sciences are requiring Christians to take absolutely seriously a fundamental aspect of the doctrine of humankind which is assumed by and required by a proper understanding of the biblical and Christian doctrine of creation, but which has rarely been taken sufficiently seriously in the actual practice of the Christian tradition. This is the fundamental axiom of the unity of human beings. The structure of the human being has physical, mental and social aspects. The studies of biology, psychology and sociology overlap more and more, and so both demonstrate and assert that these various aspects coalesce into such a unity that the drawing of distinctions with a view, for instance, of deciding what is the 'cause' of what seems to become increasingly arbitrary. This is so much the case that it is always plausible for anyone to claim that the whole structure and significance of personality must be reduced to its physical, or at any rate determined, aspects. There is a homogeneity and continuity between the 'highest' and 'lowest' functionings of the human organism. Knowledge of human 'plumbing' (e.g. of the functioning of the kidneys) can be relevant to the liberation of the human spirit. And yet, as I have argued, the logic of knowing, the experience which I have of what it is to be 'I', and the impossibility of value-free judgment about human activities requires that, together with this concept of homogeneity, we hold the concept of the mystery of the 'I'.

Christian anthropology, when it is true to its biblical basis and refuses to be led astray by the strong tendencies to dualism in the Graeco-Roman tradition, understands the human being as a creature with a purely material beginning and basis who has a spiritual purpose and destiny. This is symbolized by the whole creation myth and, indeed, by the doctrine of creation as a whole, which is simply and precisely the assertion that the material universe is related to and capable of sustaining a spiritual purpose. Hence to refuse to take physical factors seriously or to resist the implications of valid scientific knowledge is to be false to the biblical and Christian understanding of the world and humankind as created. Moreover, to resist this valid and necessary approach to the created in its material givenness is to put oneself in a false position with regard to the development and fulfilment of the creation's spiritual potentialities (the possibilities of the mystery, the development of life with God, the entering into life of God). This false position arises both because to deny manifestly given facts is to put oneself out of court as a source of relevant attitudes towards the facts as a whole, and also because to insist on remaining in ignorance of the basic grain of the structure is to persist in remaining in a primitive position with regard to developing the spiritual possibilities of that structure.

While the doctrine of creation requires the Christian to take absolutely seriously the physical basis of the structure of human personality, other aspects of the Christian understanding of humanity fix attention upon the fact that human beings must be understood as on the one hand of the utmost importance as *individuals* and yet at the same time as essentially *social* beings.

Each individual in and as himself or herself is the object of the love (and therefore of the judgment) of God. That is to say, he or she is of concern to the ultimate reality and purpose of the whole of things. We have a definite and eternal status for ourselves, although we do not have this in ourselves but in our relation to God. But as this ultimate reality and purpose is love (defined in terms of holiness and righteousness, and not of sentimentality!), the destined perfection of particular individuals can only be worked towards and ultimately achieved in terms of perfected social relationships, where the relationship with God is reflected and expressed in relationships with fellow human beings and vice versa. (The pre-eminent symbol for this notion in Christian thinking is the body of Christ.) Hence, Christianity is bound by its own understanding to welcome, as validly based and as ultimately of the utmost practical and spiritual importance, empirical investigation into the physical-mental-social structure of human beings and human society. On the other hand, despite the hindrances which Christians in practice have not infrequently offered to the development of true humanness, Christianity must continue to resist all reductionism and to demand a continuing judgment of the presuppositions and sufficiency of the procedures and evaluations of the sciences concerned, in order that the way may be kept open for the fulfilment of the mystery of personality in the direction of the freedom of perfected relationships.

For Christianity believes that to be truly human is to be truly free, and that it is in this true freedom that true happiness lies. In the Christian understanding, which requires all the corrective aid which the human sciences can give for its valid practice, the way to this freedom and happiness is to be found through entering into the knowledge and experience that we are accepted by God as we are. Therefore we may have the strength to accept ourselves and our neighbours as we and they at present are on the basis of this acceptance by God and with the consequent hope of growth into the infinite possibilities of increasingly adequate relationships with increasingly adequate persons. That this is the way forward to freedom and happiness, however, both makes possible and demands adjustment to current realities in oneself and in one's personal and impersonal environment. Because of the homo-

65

geneity of the structure of human personality, this adjustment to current realities is the necessary means of being open to and of developing into the infinite possibilities of the reality of God which Christians believe transcends all lesser realities and in which alone, so they hold, the mystery of 'I' can ultimately and only be sustained and fulfilled. Hence the practice of the Christian understanding of and faith about human beings requires, by its own nature and understanding of things, to be brought down to earth and to be given the tools for effective application in particular cases by all the tested biological, psychological and sociological information that can be scientifically made available. But for the sake of the humanness of human beings, Christianity, despite its failures in practice, must continue to insist that the human sciences do not mar *their* practice by ignoring the fact which makes them possible, that is, that the human beings which they study as objects transcend them as personal subjects.

Notes

1. Barbara Wootton, *Social Science and Social Pathology*, Allen and Unwin 1959, p.252.
2. Cf. ibid., p.221.

2 · Failed Priests and Future Servants – On Renewing the Calling of Doctors, Clergy and Carers

(1988)

The theme to be pursued in this lecture is whether the notion of 'calling' (or of 'vocation') makes sense any more. The immediate provocation to pursue this question arises from the contemporary evidence in Britain that treatment of disease and illness, together with all forms of provision for health care, seem to be more and more considered primarily as commodities whose provision is to be treated as a business in the market, with consequent implications and pressures for the professions (could we say the 'callings'?) of doctors and nurses and others associated with medicine. But the wider pressure to pursue the issues comes for me from two directions. The first is the apparent disintegration or, as I would hope and argue, the temporary eclipse of the practical idea and ideal of a caring society. For me as a citizen, the disappearance of the idea of vocation is very worrying. The second is my faith and vision, from which I cannot escape, that as a matter of simple and ultimate reality it is true that at the heart of things is a God whose concern is for promoting and sharing holiness, justice, peace and love. There is therefore an active power and an enticing promise who works for a continued and continuing connection between our human neighbourliness and God's ultimate kingdom. As a Christian believer therefore who has hopes in, and hopes from, the worship of God, I find the loss of the idea of calling a great and threatening diminishment of human possibilities and

67

human enjoyment. Is it possible and feasible, therefore, to rediscover and re-alert in a great variety of forms and vocations a persistent and humanly central calling to care for the neighbour, to share with the neighbour and to promote a fabric and a dynamic of society which tends in that direction?

It seemed appropriate to pursue this theme in a memorial lecture sponsored by the Royal Society of Medicine, the Royal College of Physicians of London and the Medical Society of London because of the intimate connections which have existed in a number of ways between the practices and beliefs of religion and the practices and pursuits of medicine in relation to human health, wholeness and happiness and in relation to facing the great challenges of human unease, suffering and death. The calling to be a doctor and the calling to be a priest have often been very closely associated. Of course the meaning, value and authenticity of these connections are matters of ambiguity, dispute and exploration, and where we are called to be in the relations between religion and medicine and in understanding how they should interact, if at all, in our facing up to problems of society today is by no means clear. I would suggest, however, that one possible line of investigation is pointed to by my title: 'Failed Priests and Future Servants'.

By this title I mean to introduce the argument or hypothesis that once upon a time people used to turn to priests in their distress and uncertainty and then they turned to doctors in their unease and disease but, by and large, these 'priests' (whether their authority was religious or medical, and whether they conveyed their pieces of, or contributions to, salvation and ease from sources which were divine, pharmaceutical or psychological) are now generally held to have let people down – or, at least, to have very doubtful performance records. (I set aside any investigation of a perfectly proper and promising line of enquiry about how we might come to an understanding and agreement about human ease, well-faring and salvation being promoted by means which were a mix of the pharmaceutical, the psychological and the divine because this lecture is not about the respective contributions of religion and medicine to the understanding of the divine and human spiritual use of the material and earthly things. It is also not about possible, practical and help-promoting collaboration between doctors and

68

clergy. In this lecture I am concentrating on a wider social issue which seems to me to be particularly appropriate to attempt to formulate and commend for further discussion in a gathering where some medical societies have invited a representative of the churches to address them. If I succeed in giving any cogency to my formulation it will be obvious that the issue I am raising extends into society generally and is not confined to people who are by profession involved in either religion or medicine. One has, however, to start somewhere and I hope I shall persuade you that the religion/medicine interface is a particularly natural starting point for the issue to be considered.)

The issue, then, is this. Where shall we find the priests that we need? That is to say, who is now going to guard, cherish and promote essential human well-being *within* society? Who has a central and representative role in guarding, cherishing and promoting the *future* of society? And who has the vicarious task of reaching out *beyond* society so that – whether there is a God or not – no pseudo-divinities dominate society or the globe, reducing human beings to functions and cyphers within any one structure of society or closing our society to the options and imaginations of change? All these things are essential if our eco-system is to survive and our spiritual possibilities are to have a chance of expanding and exploring. That is to say, priestly care, vision and some sort of authority are vital if life is to continue – and, far more importantly, life is to be worth living. (Is not London bidding fair to be as great a threat to the quality of any worthwhile life as is a famine in the Sahel? Tacitus once said of the conquering Romans that 'they make a desert and they call it peace'. When will a latter-day Tacitus observe that 'they make a traffic jam and they call it prosperity'?)

Obviously one of the classes or areas from which such priestliness should come is the living body of artists and writers who could imaginatively, demandingly and provocatively portray the realities of our present, prophesy about the threats of our future and evoke first dreaming and then working for new positive possibilities and the revival of old and worthwhile ones which have temporarily been laid aside (like working together for welfare, or regulating together for some common good or public utility). But I continue to believe that there is some especially focussed opportunity for calling and appropriate priestliness associated with, or associatable with, medicine and its allies.

Doctors and nurses handle people in their flesh and blood, in their living and dying, in their suffering and recovering. This is, surely, essentially and inescapably *sacramental* – that is to say, to do with the sacredness and the hallowing of ordinary things and ordinary people. Nothing could be more holy and more worthy of respect, of service and of loving care than the flesh and blood, the spirit and the life of one of our fellow human beings.

If one still stands within one of the communities which continue to worship God in a tradition stemming from biblical theism, or if one still stands within hearing of the resonances of those traditions, then there is the suggestion that such human flesh and blood, when it is a living person, is somehow or other 'in the image of God' (i.e. of a potential holiness and worth whose mystery is infinite and glorious). If one stands within, or still within hearing of, a Christian tradition, this is further reinforced by the faith that the flesh and blood was actually taken up and lived out by him who, in his own human person, expressed the being of God. Now to many that is plain nonsense, and to believers in God in the Jewish and Islamic traditions it is either a mistaken exaggeration or a potentially dangerous blasphemy. But for the purposes of the exploration in this lecture it at least serves to underline the potential depths and the possible extent of the sacramentality of handling human flesh and blood, which is the routine stuff of medicine and its allied workers.

My purpose in thus bringing religious and even technically religious terms (like 'sacramental') into this discussion is first to ask quite simply, soberly and practically: 'How can doctors, nurses and their aides and assistants help having a priestly ministry and avoid being somewhere near the centre of the issue: where, today, shall we find the priests we need?' This is so because they, both as a routine and at many crisis points, handle the most holy thing known to us: our own living flesh and blood. (This ascription of holiness to us in our living fleshliness is not, incidentally, to be construed as implying that men and women are the only holy and worthwhile things in the universe, still less to imply that the universe in any way exists solely for our use or is centred on us. Indeed, our very existence is so dependent on and woven into the texture of the universe that our holiness is a sign of a much more far-reaching holiness of which we are – or can be – conscious and collaborative parts. That, however, is a further part of the story of our times and the challenge of our future which can scarcely be followed up in this lecture.) Clearly in the practice and application of a medical routine those involved must be concerned with the validity, accuracy and efficiency of that routine and not be thinking overmuch about holiness. But if some underlying and over-arching sense of holiness is entirely lost – or never thought of, or never even dreamt of – where shall we be? Clearly somewhere that falls far short of being a place appropriate to what it is to be human; and also in a place which is on a way leading to greater and greater inhumanities. For must it not simply and axiomatically be taken as true, or as an overriding obligation to live as if it were true or could be made to be true, that human beings in their flesh and blood, in their experience and suffering, and in their dying and living, are the nearest thing to the sacred that you and I know (and that you and I are?)?

Which brings me to my second reason for attempting this sort of language in this sort of lecture. I am struggling to be part of renewing value words which will resonate with wonder, reverence, mystery and the deepest and most breathtaking enjoyment. For we seem to have lost any commonly shared language of worship. I fear I am inclined to say, not least after nearly five years of episcopal visiting of churches, that we have not only lost any common language of worship but we seem very nearly to have lost any resonant language of worship anywhere at all. Whatever it is that people are striving after as 'worth it' or concentrating on as 'worth it', or spending time and effort on as 'worth it', 'it' does not seem to be as worthwhile as all that.

One of the most obvious examples of our poverty of value and of spirit can, perhaps, be pointed to by quoting a once-famous phrase from the marriage service in the Book of Common Prayer. Here at the giving of the ring the husband is asked to say: 'with this ring I thee wed, with my body I thee worship, and with all my worldly goods I thee endow'. Now this is obviously archaic language and there are, and have been, many things about the actual practices of matrimony, matrimonial law, social custom and so on in this country which have demanded many reforms; there is still much liberation and equality to strive for. But it seems to be verging on the tragic that we cannot easily find a place for a phrase like 'with my body I thee worship'. Is not flesh and blood holy enough for this? And are not men and women holy enough, sacred enough, worth enough to make it urgently and possibly desirable to strive to make marriage worship-full? We have, surely, immensely trivialized our sexuality and our selves.

A second area in which we may wonder whether we have lost our sense of wonder and allowed motivations of career, exploitation and consumption to drive out motivations of calling, maintenance and enjoyment is drawn attention to by the currently fashionable issue of the environment. Here the threatening facts of so many types of pollution, the piercing of the ozone layer, the effects on rain supply of rapid deforestation and so on are compelling serious consideration of what must be done and of what international collaboration and national regulation is necessary to do it. But the discussions so far are about whose sovereignty is affected by what, whether 'they' are more responsible for this or that pollution than us, who will bear the cost, whether we can afford the costs, and whether it is right to enforce the necessary regulations and costs. Now clearly there is no other way forward. In a complex society with complex issues, long-drawn out negotiations, bargaining and planning are quite inescapable, whatever the urgency of the issue. One is bound to worry whether the process of realization and negotiation can catch up with the urgency of the issues, but this is where the maximum use of pressure groups and the maximum mobilizing of evidence is so essential.

I draw attention to this area of human concern and human survival in this lecture, however, for one particular reason. It is to comment on the absence from most of the public discussion, government utterances and industrial comments of what I want to call any note of 'reverence and repentance'. Such a note has, indeed, usually been taken as typical of the more freakish side of the Green movement. But surely more than prudential adjustment is involved in facing up to and, indeed, getting the most out of the recognition of the importance of controlling our impact on the eco-system of the world. The crisis is an opportunity to re-discover – or discover for the first time – that both the world as a whole and each and every one of our local environments are worth enjoying and sustaining in themselves. Some sort of change is both demanded and on offer, from treating everything that is around as a possession to be used up to receiving every-thing that is around as a gift to be lived with – and to be lived from in so far as we and the environment can all go on living together.

I am aware as I say this that it sounds very like those exhorta-tions to piety and goodness which are not infrequent in sermons but mostly get us nowhere because they do not engage with either the realities with which people are dealing in their daily lives or the imaginations and wills of the listeners in such a way that they are likely to be moved to do anything about it. I persist in doing it, however, for the same reason as I offered the topic of 'Failed Priests and Future Servants' in the first place. That is my conviction that the evidence steadily accumulates that our West-ern-originated high-tech industrial civilization is reaching the limits both of its sustainability and its usefulness and that to face this and to find the next profitable and hopeful moves forward for our society and for humanity we have both to face the practical evidences of these limits and to renew our sense of a value, a worth – and even a worship – which will persistently give us (or enough of us) a sense and direction of calling which will motivate and move us through the breakdowns, the breakups and the breakthroughs which can be expected as we find we have to change our ways and our life-styles. If we are living at the limits of the sustainability and desirability of a particular social and economic system, then there is a practical premium on the values which can sustain us as the limits close in on us and which can direct us as we seek for new ways of organizing a life which the world can sustain and human beings can both endure and enjoy.

The reason for inflicting this search on a largely medical audience is, as I have already explained, that while you are as much part of the system as anyone else, your very professions (which were once called callings) oblige you to handle individual and personal human beings and these are the perennial focus of – and pointers to – any values we have or ought to have.

Before I attempt to round off this somewhat diffuse exploration through the thickets of our present human and social condition – an exploration which is I believe more than a random walk but which is, I fear, by no means yet a steadily directed pilgrimage and discovery – I propose to attempt to focus what I am trying to commend to your attention and the questions which I am trying to suggest we all need to pursue by means of what might just possibly be a modern parable.

A certain bishop visited a certain steel works. The steel works was a model of its kind, generally reckoned to be highly successful, indeed a leader in its field, and obviously run at high levels of efficiency by people of singular enthusiasm, skill and dedication. The blast furnaces, the casting machinery and the rolling mills were vast and they were housed in huge sheds where everything worked to amazing precision, both as to timing and as to mixing, controlling and shaping. The number of people around was quite small and there were areas where no one was visible. However, there was at least one person high up in some control box and all was connected to a central control room. One part of the shop had recently succeeded in a smooth record run which had produced, without stopping or hitch, no less than two and a half miles of steel. Hundreds of thousands of tons were produced continuously through the year and vast quantities of coal (turned into coke), dolomite and iron ore were variously dumped, mixed-up and used. Material came from Australia and products went to San Francisco. It was magnificent, awesome and commercially profitable and there could be nothing but respect, admiration and praise for all concerned. Yet for just one moment as he stood in the inhuman vastness produced and controlled by human ingenuity, enthusiasm and skill the bishop thought he heard a whisper from somewhere saying, in a rather puzzled and wistful voice, 'But is it *worth* it?'

The answer to that is: right now, of course, it is very much worth it. It is contributing to the balance of payments; it is a centre of employment, enthusiasm and high morale in an area that is trying to recover; and people need steel. But there is a longer-term question somewhere. First, even bigger, brighter and better developments may take place in, say, South Korea, and the site may soon be derelict again. Secondly, the use of such vast amounts of material bulldozed up out of the earth will reach its limits – after how much environmental destruction? Thirdly, do we really need more big steel-framed buildings in larger cities which will have to cope with more traffic, pollution and people pressure? And, above all, seeing that less and less people are needed to work these modern wonders, what shall we do with people? And who gets the major part and control of the wealth (or at least the money) produced?

I return, therefore, to my initial question about where we shall find the priests that we need: people to insist on human well-being in human society, people to keep on reminding everybody of the issues of the future of society, and people who can help human beings to reach out beyond to some engagement with and enjoyment of what is – or might sometimes be – really worth it. Clearly the priests that we have or have had are largely failures. The sort of priest I am addresses only a decreasing minority of people with any regularity and our sort of religion looks, at the moment and too often, very much like the particular interest of particular, rather turned-inward, spiritual clubs who take up a good deal of their energy quarrelling among themselves. Artists are very eclectic and are known only to the habitues. Doctors and nurses are out there on the ground, or in there wrestling in hospitals, but the whole thing seems rather shop-soiled and uncertain at the moment. Whatever the rights and wrongs of nursing pay, the misery over regrading does seem to indicate something that is sick in our society with regard to the supporting and cherishing of the caring professions. Are the purveyors of health care selling services – services which the public should either buy at their own choice and expense if they can afford it, or which should be provided by charity to those who cannot afford to buy into this market for these services? Or is there still an ideal to be striven for that health care is service to the community at large and to all citizens which should be substantially sustained as a public service and maintained by a sense of calling which is cherished, respected, regulated of course, but recognized by general acknowledgment and support?

Everything is, therefore, very confused and uncertain, and

commonly accepted priests who can generally be recognized as both relevant and pointing to generally recognized sources of value, worth and direction are clearly in short supply. Could we therefore start looking for a new and renewing alliance of those who retain some sense of calling or are looking for some sense of calling? This would be a calling which would have to start from something as general and as simple as commitment to persons as persons, a determination to find ways of keeping this as central as possible to one's activities and concerns, and a faith that the worth that is glimpsed in all this has a depth, a mystery and a promise which goes far beyond what we usually know, feel and achieve.

Doctors, nurses and their assistants ought to be a strategic resource in rallying and renewing this sense of calling because their handling of patients is basically and potentially so value-filled. Clearly, suffering people are centres and evokers of compassion – not simply because of their suffering, but because of their potential which is impeded or being destroyed by the suffering and because of their place in a network of relationships which make them objects and foci of worth to and for other people. Clearly the activity on the part of practitioners to care for people, to relieve suffering, to give lives a chance of reconstruction, to use the best possible skills and resources to bring about what would hitherto have been miracles, is directly value-filled and a series of encounters with a worth which ought to be spread out into the world at large. And clearly medicine is an area and activity where the immense human skills and imagination of science, technology, precision and calculation are put at the disposal of human beings in their need and this is of great value and worth in itself. This remains the case no matter what are the consequent complications about decisions to use scarce resources, decisions about where life begins, ends or is switched off, and so on. Clearly people in medicine need their 'priests' to help them to deal with their own problems about calling, life and worth, as well as having a great deal to offer to priestliness in society.

It will take much more than resources from those in medical callings or those in religious callings to revive vocation and a proper priestliness right across our society. A beginning could, however, I believe be made if we could persuade one another widely that the time is ripe not only for the rehabilitation of the caring professions but also for a readiness to speak up in the form of a caring *confession*. All of us, and I am still convinced that this is most of us, who retain some idea, feeling or longing that caring for one another and living together with one another in mutually supportive and sustainable ways must be what life is about, should take any opportunity which comes our way to say loudly and clearly that quality of life is more important than consumption of goods, that cherishing people and sustaining the earth is more important than growth, and that belonging and finding meaning and enjoyment together is more important than competition and growth in money making.

Of course, that will plunge us back into all the political, economic and social arguments that go on at the moment and will go on. But just because, for the time being, our priests have failed us, we must not be put off from helping one another to restore our common sense of calling and worth as human beings and thus providing our own appropriate priests by becoming servants of one another and of our common future.

3 · *What is There to Know?*

(1965)

In the first term of a new university it may not be inappropriate to discuss the question of knowledge. In any case, I wish to do so because I am clear that it is a question which is fundamental to the present debate about God, Christianity, and very much else, including, indeed, the purposes and pattern of a university.

The basic question is quite simply this: What do you know? You may believe so and so, you may feel such and such, you may even assert this and that and take up attitudes of one kind and another, but what do you *know*?

Behind this question is another one which is not always noticed, which is: What is it to know? Do you know when you have an existential intuition? Do you know when your carefully planned experiment comes off, and do you know when you are overcome with guilt or transfigured with joy? Just what is it to know?

Perhaps we might get further on this question by asking: What is there to know? The obvious answer to this for us today is data, that which is given to us to observe and to measure. In fact, what there is to know is the subject matter of science, all that which is amenable to scientific method. It is in the picture of the scientist scientifically finding out what there is to know that we have the current model for knowing, knowledge, and the one who knows. It may well be that what we have here is a myth. Certainly, there are probably as many problems in the philosophy of science as in the philosophy of religion, but I want to concentrate on our approach on somewhere near the common sense level, at the level of what we normally and largely unconsciously find 'thinkable'.

Here the model for 'the one who knows' is 'the scientist', seen as a detached, precise and clinically operating observer with a method and a body of information supporting him (or her), which is likewise clinical, detached and precise. What scientists know is data. When they have verified their data and the organization of these data, then they know. In fact, knowing is what they do and what there is to know is what there is for them to observe, measure and articulate into law-like theories.

Important features of this way of knowing are precision, prediction and generalization, or perhaps better, universifiability. Precision is aimed at through techniques of measurement, use of mathematics, the employment of formulae and graphs. Prediction is a feature of the whole approach, because you verify that your knowledge is indeed knowledge by experimenting on the pattern that, if you observe so and so and do such and such, then you get the following predictable result. Universifiability is demonstrated by the fact that any sane person who is above a certain IQ and who has had the necessary training can be got into the same position of knowing *vis-à-vis* the same knowledge as those who instruct him or her. In all this we have here, *prima facie*, a pretty clear idea of knowing and knowledge and a manifest set of known data – and above all, this sort of knowing works.

But it is at this point of 'working' that uneasiness may arise. Certainly the knowledge of the physicist works. It produces more and more efficient fusion and fission processes, but what might be called a by-product of this is the H-bomb. Certainly the knowledge of the physiologist, psychologist and pharmacologist works. It produces more and more efficient techniques for curing mental disorders. It also gives better and better opportunities for efficient brainwashing. This sort of ambiguity may legitimately direct us to another possible answer to the question 'What is there to know?' This answer would be not primarily data, but persons. But here it is not nearly so easy to proceed with the preservation of clarity and with a steady expectation of ensuring nearly universal consent.

Precision, prediction and universifiability are by no means assured. For knowing persons raises questions of depth and value. One is moved into the field of intuitions, attitudes and commitments, judgments which seem to take one into a dangerously subjective realm, and to land one with questions which look very like those of aesthetics and matters of taste.

Therefore, with regard to the question of 'What is there to know?' we seem to have two possible answers. On the one hand data, and on the other hand persons. Data is the area of 'hard' knowledge where you know where you are, and persons is the area of 'soft' knowledge where it is very difficult to know where you are. But is not the point of knowing precisely that you do know where you are? Further, if the questions of value and the like which seem to arise in connection with knowing persons are as important as they *feel*, then is it not all the more necessary – indeed all the more to be expected – that one should really know where one is or can be in these matters? Now, those who know where they are are the data-knowers, not the person-knowers. We are therefore obliged to wonder whether the person-knower is really knowing at all. Is not real knowledge of persons that type of knowledge which is reducible to hard data, to statistics and rule-like predictions, to sociological graphs and to rules for treatment for varying types of carefully classified cases? Clearly there is a very strong case for assuming such a conclusion. Personal *attitudes* will remain, but knowledge is to do with data and persons as objects of knowledge are reducible to data.

In addition to the general pressure to come to this conclusion provided by our whole implicit attitude to knowledge which I have symbolized in the mythical figure of 'the scientist', there are two considerations which encourage this conclusion, i.e. that what there is to know about persons is reducible to data-knowledge and, indeed, is not real knowledge until it is so reduced.

The first is that truly scientific developments over the whole range from organic chemistry, through biochemistry and the biological sciences to psychology and the social sciences, have immensely enhanced our knowledge of the processes involved in being a human being. They have vastly increased our capacity for individual and social human 'engineering' – using this term in a sense which is at least morally neutral, but which tends to be morally approving.

There seems to be a strong practical case for saying that if we really know (or perhaps, rather, when we really know), we shall be able to see *how* knowing persons is reducible to knowing data.

Secondly, in the absence of strong evidence to the contrary, the natural thing to believe about human beings would seem to be that they do, as a matter of sheer fact, emerge out of the material which is the material of data-knowledge and that they dissolve back into it. As a matter of fact persons are reducible to data: 'Dust thou art and unto dust thou shalt return.'

Hence there is great pressure to conclude that *in reality* person-knowledge, if it is to be real knowledge, must be reduced to data-knowledge, that data-knowledge is the only real knowledge and that indeed all that there is to know is, in the end, mere data. The implications of such a conclusion, whether it is come to explicitly or whether it is rather more implicitly underlying one's whole approach to knowledge and indeed to life in general, are pretty far-reaching. In effect, knowledge must be thought of as a temporary (although valid) arrangement of partial (though real) data, which arrangement is the temporary possession of a purely temporary existent or class of existents. That is to say that we exist, if I may be allowed to put it so, in a situation of absolute relativeness.

I believe that although this picture I have drawn is very roughly and crudely drawn, none the less it does in rough outline represent the underlying situation as it strikes most of us most of the time. Our implicit understanding of knowledge and reality, of what it is to know and of what there is to know, is back, for all its necessary modernity, to that of Heraclitus: *panta rei*, everything flows; we have absolute relativeness.

A variety of consequences, some of them logical, some of them practical, follow from this. Among them I may mention the following.

First, as far as reality goes, neither persons nor knowledge matter. The 'stuff' of the universe, the data of knowledge, what really is 'there' to be the object of 'real' knowledge is quite indifferent to knowing persons and to what they do or do not know. As objects of knowledge persons are reducible to data and, as a matter of fact, knowing persons are ultimately reduced to data. When that has fully happened there are no knowing persons and therefore no data. In this sense reality is absolutely indifferent to persons and knowledge.

But, of course, knowing persons do not share this indifference! So certain practical reactions follow, of which three strike me as particularly current and important.

First, there is the response of *commitment*: we must individually make some limited area of reality or sector of experience significant by our commitment to it. The commitment proceeds from us, and any value there is in it lies in the commitment as such. Hence the vogue for words like commitment, relevance and freedom, used absolutely.

Secondly, there is a response which is particularly prevalent in academic circles, though not confined to them. You sell yourself to one approach (naturally that discipline or science in which you yourself are, in however minor a way, a luminary), and you stick to this approach as providing *the* unifying force and the explanatory key.

It used to be physics; now it is much more likely to be the biological sciences, psychology or sociology.

This is really only a form of the general reductionism we have been discussing, but one can keep oneself sufficiently busy in a sufficiently significant way not to be troubled by this.

A third possible and common reaction is to be concerned not with any particular commitment nor with any particular pattern of co-ordinating and making sense of human life, but rather with immediate reactions to and experiences in the moment. *This* is typified in much current literature and drama and expressed in a great deal of current discussion of morals. The utmost possible significance or satisfaction or forgetfulness or what you will is to be obtained by seeking unrestrained self-expression in whatever circumstances happen to be obtaining or in whatever opportunities happen to be offered.

The effect of these and kindred common trends is to produce much fragmentation of knowledge, many tendencies to intellectual imperialism and a great deal of sheer moral anarchy.

With regard to fragmentation of knowledge, we can see it reflected in answering the question 'What is a university?' and by the doubts which this raises in our minds as to whether there can be such a thing nowadays, in the sense of something that is corporately concerned as a whole with knowledge as a whole. With regard to intellectual imperialism, I should perhaps not make specific charges without careful documentation, but I would suggest that we should easily find examples in the works of some sociologists, in such a field as that of criminology, and in the works of some psychologists, especially perhaps those concerned with the behaviourist approach. As to what I mean by moral anarchy, this is sufficiently indicated by the easily recognizable fact that the one rule which is universally applauded in the sphere of human activity is that every man and every woman should do that which is right in his or her own eyes.

I am arguing (or perhaps rather suggesting that it could be argued) that all this and much more like it follows from the assumed position with regard to knowledge. If one is looking for a knowledgeable approach to things, where can one start from? What assumed or authoritative basis is there for making sense of life and experience or for living one's life realistically? You simply have to start from wherever you happen to be.

If you have landed in an interesting discipline of experimentation and practice, medical, biological or sociological, then the thing to do is to stay busily in the middle of this. It is necessary to stay in the middle to avoid being confronted with questions which are too difficult, i.e. which cannot be answered in terms of your own discipline. But you can give yourself a methodological reason for what might be called this intellectual cowardice by saying that questions which cannot be answered within your own disciplines are not real questions.

Or, if you have more courage (belligerence?), you can proceed from your discipline to claim that this discipline *is* the arbiter of what is knowledge, of what is real, of what is truly human.

Or if you have no taste for the routine of intellectual disciplines and no stomach for intellectual empire building, then you must clearly start always from your immediate reactions. There *is* no such thing as a *knowledgeable* approach – there is just *my* approach.

And who can suggest a better one? Clearly there are *others*; but on what grounds are they *better*, at any rate, for me?

Now this is where, as I understand it, Jesus Christ comes in. A Christian is someone who is convinced that there is an answer to the question about the possibility of a knowledgeable approach to reality – and that this answer is both a given answer and a potentially universifiable one.

Where can you start from? From Jesus Christ – or rather from Jesus of Nazareth who was recognized to be the Christ. We have here a matter-of-fact starting-point, the datum of a particular person who establishes himself as the basis for a particular understanding of the reality of the world, of the reality of human life in the world and of the possibilities involved in human life by virtue of that reality.

The manner in which Jesus of Nazareth establishes himself as the starting point for knowing and evaluating the reality of the world may be briefly indicated as follows:

1. We have a given historical reality, the Jewish people, with their tradition of an experienced living God known to them through the ups and downs (mostly downs) of their intensely varied history.

So confident were the Jews that the living God whom they had experienced was really God and really living that there had grown up among them a messianic hope. The forms of this hope varied, and it was naturally expressed in imagery drawn from their history and given shape by their particular experiences. A clear example of this is the form of the messianic expectation which took its shape from King David. He had indeed been the Lord's anointed in that he was a king, and particularly favoured – particularly associated with the establishment of Israel. Now the Jews were sure that these experiences of God in the past could be vindicated in the future.

God was the Lord, living, powerful *and* consistent in his purposes and attitudes of holiness, righteousness and love. Therefore they expected him to send another decisive anointed king, a son of David, one analogous to David in God's purposes for his people, but greater than David in that he would bring about the decisive settlement of the affairs of the world in accordance with the reality, the character and purpose of the Lord God.

Confidence in God, assurance of his reality, was thus expressed in this and other forms of messianic expectation. With regard to the establishment of Jesus of Nazareth as the decisive starting point for understanding the reality of the world this tradition, assurance and hope of the Jews forms the *context of recognition*.

2. In this tradition there appears the historical individual Jesus of Nazareth, about whom one thing is as clear as any historical fact can be, i.e. it is not provable beyond all shadow of doubt, but it is 'morally certain'. Jesus of Nazareth believed that he had a mission connected with the kingdom of God. That is to say, he had a calling from God which placed him somehow very close to the centre of the purpose of God relied upon by the Jews in their messianic expectations. Real experience of the real God had shown that he was indeed 'there' and had purposes of holiness, righteousness and love. As he really was God and was a God of this nature, he was bound sooner or later to establish his kingdom, i.e. show that he was God, by aligning everything in accordance with his character, his goodness. Jesus of Nazareth was convinced that he was called to play a part in God's establishing of his kingdom.

'The kingdom of heaven is at hand.' In obedience to this calling, he taught, collected disciples, and followed a policy which brought him, not without shrinking, but eventually by deliberate choice, to the death of the cross.

Jesus of Nazareth was undoubtedly a man for God, a man with a mission concerning the kingdom of God, and in pursuit of this mission he died.

3. His disciples had accepted the fact that Jesus had this mission in connection with the kingdom of God; they had placed him in that context of recognition which at least associated him in a central and decisive way with the fulfilment of the messianic hope of the Jews. But they were brought to a full stop by his death.

The reason that any claims are made about the significance of Jesus of Nazareth for an evaluation of reality is that this full stop was removed. For some reason the disciples became unshakably convinced that death had not put a stop to Jesus and his mission. They were convinced that, as a plain matter of fact, as matter-of-fact as the fact of Jesus' calling and Jesus' death, Jesus was once again alive. The incidents and experiences which partly produced

85

and partly reflected this conviction are to some extent mirrored in what we call the narratives of the resurrection. The *central* conviction was – and is – that Jesus' calling and Jesus' mission for which he had died were vindicated. Jesus had died in obedience to God, and God had shown that this was obedience by 'raising him up' – establishing him as not dead, not brought to a full stop, but alive and fulfilling his mission.

This matter of the resurrection and its credibility must be returned to. But first let me complete the historical sketch of the way in which Jesus of Nazareth was established as the criterion of knowledge and reality.

Jesus had identified himself with the general context of the messianic expectation of the Jews and followed a calling connected with the coming of the kingdom of God. In following this calling he had been crucified. His disciples were convinced that God had raised him up. Therefore,

4. Jesus of Nazareth was to be recognized as the Christ. Jesus' mission concerning the kingdom of God had been vindicated by God's raising him up.

Hence, the way Jesus had carried out his mission, with its pattern of teaching and service leading through his death to resurrection, was to be received as the pattern by which God established his kingdom.

Once Jesus has been recognized as God's Christ, the particular details of his approach to life and his encounter with death have now to be understood as the essential clues to the way in which God arrives at his purpose – indeed as the essential clues to the shape of that purpose.

To recognize Jesus as the Christ requires the *context of recognition* of Judaism and the Old Testament tradition of faith in God. But once Jesus is recognized as the Christ, he himself becomes the *context of definition*. This is expressed by the well-known and extremely primitive Christian confession, 'Jesus Christ is Lord'. That is to say that the dominating and decisive factor concerning the understanding of God and the world is Jesus Christ. This is where we return to the question of the credibility of the resurrection.

It is not a question which can be settled by the immediate

application of criteria relating to what we or anyone else habitually find thinkable. For the whole point about the proclaiming of the resurrection of Christ is that it is a claim to *define what is thinkable*.

We have, as a matter of history, the tradition of the Jews with their faith in a living God distilled from their corporate experience and producing their messianic hopes. We have also as a matter of history Jesus of Nazareth, who believed himself to be called to serve the kingdom of this same God in whom the Jews believed and whom they thought they knew. And we have as a matter of history, Jesus of Nazareth crucified in the course of this mission and his disciples convinced that the God whom Jesus served and for whom Jesus had died had raised him up.

We are therefore faced with deciding whether what *we* think to be reality swamps Jesus Christ or whether Jesus Christ defines reality. It is the old question of whether or not Jesus Christ is Lord, and it is a perfectly proper question. It is not a mythological or superstitious or religious one. It is simply a question about reality, directly related to the questions 'What do you know?' and 'What is there to know?' For if Jesus Christ is Lord, then – starting from him – we may be clear that God is, that he is properly thought of as the Father with purposes consistent with his holiness, righteousness and love, and that God the Father can be relied upon as being involved in this world with a view to bringing his purposes out of it.

This being so, we return to our discussion of questions of knowledge in a very different frame of mind. It becomes clear that we have to tackle the whole matter of the relation between data-knowledge and person-knowledge with the conviction that persons are not, in the end, to be reduced to data.

Rather, data exist to serve and to develop persons. With *that* assurance we must then be extremely careful to see that every possible piece of data-knowledge is treated with the respect it deserves and made scientifically available for the service of personal purposes.

We must be clear that commitment is indeed demanded if we are to experience worthwhileness and serve worthwhileness, but it is not undefined commitment or mere commitment. It is commitment to all that promotes personal purposes and the development of persons as defined by the holiness, righteousness and love of God. As to attempts to articulate particular disciplines into arbiters of what reality is and what is truly human by way either of limitation or of possibility – we must be clear that no system and no theory can be of more than limited use. For the context of the possibilities of human beings is the infinite and transcendent reality of God, and anything which shuts human beings into any theory or framework whatever is an enemy of their eventual humanness. It is, incidentally, important to notice that this applies to theology too. The only theology which does justice to the reality defined by Jesus Christ is a broken theology in which all theories are systematically and constantly being broken up so that they may be open to further possibilities.

And finally, in relation to self-expression, in relation to the question of everyone doing what is right in his or her own eyes, in relation to the question of the freedom to be oneself, it becomes clear in the light of Jesus Christ as the definition of reality that all self-expression is deceitful and destructive unless and until it is aligned on the expression of oneself in love. And love is to be defined not by the impulses of the moment or the instinctive reactions of an animal make-up but as love which harnesses these impulses and directs these instincts in the direction of that total self-giving for the sake of the personalities of others which was demonstrated by and vindicated in Jesus Christ.

I fear that I have attempted the impossible and my over-reaching has brought its own destruction. But perhaps I could sum up the thesis I have attempted to set out like this:

The answer we give to the question whether Jesus Christ is Lord makes literally all the difference in the world and to the world.

Neither Christians nor non-Christians have begun to assess Jesus of Nazareth until they have begun to face up to this.

4 · *Christians and Other Faiths*

(1968)

On the question of how a Christian stands with regard to other faiths, I find that I have to begin at the beginning and ask myself how indeed one does approach this question, which has obvious theoretical implications and increasingly practical ones. We are forced to begin at the beginning because one of the really splendid things about the present situation is that we cannot escape realizing that we are in one world. Consequently it cannot be the case that one can have one's understanding of the world, one's understanding of one's self, one's understanding of one's commitment dictated by something which is of purely local interest. Even if our faith in Jesus Christ has been a purely local matter, conditioned, say, by our cultural life in a part of Western 'Christendom', it cannot now remain so. We are faced with a question very similar to that which arose for the first Christians. In a Judaic culture, localized for them in Palestine, they discovered that Jesus was the Christ. But was it the case that Jesus was of significance for the whole Hellenistic world? Was he truly Jesus Christ the Lord in that wider world? So now we are faced with the question whether Jesus Christ the Lord is indeed in any real sense the Lord of the whole earth. And this is being forced upon us in a way which really, in one sense, threatens us, so that we are therefore forced to real exploration.

How, then, does one start on this exploration? First of all, we must be quite clear that traditionally Christians are entirely exclusive and absolute about Jesus Christ. This is well symbolized in that symbol of the Christian faith, that sort of distilled summary of Christian experience, the creed, where Jesus is referred to as being 'of one substance with the Father', one of those apparent pieces of mumbo-jumbo which either points to a mystery, or to nothing. And if one investigates what it points to, one is faced with the fact that this is a claim that in Christian faith and understanding, in the understanding of the world provoked by Jesus, in the understanding of man focussed on Jesus, Jesus is known to be of the very stuff of God. What we are up against in Jesus is God. Jesus is God's decisive act, his decisive act to bring in his kingdom. That is to say that Jesus is what God does to establish everything in the world in accordance with his own reality. God is the living and the active God, he is the God who cares. This he has made clear to his people and through his people, and because he cares, he will act consistently with his caring. And God does act, such is the Christian understanding: he sends his Christ, his Christ is Jesus. So Jesus turns out to be God's decisive act.

Or another way of putting it is: Jesus is what it is all about. We may symbolize this by speaking of him as the word of the creator; that is to say, he is the embodiment of the pattern and of the purpose of the universe, and therefore he is what it will all come to. We may symbolize *that* by saying that he will come again to judge both the quick and the dead. What did it all start from? That pattern in God's mind which is seen to be embodied in Jesus. What will it come to? That pattern which is seen to be embodied in Jesus. Jesus is the stuff of God, a God who is love. He embodies what God had in mind at the beginning; he is God's word, he is the shape of things which will dominate in the end. Jesus is Lord. That which is embodied in him is that which will overrule all things in the end. And therefore in Jesus Christ we have what we may say is God in person: God in person showing us what human beings are, showing us what human beings will be, showing us what human beings can be, and further showing us that the ultimate reality of the universe, that which is at work in, through and beyond the stuff of the universe, is at work to bring us to this fulfilment, to this shape, to these opportunities, to the enjoyment of the possibilities which are embodied here. And therefore for Christians, here in

Jesus Christ, as far as our understanding of ourselves goes, is the clue to reality. This is what I have a chance of becoming, this is what we all have a chance of becoming, and what is more, this is related to the very stuff of the universe. Here is the transcendent in the midst.

Further, Christians hold, this is not a theory. There are all sorts of theories which can be based on Christianity, there are all sorts of deductions which can supposedly be drawn from it, but the centre of the matter is a happening, is a man, is a piece of history. And consequently Christianity is not a view of life, not a theory about the universe, but a basis on which one will have to work out all sorts of views on life. It is a point of vantage from which one will have to wrestle with all sorts of theories about the universe. Basically it is a reaction to the happening who was Jesus, and it is believed to be continued because it is a reaction to the reality who is Jesus. It is a reaction to this happening who is Jesus, and all that led up to him, and all that follows from him. The scope of this is believed to be total, because all that led up to him goes back to the creative purpose of God and all that follows from him goes on to the fulfilment and very end of all things. The first point, then, is that Christians are committed to absolutely exclusive claims about Jesus Christ. Reality demands this. This is how things are, and therefore this is what always must be taken into account.

One proceeds from the first point to the second. Which is this. It follows, therefore, that anything in other faiths which contradicts Jesus Christ, anything in other faiths which goes against the reality of Jesus Christ, in the Christian view is wrong. And it is wrong, not as a matter of intellect but as a matter of reality and practice, so that it must be combatted. It must be stood up against for the sake of reality, for the sake of the truth of things, for the sake of the development of man. Now to state it this way is such a scandal, such an occasion of stumbling, that we need to pay very careful attention to the true implications and the true applications of this. My second point is that anything in other faiths which contradicts or goes against Jesus on the Christian view is wrong and must be opposed. I do not agree for one minute that everybody is going the same way, or believes the same thing – I believe that is wholly contrary to the situation and the logic of the various faiths. This may mean that Christianity is false. But one must at least be quite clear about the situation. And in order simply to make the point I shall have to give a series of examples of the sort of things which might be involved. Pressure of time forces me to put these examples extremely crudely, and therefore very probably offensively, but I see no way of avoiding this.

For example, then, it seems to me that the Christian is clear that Jews are wrong. They have failed to identify the essential clue to the way their God and ours worked for and among human beings. And one of the results of this is Zionism, Zionism with its consequent misery which arises from the assertion of the wrong sort of power, in the wrong sort of situation. Zionism has even become a religious failure, because nowadays, in Israel, many Israelis are prepared to assert that they are Israelis and not Jews. This point must be picked up later, because it must be noted that one of the causes of Zionism is clearly Christian persecution. But our concern at the moment is that it seems quite clear that the Christian must understand that Jews have made a fatally wrong mistake here.

Similarly, if Islam is wedded to a rigoristic view of law, if Islam is wedded to a performance of religious duties which is based on this understanding of the law, if Islam is wedded to the view that understanding of God is wholly transcendent so that one is ruled by a predetermined fate, if all this is true, then Islam is wrong. The reality of God is not so.

Human beings are not to be fulfilled in the way in which the religious duties of Islam point. There is too much rigidity here to cope with the demands and opportunities of science and to respond to the true situation of humankind in the world under God.

Again, if the teaching of the Buddha is basically atheistic, that is to say, makes it clear that there is no God of concern, if the teaching of the Buddha interprets men and women as needing to escape from rather than to fulfil their personality, if the teaching of the Buddha holds the world to be a fantasy and an illusion rather than the very material of human life and development, then the Buddha is wrong. This is a false reaction, which goes against the grain of reality, which wrongly faces the possibilities of science and the challenges (and, admittedly, the threats) to humankind. Again, if Hinduism dissolves the significance of individuality through a reincarnational circle, if Hinduism finds room to worship both the evil and the good aspects of what is manifested to us, then this is presenting a gross distortion of the truth, a distortion from which humanity in Christ's name needs to be rescued. I must stress that I am simply using these things as examples of the sort of thing that seems to me would follow from point one, if my brief examples from other faiths did not turn out, on closer investigation, to be simply misrepresentation.

I believe that there is bound to be the possibility, and indeed at times the necessity, of a sharp clash between the following of Jesus Christ and all these religions and faiths, and others which I have not time to mention (and I particularly leave aside what might be called faiths – Marxism for example, and secular humanism – because I think we do not want to concentrate on the faiths of the West). As I observed at the beginning of this second point, where anything contradicts and goes against Jesus Christ, it must be opposed as wrong.

To proceed, therefore, to the third point. Here we come up against a strong caveat, a very big '*but*'! My subject is Christianity and other faiths, and so far I have not spoken about Christianity at all. I have spoken about Jesus Christ. It is very important to be clear that Jesus Christ is not to be equated with Christianity, that is to say, with the particular cultural and institutional embodiments which have so far historically arisen as attempts to respond to him. This is quite vital. Jesus Christ is not to be equated with Christianity, where 'Christianity' means the particular cultural and institutional embodiment which has so far historically arisen as a consequence of attempts to respond to him. There is a good deal of Jesus Christ in these things, but they are not equivalent to him. The whole of him is certainly not in them, and quite a lot of them do not coincide with him at all. This may perhaps be made clear by discussing the distinction between Jesus Christ and Christianity as affecting the relationship between Christianity and other faiths.

First, nothing I have said so far denies the necessity of dialogue with other faiths. In my view, quite the contrary. For what, *in fact*, contradicts the reality of Jesus Christ? On the Christian belief, Jesus

Christ is the embodiment in history of the ultimate reality God, who is before all things, and who brings all things, and all men and women, to fulfilment. Jesus Christ is the man in the middle who is related to the beginning and the end of things. It is impossible, therefore, on the Christian understanding of Jesus Christ, for any present understanding to have the monopoly of the reality of Jesus Christ, or indeed for it to embrace the totality of the reality of Jesus Christ. No matter how carefully any present understanding is built on past understandings, there must be more to discover, to embrace the totality of that reality. It therefore seems quite clear that we need the help of all men and women to learn about and to expose the reality of Jesus Christ. And those who have tried to respond to reality, those who have tried to explore the human condition (along the ways it may be of Islam, of the Buddha, or of many others), such individuals, we may suppose (and it seems to me that there is much evidence to force us to that supposition if we were reluctant about it), have achieved experiences and insights into the possibilities of the world which are clues to the true reality of God. Loyalty to Jesus Christ requires us to be exposed to these insights; requires us to enter into fearless and faithful dialogue so that we can together learn more of what is truly involved in seeking to become really human, more of what is truly involved in the human condition and the possibilities of the human condition in the world, in the world in which Christ lived, died and rose again. I believe that Jesus Christ does, at some essential points, if I may state it shortly, put all religions in the wrong. But Christians must be clear about two things here. First, that he puts much in Christianity in the wrong. And secondly, that he does not therefore condemn all other religions. Although he puts much in the wrong he is to be related to, and he is to be understood, through many insights of many individuals in many other religions, which sometimes reflect his reality better than so-called Christian understandings. Therefore the absolute claim of Jesus Christ does not forbid, but rather requires, dialogue with other faiths. That is the first point. And it moves on to a second point.

It is not really Christianity and other faiths with which we ought to be concerned. Rather, our concern is men and women exploring and responding to reality as Christians, Buddhists, Jews, Muslims, Hindus. For surely Jesus Christ makes it clear that not doctrine but human beings are basic to the religious quest, are basic to human living. And, consequently, these absolute claims of Jesus Christ are to be received primarily and centrally and decisively in terms of obedience, in terms of response to the possibilities revealed, in terms of practice in our relations to our fellows and to the world at large, in terms of commitment to explore further and more deeply the sort of things that we are put on to. The questions which therefore have to be faced are of the type: 'How are we to love our neighbours?', 'Who am I?', 'Who are you?', 'What are the possibilities involved in our existence and in the context in which we operate?', 'What resources are available for being human in the world as we now have to face it?' And, 'How can we go more deeply into what is involved in what we allege to be our faith? How can we respond so as to get a better understanding both in heart and in mind to those things which our faith, which our religious understanding, begin to give us glimpses of?' Dialogue between religions which is consistent with the reality of Jesus Christ must take on this form of concern for practical truth, for commitment to response, for going deeper into the reality which we believe we have so far seen. That makes it clear that there must be no question in any dialogue between faiths of any kind of intellectual or cultural imperialism. It is a conversation between human beings about human living.

This brings me to the third point, which is really my summing-up point in the question of the nature of the dialogue of faiths. We must learn (and it is going to take some learning, to get clarity into our system and systems) that what has been called Christendom is not Jesus Christ. The ways of thinking of the West must not be identified with Christianity, still less with Jesus Christ. One of the ways in which it will appear whether or not Jesus is Lord, in the broader sense which our present situation now demands, is whether the faith of Jesus Christ and the life in Jesus Christ remains clearly a living option when it is quite clear that the West no longer dominates. If Jesus is the Christ, if Jesus Christ is Lord in the way in which I believe he has been proclaimed to be at the heart of Christianity, then there must be a disentanglement of Christianity from the cultural taken-for-granteds, if I may so put it, of the West. For the sake of Jesus Christ and in the name of Jesus Christ, cultural equivalence between a form of Christianity and Western society has finally to be broken down. One of the splendid things is that Western atheism is finally assisting in this. But it is surprising how far Western atheists are often Christianly cultural imperialists at heart. They may be atheists, but they are still Christian ones, in the sense in which I am using the adjective here, related to cultural realities and embodiments which at some stage in the history of things were a proper response to, and a means of, passing on the Christian gospel, but have now become fossilized misidentifications. And that is why, basically and fundamentally, dialogue with other faiths, which are many of them rooted in other cultures, is quite essential. For if Jesus Christ is what I believe him to be, then he will challenge all. He will challenge all Western particularism and imperialism which has got bound up with a thing called Christian society. He will challenge all oriental pessimism, which goes deep into the culture which is bound up with Hinduism and Buddhism. He will challenge all Jewish particularism and so on, just as he will bring out the insights in Buddhism, Hinduism, Judaism and Christianity which we all need to be human. Certainly in many ways Christianity, as a religion, is in the same position as other religions. It has much to be set free from, it has many authentic insights, it has much to repent for.

Here I must return to my perhaps brutal remarks about Jews earlier, because it is surely clear that whatever sin has been committed in connection with the state of Israel is really the sin of the world. That is to say that any misunderstanding of national power or of national possibilities which has misled Jews in connection with the founding and developing of Israel is the sin of Christendom. For why must they turn to having a national home of their own? Because they have never been safe anywhere else? But that is not their sin. Speaking as Christians, it is our sin. Therefore it is quite clear that in the dialogue with other faiths there must be no self-righteousness. One of the things that becomes more and more striking is the way in which the Bible so often turns out to be true. On reflection it is so justly clear that 'all our righteousnesses are as filthy rags' (Isa. 64.6), and they do not clothe us for the future. So there must be no self-righteousness; rather there must be solidarity in penitence, in search for forgiveness and for grace, solidarity in mutual service for reconciliation. For loyalty to the reality of Jesus Christ, which is also loyalty to the reality of humanity, does not require imperialism, but service. The very shape of Jesus Christ, his living and his dying, his cross and his rising again, surely makes this clear, though it is the sort of clarity to which we do not readily respond. Jesus Christ, therefore, is not to be equated with Christianity. This is the third point, and there is just a brief postscript.

The above is the merest outline of a possible approach to the question of Christianity and other faiths. In closing, I wish to draw attention to the perspective within which all our thinking about Christianity and other faiths should be done. The authentic Christian viewpoint is, surely, given by the phrase in Ephesians about it being the good pleasure of God to 'sum up all things in Jesus Christ' (Eph. 1.10). Christians are called to see, and to help others to see, that Jesus Christ is the shape of the future – God's future and man's future. And this future has to be entered into. It has to be entered into by Christians and by Christianity as well as by other faiths and non-faiths.

This future, because it is the future of the God of the whole earth who is also the father of Jesus Christ, must hold the fullness of the primal vision of Africa, the fullness of the wisdom of China, the fullness of the riches of orientals who have lived through cultures so different, and in many ways so much older, and so much richer than our own. It will embrace also the fullness of the purified riches of Western Christendom and of the churches of the East. We are offered a vision. The vision is that of the one true man in Christ Jesus who would have in him as a community some of the things that one is enabled to glimpse through one's African friends, some of the depth that one is offered through one's Indian friends, some of the struggles of the Chinese, some of the simplicity of the Aboriginals, some of the multiplicity of resources of the Europeans, something of the Amer-Indians, and much more. We need one another in our human and in our religious explorations, and in our living. We need one another, just as we cannot be fulfilled without one another. Loyalty to the absolute and exclusive claims of Jesus Christ, a loyalty which is shaped by the reality of Jesus Christ, requires absolute openness to all the human faiths, and complete readiness to serve in a common exploration and in a common living.

5 · The Reality of God and the Future of the Human Project

(1988)

It is commonplace that we are now one world, and as such a limited world and a threatened world. It is commonplace, but the knowledge, the reflection and the inescapable assumption of being one world are given no common place in practice in the actual pursuit of politics or industry and commerce or religion. Everyone gets on with doing their own thing, in religion as much as anything else. Further, in religion they do this with a singular additional paradoxical twist because in most current and developed religions the alleged object or subject of the religious quest, practice and claim is, in some sense or other, claimed to be the one true God of the whole earth and, indeed, of the whole universe – or the fundamental spiritual principle and insight thereof.

I have therefore taken the honour and opportunity of your invitation to me to give a lecture under the auspices of the Chair of Judaeo-Christian studies here in Tulane University to offer the absurdly wide and possibly pretentious title of 'The Reality of God and the Future of the Human Project'. I have done this in order to focus on one particular question which is now posed with especial sharpness and urgency to all Jews, Christians and Muslims. It is a question which has been around at least potentially since the time of Moses and has emerged in various actual and historical forms with the split between Jews and Christians and then with the life of Muhammad and the rise of Islam. However, as I shall try to show, it is singularly pressing now and can be argued to be a question which is urgent not only for the adherents of Judaism, Christianity and Islam but also for the whole human race. The question is: 'Can a faith in the one true God which arises out of the tradition of monotheism arrived at in the Jewish scriptures and/or in those scriptures with the Christian scriptures added to them be anything but exclusivist and therefore necessarily in conflict with any other tradition of monotheism so arising?'

To put the issue more bluntly and directly: is it the inevitable logic of Christian faith that Christians must expect, in the name and power of God, to convert all Jews and Muslims? Is it in the inevitable logic of Jewish belief in God that Jews must survive *exclusively* as Jews until God mops up the Christians, the Muslims and the rest? Is it the inevitable logic of commitment to Allah through the Quranic revelation and obedience dictated to Muhammad that Muslims must be ready for *Jihad* until Islam is victorious against all enemies and unbelievers? And does this inevitability arise because of the very sense of calling by, encounter with and revelation from the one true God which constitutes the defining characteristic of the various faiths?

If so, the outlook for the world and the human project within it is poor, for the world needs some powerful and yet open form of human unity. Also, the outlook for convinced and convincing belief in one true God who truly exists and truly is God is also poor. For his professed and devoted adherents contradict one another and, in actual history, sometimes destroy one another. At this juncture in our human affairs, therefore, does God have any relevance to the human future and, if so, what is that relevance? You could, of course, turn that question inside out and ask: 'Given the history of the monotheistic faiths derived from the influence of the biblical tradition and given the pressures that are now upon us in our one and limited world, would we not be best advised to work and to do the equivalent of pray for the establishment of a realistic and open atheism?' The question in that case would then be: 'And where shall we find ourselves if we succeed in doing that?'

Clearly, the reality of the situation with regard to the existence, nature and activity of God is exceedingly unclear, not least because of the behaviour, claims and history of his self-styled faithful, whatever their tradition or form of commitment – or rather I should say, whatever our tradition of faith and commitment. For I am myself a convinced and committed Christian who has a strong and increasing sense of calling to the job I am at present doing and to the representative role I am at present occupying.

Those of us who are caught up into the practice and pursuit of a faith are therefore confronted with the actual practical effects of people holding and expressing what they believe and claim to be 'true faith'. This is a very ambiguous term. Presumably it takes its legitimizing role among religious people from its implication or claim that the faith being held, celebrated, expressed and lived out is an authentic and appropriate response to the way things are and will be and, in particular, to the being, nature and purposes of God in his relation to the totality of things. In practice, however, to show 'true faith' seems to be a matter of commitment, of readiness to make demands and readiness to take urgent action of some sort, independently of the truth, coherence or appropriateness of the religious story, theory or system which forms the background to, and the basis of, the religious tradition within which the 'true faith' is being expressed. Religious renewal or revival seem most frequently to be associated with heightened fervour, increased demands and readiness for distinctive and decisive actions, and strengthened dogmatism or even fundamentalism. All this gives increased coherence to the group involved but accentuates their exclusion of, and difference from, their neighbours in general or from their co-religionists in particular.

Of course, if religious faith kindles no fervour and makes no difference then there would seem to be little point or power in it. At the heart of any tradition of religious faith is the conviction or hope of what might be called a saving impact. God is the saving resource and promise. Being saved involves being saved from something and being saved for something, and that must involve producing a difference and making a change. Hence, in principle, we should expect people who are caught up in a 'true faith' to be different, to be changed and then to be agents of change. But when we see how religious devotees and enthusiasts are in fact different, and what they are changed into and what changes they seek to bring about, we may well be inclined to come to the conclusion that if religious faith reflects something to do with salvation or with being on the way to salvation, then whatever the salvation saves from the cure is worse than the disease. Indeed, there are good grounds, both in history and in contemporary experience, for regarding religion as part of the pathological and diseased side of human life.

Yet we who are caught up by and into a religious faith or, as we might dare to say and feel compelled to say, caught up by and into God, cannot accept this diagnosis. How then shall we face this challenge? I suggest we might find a way forward by pursuing the question 'Does God have favourites?' If we find that our tradition of faith and our practice of faith obliges us to answer this question 'Yes, God does seem to have favourites', then it would be necessary to press the question 'And what does God have favourites for?' This question, I believe, would bring us back to my topic, namely: 'The Reality of God and the Future of the Human Project'.

I will therefore pursue my Christian self-questioning thus. The issue of the reality of God may, on reflection, and on reflection on the behaviour and claims of the various faithful worshippers of God, appear to be very uncertain and possibly unhelpful or even harmful. The reality and problem of our *one world*, however, is both clearer and more plainly and evidently universal in scope than any religious tradition or self-styled true faith.

We all know now that we live on a small and limited planet which we are both overcrowding and overusing. The picture of the earth relayed back to us from space provides the unforgettable concrete image and symbol of this. The world is now one financial system, and the system is highly volatile and fragile. It is overburdened with debt. In your rich country you have the double deficit of both budget and trade. Among poor countries of the Third World there are those which are getting more into debt in order to finance the interest on the debt they already have. Moreover the system is now linked up on computers in such a way that it is programmed to respond to its own responses. This is clearly a structure made for turbulence and collapse.

Moreover what keeps it going is growth in both production and consumption. But this sort of growth has already produced ecological erosion of very threatening extent. We can now all know clearly that we are steadily using up the non-renewable resources and even the very substance of our strictly limited and heavily populated planet, at rates which are debatable with regard to each particular resource but in an overall way which is undeniable. Forests are being felled without restraint, despite repeated warnings, and this not only destroys the possibility of a steady growth of further trees but encourages atmospheric changes which lead to deserts, which are also encouraged by the erosion of soil when the trees have gone. The ozone layer which helps make sunlight healthy and life-giving when it reaches us is under threat from our pollution and is as good as pierced already in some recognizable spots. The disappearance of living species proceeds apace and the encouraging and multiplying efforts of conservation are, nonetheless, at the same time further symptoms of how we are turning the world into a desert. Even our love for the countryside threatens it, as the recreational invasion of our wilderness makes increasingly clear. So our method of keeping our finances and economics going threatens the very ability of our world to sustain itself and support us.

It also threatens any sort of viable and sustainable community in the world. This is vividly illustrated for me by what I have come to call the barbed-wire divide. This symbol came into my head and has stayed hauntingly with me ever since I happened to see a short sequence on television news which showed Archbishop Runcie visiting Soweto with Archbishop Tutu. One sequence was filmed, so to speak, from outside in, and running across the centre of the screen was a barbed-wire entanglement: to mark, as it seemed to me, the need to defend white prosperity from black poverty. About the same time I also saw a brief moment of a film about the United States border with Mexico and the need for ceaseless vigilance and pretty violent measures to protect that border against the steady flow of poor people from the South pressing into your dreamt-of Eldorado – and incidentally running, some of them, drugs and committing other illegalities. The film implied that nothing would actually keep the tide back. Again I had the sense of the have-nots pressing desperately, although as yet not with any organized violence, into the land of the haves – where they would, of course, find many fellow have-nots. For the 'barbed-wire divide' is also symbolic of increasing divisions, certainly in both the United States and in Britain and, I believe, in other Western countries. There is a clear, and worsening, division between those who are in the system and can increasingly purchase its benefits, and those who are out of the system who can never get the chance of either forming a market or joining in a market. Will it be necessary to hive them all off into ghettos, surrounded by barbed wire and patrolled, I suppose, by increasing numbers of police and soldiers? So we have 'Third Worlds' (as you might say) both within us and all around us.

On top of this it seems almost too much to add to the apocalyptic pressures by bringing in the threats of nuclear war and the uncertainties of nuclear power, but they must clearly never be forgotten. It may be that these threats are at last being seriously reduced, and it may be that nuclear power can be handled in sufficiently positive and safe ways, but to do either of these things successfully requires great trust, great patience and great collaboration. Shall we get this in a world made so unstable and uncertain by global financial instability, by ecological erosion and by the barbed-wire divide? The pressures upon us all in our one world to recognize our unity within the limits of our globe and to work together to discover new ways of organizing our lives and systems so that Third World countries can develop an economic independence within which they can work out their own sustainable ways of flourishing and so that First and Second World countries can settle down to ways of life which are saved from excessive consumption and thus sustainable, renewable and shareable, are clear, urgent and ought to be irresistible.

But the human race as organized into states and nations seems to have no more practical sense of what is required of it, and offered to it by way of global survival and sustainable and shareable life, than religious people who are organized into various traditions, communities and churches seem to have of the practical and spiritual implications of the transcendent oneness and mystery of God, if he exists and is indeed God. Might it be possible, therefore, that the ignored threats to our one world and the apparently self-contradictory practices of our 'true' faiths could interact in a positive, creative and future-enhancing way?

From within one of the faiths which have grown out of the biblical tradition this is not only a proper, but also a necessary, question to ask. First, it is of the very essence of a religious faith to be a 'true faith'. As Kenneth Cragg puts it in a magnificently stimulating book: 'It is not in the nature of religion to consent to be indifferent about its own claims.'[1] To be caught up in faith in God within any religious tradition, community, story and framework is to be caught up in offers of finality, demands of totality, experiences of utter but gracious dependence and promises of over-riding and invincible joy and love. There can be no half-measures about the offers, demands and implications of God. There can be, and there of course is, a sad and nearly infinite variety of half-measures, no measures and inappropriate measures by which the would-be or self-styled 'faithful' respond, or fail to respond, to God. Everybody sins, and religious people sin religiously. This very obvious and deeply troubling fact can be transposed, from the perspective and problematic of this particular enquiry, into the statement that all we faithful sin faithlessly: both as individuals and in our various groupings, communities and institutions. The question is whether this practical and long-continued contradiction decisively destroys any claims to reality or truth conveyed in, or pointed to by, the 'true religion' of whatever tradition. Or are the human contradictions of the faithful religious in the practice of their religion one pointed, distressing and diagnostic case of that whole range of human contradictions of, and fighting against, the true, the good, the hopeful, the beautiful and the loving which make us, despite our being so great a resource for love, discovery and progress, yet our own worse enemies? This is a fundamental religious and human question, a question about the ultimate nature of things and about what resources there are available to us for life and human living in, through and beyond the universe. It is, in fact, the question of God to which all 'true faiths' are a joyously positive and potentially all-demanding and all-embracing response. Therefore, faithful believers (and every appropriate institution within the tradition of each one's faith) are bound to respond to the contradictions of their faith from within the resources of their faith, however far outside the presently understood boundaries of that faith such a contradiction and challenge may take them or us when properly, hopefully and graciously faced.

So a contradiction to a true faith – or to the very idea of there validly being such a thing as a true faith – has to be faced, by believers, from within the resources and truth of their faith. After all, for a believer, a faithful and faith-seeking believer, there is nowhere else to turn – and nowhere else to which he or she should, would or could turn. But there is a further point from within the particular tradition and faith in which I myself am caught up and to which I remain wholeheartedly committed by renewed and reflective choice, as well as, I believe, by divine graciousness, which is an infinitely greater and more necessary cause than my own weak will and limited intellect. This arises from what I will call the prophetic insight and tendency to discern if not the hand of God, then the touch and the invitation of God, in certain convergences of events and experiences which call our humanity, our faith, our religion and our world in question. Judgment to condemnation is opportunity for renewal. Death is the way to life. The undermining of the old and the oppressive is a breaking out into newness and liberation: if faith can discern, obedience can respond and grace be received. Thus the coming together of a recognition of the failure of the witness of our respective 'true faiths' to the glory, reality, demands and offers of the one true God with a recognition of the urgent threats to our one world would seem a wholly appropriate pressure, provocation and promise for prophetic discernment and for religious repentance, obedience and renewal. Might this not be the proper and urgent way forward for the sake of him who is the worship of all our faiths and in the service of the world which is his and of all humanity who are his?

As I wrote this, and as I say this under the specific auspices of a Chair of Judaeo-Christian Studies, I could not and cannot but be aware of a very particular calling in question which we who are Jews and we who are Christians must be confronting as we seek for effective renewal of faith, prophecy and action at this very moment in this very world. This is the reality of Auschwitz and the reality of anti-semitism to which Christianity has made such a major contribution. I have no time here to refer to the great amount of most important and challenging material which has been produced and is being produced around this theme, save to say that any following up of the agenda which is being pointed to in my lecture will require the most serious study and digestion of this material. For now, I make just one point, as follows.

Both Jews and Christians exercised the sort of prophetic discernment I am talking about on the fall of Jerusalem in AD 70. This is well put in an early chapter of *Approaches to Auschwitz: The Legacy of the Holocaust*:

> Both the Jews and the Christians were nurtured spiritually by scripture to believe that God is the sovereign lord of history who controls the destiny of all nations. Both believed that God had entered into a covenant with the chosen people and that Israel's ruin was explained by both as due to a failure to keep the covenant and God's inevitable response. Where they differed was in the view they each held of the sin by which Israel had been chastized . . . the Christians believed that Jerusalem fell because the Jews had rejected Jesus Christ. For the rabbis Jerusalem fell because the nation failed to obey God's commandments as they were interpreted by the Pharisees.[2]

This way of proceeding has been devastatingly called in question by what has actually happened. On the Jewish side it would seem just possible to contain the fall of Jerusalem within an understanding of the just judgment and the loving providence of God. Can this possibly be done with the Holocaust? On the Christian side it might have been just possible to contain a Christian understanding of God's temporary judgment on the Jews within a loving and obedient response to a merciful and gracious God if we had taken with absolute and consistent seriousness Paul's sure and certain vision in Romans 11 that, in God's mysterious purposes, Jews and Christians would ultimately share in one salvation and fulfilment and that this was necessarily so because of the very nature and being of God. But in practice the 'prophetic' discernment turned into charges of deicide and justification for pogroms, persecutions and persistent practices which make such sickening reading that few of us Christians even know about them, let alone begin to face up to them. The stain and damage would seem well nigh ineradicable, even without its climax in contributing to making the Holocaust possible. Maybe we should say that in their use of prophetic discernment the Jews were sadly mistaken and the Christians more wickedly perverse, but in either case, or putting them both together, is not the whole procedure permanently discredited?

Perhaps then we should cede the living remnants of the biblical tradition of monotheism to the Muslims. At least they are clear that God must be visibly victorious. This is why Jesus is second to Muhammad as a prophet and servant of God. Muhammad succeeded, while Jesus failed. Because Jesus was indeed a prophet and servant of God, God did not allow death to seal Jesus' failure; rather, he was 'raptured' away from that death – but the future of God's purposes lies with the followers of the Prophet. Yet here again all did not go as the first followers and readers of the Quran might have expected. In today's threatened and precarious world it is by no means clear that as the followers of the Prophet pursue their understanding of the purposes and calling of God for the world they will avoid precipitating the blowing up of that world.

Perhaps, therefore, we should cede the whole pursuit of spirituality in our crises of humanity and the world to the Hindus and the Buddists. They have always known that the whole trouble is Illusion – about the reality of the world, about our separate selves, and about all the things that trouble and threaten us. If we are convinced that we must not do this because, despite all contradictions, threats and uncertainties, we are held by the richness of the world, the richness of persons, and the glories glimpsed through and beyond our traditions so that we must persist in praise, in suffering and in hope, then we must still clearly face the atheists. What can our struggling on be but self-deception, and what can our bursts of praise be but whistling in the dark? The whole notion of making ultimate sense, of there being a human project which comes from anywhere, or is going anywhere, and the whole notion of going beyond all projects and ultimate sense to Nirvana are all alike pieces of semantic nonsense. Why continue to play with them when we require all our spiritual, mental and physical capacities to preserve what world we have for what hope we can enjoy?

But supposing our faith, our spirituality, our community, our tradition, our worship and our experience, both individual and corporate, of what we must call God and which will not let us go, all insist that we should carry on: as Jews, as Christians, as Muslims and as Jews, Christians, Muslims of our particular and perculiarly devout sort? Shall we then fall back on sectarianism? God *has* his favourites, and they are to be found above all among ourselves, strengthened, defined, upheld and continued by what has been given us in our tradition, history and faith and in its special and particular peculiarity. It is this very favouritism which allows us to exist and to continue to exist. God calls us to be what we are and God sustains us by keeping us what we are. So, of course, out of the very essence and practice of our existence and calling we must exclude other claimants to favouritism, either as against us or at least as not of us. How else can we survive – or be true to that which has given us existence and enables us to survive? Whatever may be the practical and functional truth in this claim and experience of favouritism in relation to calling, encounter, inspiration and revelation, surely it must all be placed in a much wider context than where we 'religiously', in all our traditions, hold and confine it, thereby distorting it. We must be challenged again and again – and more and more deeply, painfully and sharply about such 'favouritism'. Maybe it does reflect a real, vital and important way of God's working and of God's making himself known. But what is it actually for?

Can there be any creative and realistic way forward, given the needs of the world, given the flawed histories of all of us, given the reality of God which we all claim and acknowledge – and, as some sort of immediate prophetic and demanding symbol to us, given what is going on in and around Jerusalem and Israel at this very moment? For Jews and Christians Israel/Palestine is the holy land. Jerusalem is our holy city and in it are the holy places of Islam. Yet, at the moment Jerusalem and some of the parts of Palestine/Israel are, perhaps, one of the most unhappy and unhallowing areas in the world. I cannot even use geographical and state nomenclature without causing offence to some community or other and seeming to take sides in a bitter battle. Here hitherto oppressed Jews are behaving as oppressors or looking like oppressors, however much they are forced into this, or claim to be forced into this. Here Muslim sensibilities are being outraged, Palestinians are being killed and Arab inhabitants are being displaced and forced into being, or remaining, refugees. Here local Christians are among the Arabs and foreign resident Christians seem to be utterly confused and still, if reports are to be believed, to be keeping up their internal quarrels about who shall maintain which part of the Church of the Holy Sepulchre. Moreover the quarrels in, and the quarrels about, this holy land threaten to embroil great powers and the whole world and certainly have repercussions among the great powers and throughout the whole world. Are we to interpret this in a sectarian way as threatening (and as some fanatics believe, promising) Armageddon and the end of the world? Or are we to see it as an urgent divine demand and an immediate human plea to all of us, Jews, Christians and Muslims, to work out a speedy, practical and common repentance which is worthy of our deepest religious convictions and our truest knowledge of God? All the more so as our Mediterranean 'holy land' is *not* the holy land of the East? Is our distracted and distorted 'holiness' to be their and our destruction? Is that what he whom we all believe to be the God of the whole universe wants his quarreling and divided 'favourites' to do for him and offer to him? Is this the meaning of our calling, our devotion, our worship and our hope?

I judged that I had to raise these questions and draw attention to this agenda because the threat to our one world is so urgent, because the need for a reconciling unity of faith, resource and vision is so apparent, and because I cannot myself escape glimpses of the glory of God, however much he seems to be hidden, contradicted and ignored in practice, and however ingloriously and even shamefully I and my fellow co-religionists seem to respond to him. As you would expect from what I have said previously I can respond to the judgment, the crisis and the opportunity we are all in only from within the resources of my own tradition.

A final brief word, therefore, formulating the dilemma and the opportunity as I see it around the name and tradition of Jesus, whose name and what it should be taken for is, of course, a matter of contention among us. I offer the formulation first and principally as a challenge to us Christians to take up the dialogue, the disturbing investigations and, then, the practical actions which the questioning agenda I have been outlining above would suggest. I also hope it might be able to be offered, in the second place, to those Jews and Muslims who also find themselves to be called in question in order to see whether they could propose a corresponding and resonant formula from within their own faiths, traditions and devotion so that, however tentatively, some of us might begin to take steps together in moving beyond our mutual exclusiveness and our mutual conflicts to a more appropriate worship of our one God and more creative service of our one threatened human race.

The formulation is this: from a Christian point of view the present tragedy of the world and the present call to biblical monotheists might thus be described. The Jews have failed to recognize Jesus as the Messiah, the Christians have failed to obey Jesus as the Messiah, and the Muslims have chosen a warrior prophet instead. What that means is that we have all got God, to a large extent, wrong and so we are in the gravest possible danger of being one of the destructive threats to the future of the human race rather than God's offer of service to and for the whole human race. God is not principally to be conceived of as a mighty warrior or a dominating potentate to be served with exclusiveness and on one set of demanding and enforceable terms which are known to us alone (whichever of his 'favourites' we are). God is himself (or himself and herself and itself – for God is anonymous and beyond all naming) the presence, service and power who is love, persuasion, endurance, suffering and joy which cannot and will not be fulfilled until all is fully shareable and fully shared. Hence, eventually, our dialogue, repentance and moving into appropriate actions must not be only among Jews, Christians and Muslims but also reaching out to, and in human pursuit with, Hindus and Buddists, atheists and agnostics – and all searching, suffering and hoping human beings. But 'judgment must begin at the house of God' (I Peter 4.17), so the first challenge is to us who believe we are, somehow or other, God's chosen favourites, chosen particularly for God's universal purposes. That is to say that the first challenge concerning the reality of God and the future of the human project is to us Jews, Christians and Muslims.

So I must leave you, as is so often the case with sermons, and I fear sometimes the case with lectures, at the precise point at which we all ought to begin. Perhaps, because we all agree in confessing that God is merciful and gracious, we should help one another to cast ourselves on that grace and mercy so that we can find out what God wants to make of us, instead of continuing to insist on what we want to make of God.

Notes

1. Kenneth Cragg, *The Christ and the Faiths. Theology in Cross-Reference*, SPCK 1988, p.319.
2. Richard L. Rubenstein and John K. Roth, *Approaches to Auschwitz. The Legacy of the Holocaust*, John Knox Press and SCM Press 1987, p.41.

6 · God, Truth and Morality: Some Shared Questions for Jews and Christians in a Bewildered World

(1988)

I am both honoured and touched to be invited to give this twentieth lecture in the series supplied alternately by Jews and Christians in memory of the honourable Lily H. Montague, her broad social interests and her pioneering work in the field of Jewish/Christian relationships. The invitation touches me because, as I seek to be some sort of faithful responder to, and servant of, God in the way of Jesus, and as in this calling and search of mine I try to face up to the realities, confusions and opportunities of our common and threatened world, it seems to me more and more urgently necessary that Jews and Christians should find practical and purposive ways of getting together around the issue of God.

I realize that this is a very difficult and sensitive matter and will, in the first place, only be taken up persistently by a few, who will almost certainly be viewed with a good deal of unease and suspicion by their fellow faithful in our respective faiths. One of the mysteries about people who believe in the universal God is that they tend to show signs of panic if there is any question of universalism! The difficulties and sensitivities lie in two principal areas which need to be taken with the utmost seriousness. The first lies in the area of being worshipful and the second lies in the area of being practical. As to the first, God, primarily and basically, is not the object of questions and discussion; he is the subject of worship, reverence and obedience. As to the second, we all know – or think we have good reason for knowing – that 'getting together around the issue of God' tends to produce something called 'theology' which a few Christians have perennially dabbled in to the grave discomfiture and division of their churches and to the deep disapproval of 'men and women in the pew' who need worship, guidance and comfort for their daily lives. Jews, as I understand it, have always been clear that theologizing simply is not part of the mainstream of worship, practices and habits of Judaism. The difficulty here, therefore, is to see with any clarity or urgency what is the practical point with regard to worship, religion and faith in 'getting together around the issue of God'.

The whole matter is made even more questionable as a worthwhile or needed undertaking by what seems to be the prevailing climate of opinion in Britain – and in Western culture generally? – which is against exploratory thinking in personal, social, political and religious matters. I believe it was Dorothy Sayers who said that 'most Englishmen would die rather than think – and many of them do'. It may therefore be that this attitude is peculiarly endemic in Britain. We are, however, now confronted with phenomena like the emergence of 'liberal' as a pejorative and dismissive adjective in the United States Presidential elections and with the link-ups that are being worked out between 'Moral Majority' groups from the United States and groups in Britain who hold that what society urgently needs is the authoritative statement and social enforcement of certain basic and simple moral requirements, largely in the field of individual responsibility, sexual mores and familial requirements (to do, that is to say, with the normative nuclear family). It is claimed that more thinking is the last thing we want or need. What is required is clarity and simplicity about moral injunctions – linked, if possible, to clarity and simplicity of religious faith-statements. We need a clearly presented authority which can indicate, exact and, perhaps, enforce a clear and simple individual personal and social code and pattern of behaviour which will restore our social cohesion and contain our social disorder. Exploratory thinking, it is claimed or assumed, is counter-productive to this.

The issue is therefore frequently presented as one of the restoration of *authority* whereby we may receive personal guidance, social cohesion and religious comfort. But is this not precisely where Jews and Christians need to get together around the issue of God? For what is the connection between alleged authority, required obedience, offered comfort and *truth*? This question arises because of claims to revelation from God, claims to encounter with God and claims of call from God. Both Jews and Christians are involved in claims about these matters and both Jews and Christians would have to agree that their claims, however they may overlap in one way and disagree or conflict in another, involve claims about the same God. This is pragmatically and historically so because of the way Christians first emerged as a Jewish sect and it is witnessed to by the Christians retaining, as their 'Old Testament', what are substantially the Jewish scriptures. But the claim about being in touch with one and the same God is also theoretically, theologically and absolutely inevitable because both Jews and Christians are decisively clear that there is only one true God who is the subject of the revelation, the encounter and the call with which both Jews and Christians in their varying ways have to do.

This necessary claim to be engaged with the one, true and only God cannot be abated or turned aside by the evident, paradoxical and disturbing fact that Jews and Christians are in serious opposition to one another about at least some of the content of God's revelation, of the nature of the encounter with God and of the scope and aim of the call from God. The undeniable and obvious common fact, faith and claim continues to be – and must continue to be – that we have to do with the one and true living and glorious God who is the only God that is, the maker and sustainer of all things – and who is God indeed.

Now if God is indeed God, then we who believe we are within hearing of a revelation of God and from God, we who count ourselves belonging to those who have a tradition and experience of encountering God and we who are convinced that we belong to a people who are called to serve, know and receive from God in some special way, cannot avoid facing the practical implications of all this for ontology, eschatology and value.

I am rather proud of this sentence as an example of how to start on a high note and then to end with a complete anticlimax – not a coming down to earth but just a dull terminological thump! However, I decided to put the issue and the search I am to place before you in this somewhat pompous and technical way because I am sure we need to hold it at a certain distance and look at it in a rather detached, tentative and provisional way before we can take some steps to come together to pursue it. Technical terms and the use of language which is more likely to be off-putting than emotionally and spiritually engaging (and therefore, also, emotionally and spiritually disturbing) are probably the best way into public exposure of matters which must, in the end, be of the most profound and engaging concern for us all.

The point is that if God is God, then he must make a difference to what there is ('ontology'), to what there will or might be ('eschatology'), and to the worth that is or could be available in what there is and what there will or might be ('value'). If God has offered any revelation, any encounters and any call which truthfully affect our knowing of him, our responding to him and our service of him, then the knowledge, experience and hope built up out of this must have a bearing upon proper types and uses of authority, appropriate obedience as persons, citizens and worshippers, and the offers of a comfort which is realistic, humanizing and liberating rather than the seduction of a comfort which is hiding from reality, self-indulgent and confining. God, if he is God, has a bearing on everything and everyone and it is a bearing to do with truth, value and hope.

Here, I think, it is necessary to refer to something which I take to be at the heart of both Jewish and Christian worship of, belief in, and understanding of God. This is that however God may involve himself in the affairs of the world and however those who are called to know God have to pick up this knowledge through the events, the facts and persons of the world, nonetheless God is independently God and the bearing he has on truth, value and hope for persons and within the world stems ultimately and decisively from his being God and not from his relevance to or, even, use in, the world. That is to say that at the spiritual heart of our respective faiths is the worshipful conviction that all of God's immanence in and involvement with the world, including his calling of us, stems from and is directed by his transcendent being, nature and glory.

Of course, the rightfulness of this conviction, indeed whether it can have any meaning, is itself a matter of perennial dispute. This is a dispute which is always on with the company of atheists outside and over and against our faiths. But, nowadays, it is also a dispute with people whom we are bound, I would think, in some sense to recognize as 'co-religionists' within our faiths or at least as some sort of fellow-travellers who form part of the whole of our faith as it exists communally, historically and socially. If I understand the situation rightly, Judaism has for a long time, at least within the modern era, reckoned with a spectrum of belonging and practice which stretches from a self-defining orthodoxy through the usual spectrum of variations to that of a liberalism about which there is always debate as to how strongly it belongs or fails to belong. The spectrum then continues – and this is the point at the moment – to include Jews who religiously are agnostic or atheistic but who are consciously and active Jews nonetheless. (Dr Raphael Loewe has coined the term 'Judaicity' to refer to this latter end of the spectrum; but I am afraid I do not know how widely recognized this diagnosis and coinage of his is.)

Christians have always really had an analogous and parallel problem, although the reasons for people being concerned partially to conform and fitfully to belong to the Christian community, even if they find themselves more and more out of sympathy with the religious core of that community, has never been so clearly and simply related to peoplehood and ethnicity as with Judaism – for obvious reasons. Now, the case for continuing as a member of the Christian community, including doing so for religious and worshipful reasons, although an atheistic position has been reached, is being put and is gaining a good deal of sympathetic hearing in some quarters.

All of this points to a case for some Jews and Christians getting together around the issue of God for at least three reasons, which converge on my final and principle reason for posing the questions and hinting at the programme which I am sketching in this lecture. I will come to the final and principal reason after I have indicated the three preliminary reasons implied in, or derived from, the immediately preceding discussion.

The first reason is that demands for simple authoritative statements which will put moral and religious authority behind clear and obvious efforts to restore social cohesion and restrain social disorder look as if they assume that God is there to be used for our social and personal purposes. The existence and formulation of the demands are evidence of the bewilderment, uncertainty, distress and disorder in our society. As such they must be taken with full seriousness. But a religious response to this in the name of God needs very careful consideration and expression. On what tradition of truths about, and experience of, God are these responses to be based? Is God regularly, deeply and reliably known as the one who props up and maintains a given social, political and religious order simply because it is a given and existing social, political and religious order? Does God regularly and consistently meet people's needs as they express, feel and define them or does God meet individuals, groups and social orders with an offer which is a mixture of compassion and judgment, forgiveness and holiness, offers and demands, which requires – and enables – vision, change and newness? This may take us out of our current needs and current selves in the direction of becoming the best we have it in ourselves to be, a best which being in the image of God transforms our current needs and wants into longings, desires and visions which promote an ever-widening neighbourliness, an ever-deepening responsibility of stewardship and an ever-growing sense of community. There is a grave danger that we may succumb to an invitation to use authoritarian religious statements and simplistic moralizing statements to protect people from questions which need to be faced and to preserve the power of those who benefit most from the current *status quo*.

Surely we who remain by conviction, devotion, longing and worship theistic and religious Jews and Christians would do well to consider together how we face these common challenges of the modern world which seem to want, not least in Britain, to make use of an idea (surely a *false* idea?) of 'God' to prop up and promote what those who demand this use of religion see as requirements of society, survival and power at this particular juncture in history, culture and politics. It would seem to be a denial of our shared understanding of the living God to suppose that religion is for the use of society – whatever may be the relevance and bearing of religion and the worship of the true God on the uses, disorders and longings of men and women in society.

This sort of question makes the second reason all the more urgent. This is the danger that we are, in our respective ways, searchings and responses, 'losing our grip on God', if I may so put it. Would it not be true to say of both the Jewish and the Christian understandings of God – which, surely, are deeply shared and come from the same roots and sources – that in this tradition and worship *God is nothing if he is not himself*. God is so mysterious and so glorious that we doubtless do well to have among our 'co-religionists' and fellow pilgrims men and women whose overt and explicated atheism challenges the pettinesses, trivialities and simply honest mistakes about God which religious people are given to producing. Further, the human response to God clearly must go well beyond the bounds of our respective traditions, faiths and personal experiences. But just because of this, it must surely be the case that to be faithful to the way we have so far come as Jews and Christians and to the God who we believe has encountered us and kept us going in this way, we must be deeply concerned to keep a grip on the godness of God – or, to put it more appropriately, that we should respond to God's grip over and offer to us. I see, therefore, a strong and urgent spiritual case for some of us to find ways of getting together on the issue of God at just this juncture in the history of men and women in the culture and confusion of both our particular society and the world. What do we mean by God? And what must God mean to us? God might have much of great and moving significance to show us through one another.

Which leads me into my third preliminary reason *en route* for my principal reason. Surely we who seek devoutly, honestly and obediently to worship the one true God, whether we do so as Jews or as Christians, are faced right now with what I can describe only as hellish problems on the ground of this world about the next stages in our respective faiths? Let me just mention one which seems to me to face Christians and one which seems to me to face Jews – and both of which face us all as human beings together, let alone as those who seek to worship the one true God. I just mention both of them; for they are so delicate, explosive and divisive that I see the only way of pursuing them would be to subsume them under my final point to which I will come in a moment.

The question facing Christians is this. How do we serve the saving purposes of the one true God of the whole world for the whole world when our insistence on the absolute metaphysical and theological uniqueness of Jesus Christ necessarily puts us at odds with, and divides us from, all other men and women of religious devotion, human commitment and divine pilgrimage – let alone keeping us occupied with something the interpretation of which divides Christians among themselves again and again? And yet – this uniqueness of Jesus Christ is both our distinctive point of identity and our deeply held, profoundly felt, point of salvation.

The question facing Jews is this. How do you serve the saving purposes of the one true God of the whole world when your building up of the state of Israel has brought you to a perpetual conflict with the Arabs (a conflict which seems insoluble unless one side totally destroys the other – which is, presumably, as unthinkable as it is unachievable), a regular daily pattern of happenings which are morally and humanly debilitating and distressing and a continuing instability which super- (and other) power meddling could escalate into a third world war. And yet, the existence and uniqueness of Israel is both your distinctive point of identity and your deeply held and profoundly needed point of salvation or, at the very least, point of protection.

Can God save us from the contradictions of God to which our respective followings of God seem to have brought us? Presumably, if he is God, he can and he is willing to do so.

So under pressures such as these some Jews and some Christians ought to get together around the issue of God. The more so as we are all, Jews and Christians, with all the rest of contemporary humanity, faced with, and part of, what surely must be described as a fragile and threatened human project. Which brings me to my final point and question. Do people who know themselves to be called to worship and serve the one true God have, whatever their differences and conflicts, what might be called a common theistic responsibility to society at large, to the world at large and to their neighbours – a common responsibility which stems from their commitment to the God who calls them/us to his knowledge and worship?

The context which provides the pressures for asking this question is well known and includes such things as the nuclear threats to us all; the ecological erosion of our shared and limited world (created, as we biblical theists claim, by God); the idolatry of market, of consumption, of individual choice and wealth which splits up everything into separated individuals who are then defenceless before aggregations of market power or political manipulation or the poverty which afflicts left-outs. There is also the consequent threat to democracy and freedom because people are determined to pursue what they identify as feasible and desirable in totally fragmented and turned-in ways which reject any notion of the all-embracing transcendent and any vision of an all-encompassing community.

What then of God's covenant with humanity? Does God have one – as well as his covenant with us about which Christians and Jews are both convinced and yet often at loggerheads? Presumably God does have this covenant with humanity and any covenant he makes with 'chosen' people must be somehow or other relatable to his purposes for all. I am not sure where to go from here. But I am pretty clear that here is where we are and that it has the features to which I have sketchily drawn attention in this lecture. It seems urgently necessary that some Jews and Christians should therefore get together to consider how the issue of God is in all this, affects all this and offers a way forward through all this.

I would suspect that it would be no good to get together to consider the issue of God 'head on', so to speak. Who could do such a thing? ('My face you cannot see.') But it might be a way forward if some Jews and Christians in some places can get together to share and explore two matters. The first would be to do with spirituality and worship. How do we understand our personal pilgrimages, in the context of our faiths and the people and community to which we belong, in relation to the one God and to his one world? The second area would be to do with what we now see to be required concerning the worth of the neighbour. For is not God's covenant and election love related and relatable in some way to his universal love? And are we not agreed that we are all called to love the Lord our God with all our hearts, minds, souls and strength – and our neighbours as ourselves?

7 · What is There to Hope For?

(1969)

I find it odd. I become more and more sure that the people who said that Jesus was risen from the dead are quite right. Risen he was and risen he is. There is a fact here which is a fact of the world and a fact for the world. My intelligence and my imagination seem to be more and more ready to accept the resurrection as a fact of the past. But (and this is what I find odd, disturbing and provocative) I do not seem to be able to get to grips in the same way with what presumably follows, that is with the resurrection as a fact of the future.

I know, of course, that people who are not Christians are quite clear that the resurrection of Jesus is in no sense a fact. I know, too, that Christian belief is alleged to be on the wane. I am further aware that very many people who declare themselves to be Christians, and whom I, for what it's worth, would certainly recognize as such, hold that the resurrection is not a fact but a symbol. All this, and all the argumentation that lies behind it, is very weighty. I can quite see why Paul should have been laughed at when, on Mars Hill in Athens, he got to his talk about Jesus and the resurrection. But – although this still rather surprises me – I think that Paul was right and that those who take a contrary view are wrong. Jesus was dead and God raised him up.

At Easter I am not really concerned to argue for my faith in Jesus and the resurrection but to try to face what at present I see involved in that faith (in particular this matter of the fact of the resurrection, past and future), but I still find here an argument with myself. I consider my study of the Gospel narratives of the so-called resurrection appearances. I compare this with the shape of the preaching presented in the Acts of the Apostles and with the relevant references in the Epistles. Scholars, of whom I suppose I might count myself one, argue back and forth about how to evaluate these writings. At times one wonders how so few New Testament words can sustain so extensive a volume of scholarly sentences. But through it all I find a simple conclusion emerging. We can be pretty clear about what the first disciples believed had happened.

Some of them were familiar with the shape of Jesus in his living, that is to say that they knew him as a person. Some of them were well aware of the shape of Jesus' dying. He had become involved with the Jewish and Roman authorities and was killed. Some of them were equally aware of a new living of Jesus, a living as real and actual as the living of Jesus from Nazareth to the cross and a living as much present, and as much to be reckoned with, as the dying, becoming a corpse and being buried. Further, Jesus had directed his living, the Jewish and Roman authorities had directed his dying and God had directed his new living. This was so concrete and fact-like that it was perfectly appropriate to include in the story of the incidents which led to the discovery of this new living of Jesus the incident of the empty tomb. I cannot, for my part, decide whether the actual discovery of the empty tomb was one of the preludes to discovering Jesus to be alive or whether the story came to be told as a symbol of the discovery that Jesus was alive. But either way, the shape of the discovery and of the belief seems to be clear and one and the same. The burying was real and the being alive again was real and both are in the same category of reality. The fact of Jesus' death had been taken up into, and overcome by, the fact of Jesus' resurrection.

Jesus had lived, men had killed him and God had raised him up. This is what had happened. And from now on the responses of our living and the expectations of our living are to be made and developed in the perspective of these happenings. I can see no escape from the awkward shape of this belief of the first Christians, of this belief which constituted the first Christians. I get no escape from the awkwardness by transposing the statement 'God raised up Jesus' into the statement 'there arose a belief that Jesus was as good as alive'. If this means that the disciples spontaneously persuaded themselves to carry on in this manner, then we are dealing with a delusion of considerable historical and, it may be, pathological interest but of no ultimate religious and human significance. Further, we are doing quite impermissible violence to the logic and spirit of the New Testament simply considered as a literary work. No literary or historical critic of any integrity would permit such a violation of any other document. A piece of writing must be allowed the authenticity of its own approach and its own errors, whatever conclusions this may force us to about its value. As I say, I am unable to escape the conclusion that the shape of what the first Christians believed to have happened is clear enough.

If, on the other hand, by 'there arose a belief that Jesus was as good as alive' we mean that God enabled some men to perceive the lasting significance of the shape of Jesus' personality, then we are back with talk and belief about God acting. To cause a belief, and *a fortiori* to cause a true belief, is just as much a happening as, say, raising up Jesus.

So, try as I will, I have not been able to avoid the conclusion that I am presented with the resurrection of Jesus as a fact of the past. Indeed, I now find that, far from wishing to avoid this conclusion, it is resuming its place as part of the basic stuff of my Christian faith. Paul wrote that if Christ be not risen then Christian preaching is vain and so is Christian faith. Right now it is not conceivable to me that the faith which I share with my fellow-Christians is vain. I find it too much of a gift, too much of a resource, too much of a personal presence and provocation. Of course, I am intellectually aware that all faith may be folly, but my only concern now is to try to be clearer about the shape of Christian folly, the implications of Easter foolishness.

God raised up Jesus, dead and buried when Pontius Pilate was procurator of Judaea, and established him in his person, in his achievements, in his continuing significance. Since this has been done, what will be done? Paul, with whom I have been daring to agree – with some surprise – has a short and strong word for anyone who asks 'How are the dead raised up? And with what body do they come?' (I Cor. 15.35). It is *aphrōn* – mindless, ignorant, 'Thou fool!', as the Authorized Version has it. But I shall persevere with the questions and accept the epithet. For I seem quite often to find myself caught up in a sort of expectant puzzlement between being more and more sure that I have been given something to believe and being less and less sure that I know what it means.

God did raise up Jesus. What then will he do through and in the spirit of Jesus? What am I to expect, what am I to look out for now and to look forward to in the future? Death and resurrection, I suppose, dying and rising, confronting being brought to an end and discovering offers of a new beginning. But this will have to have specific meaning through and in relation to specific happenings if the resurrection is a fact of the future as it is a fact of the past.

The resurrection means that God acted to establish Jesus in his person, in his achievements and in his continuing effect. Hence, it must be possible in fact to discover the shape of Jesus Christ in and through the events, circumstances and persons with whom I get involved, and it must be possible to see any set of persons, events and circumstances in the perspective of this shape of Jesus Christ. Further, must I not expect ultimately to see the shape of Jesus Christ established beyond and over all events, circumstances and persons?

I think that this must mean inextinguishable hope *in* the world and a final hope *beyond* the world.

For by 'the shape of Jesus Christ' I mean the person that he was, the expectations which he aroused and the promises which were thereby held out. The resurrection as a fact of the past is God's re-establishing of *this* person, that is of Jesus Christ, in his own personal pattern and presence, through and beyond death. The particularity of the resurrection seems to be an essential part of its meaning and its universal significance. It was Jesus who was known to be living again, not the spirit of Christ, nor the essence of love nor the embodiment of humanity. The resurrection is a preservation of identity and a declaration of identity. In raising up Jesus, God makes it plain that his resources are at work for, and are at the disposal of, the establishment, development and liberation of human identity. This identity, moreover, is your identity and my identity. We are meant to have our own proper names and it is those names, not our surnames or class names or categorizing labels, which are our real names and which denote the real in us which is offered the possibility of establishment and fulfilment.

Here something in me joins fiercely with much from outside me to say 'nonsense' – look at the world, look at the news, look at your neighbour, look at yourself. But this seems to be precisely the point of the resurrection of Jesus Christ. His identity is established and declared through and then beyond everything that counted against it. It was a rising again from the dead. Hence all human endings and all inhuman absurdities are put in question. The last word is claimed by God as the establisher of identity.

Not that this identity must be confused with mere individuality. For the shape of Jesus Christ is not merely the person that he was but also the expectations which he aroused and the promises thereby held out. These expectations and promises are all to do with the fulfilment of the life of the people of God; they have a communal dimension and they are concerned with relationships. The love which Jesus embodied and the love which he encouraged saw every man in need as my neighbour, prayed that we might receive the same forgiveness from God as we extend to those who trespass against our identity, and had a vision of a body in which unity overcame all differences of class, status, sex, nationality or religion. Hence the establishment of identity, which is declared in and promised by the resurrection, is also the establishment of community. The resurrection of Jesus Christ promises that I shall be me, but only and excellently in oneness with all men and women.

Perhaps, then, it is not so very odd that while I find my intelligence and my imagination increasingly accepting the resurrection as a fact of the past I do not find a corresponding increase in my understanding of the resurrection as a fact of the future. What will my identity be when it is fully established in openness to all men and women in God and to God in all men and women? How will the dead be raised up and with what body will they come? The only answer can be that they will be raised up by the God who raised up Jesus and that they will come with the body and in the body of Jesus Christ. This will be the establishment and the declaration of an identity and a community in a way that is now unidentifiable.

But although we cannot visualize how we shall enjoy our identity in this community, the establishment of this community is assured. The definiteness of death no more puts a limit upon the possibilities of our human identity than it did upon the identity of Jesus Christ. Our hope, therefore, goes beyond the world into the future which is the future of the God who raised up Jesus. But this hope stems from the resurrection as a fact of the past and of the future. Such a fact must also, in bridging past and future, have its existence in the present. If there is anything in these wonderings and wanderings of mine, then the reality of the resurrection should be looked out for and expected wherever we are offered possibilities of, or faced with problems about, identity and community. This is where we shall find possibilities of dying and rising, of being brought to an end and of discovering offers of new beginnings which are reflections and realizations of the power of the resurrection.

Every threat, as I receive it, to my being me can be received as an opportunity to discover some new way and some renewing way of living. Dying itself is the opportunity to discover that life can be received only as a gift, in total and unmitigated dependence on others and on the source of life beyond all others. Every opportunity to be me can be received as a step towards a greater openness of community and a greater opportunity of sharing in the one bundle of life into which we are all called for the fulfilment of all. Similarly, every threat to community, at whatever level we are involved in it, can be received as a challenge to live into the resurrection, to be part of a bringing of death to that which impedes community, to suffer with and for the bringing to life of that which develops community. Every development of community is itself a sign of the resurrection to be received with thankfulness and hope and to be used for still wider building and sharing.

But there will come a time when we find our identity finally threatened by the inevitable fact of death. Our hopes of building community will seem decisively checked by the ineluctable facts of human nature and the tangles of politics, indifference and greed. It is then that our faith in the resurrection will be finally put to the test. If God has raised up Jesus, then we shall find that it is the threats and the checks which are temporary and the identity and the community which are final and everlasting.

8 · *Easter Sermon*

(1989)

'When Christ, who is our life, shall appear, then shall ye also appear with him in glory' (*Colossians 3.4*)

This verse from our Easter epistle is one of many in the New Testament which makes it clear that the resurrection of Jesus from the dead is *not* a sign that individuals have a chance of surviving death. Rather the raising up of Jesus from the dead is a declaration by God that the last day is at hand, that Jesus will be the judge at that last day and that those who believe in Jesus will share the glory of that last day and escape the destruction of that last day. 'When Christ, who is our life, shall appear, then shall ye also appear with him in glory.' In other words the resurrection of Jesus from the dead is an eschatological declaration!

I use this rather clumsy sounding word 'eschatological' deliberately, partly because it is the *correct* word to use when considering the meaning of the resurrection in New Testament terms, but mostly because I expect that, like myself, you do not really know what the word 'eschatological' means. I therefore thrust the word 'eschatological' at both myself and all of you in the expectation that we shall not understand what it really means and therefore be reminded here, in the faith and glory of our Easter worship, that we do not really know what the resurrection of Jesus Christ from the dead means.

It is, surely, a cause for concern to those of us of Christian faith that talk about the resurrection sounds more and more like Christians discussing a shibboleth which bothers them rather than an exploration by faithful human beings who are trying to understand and proclaim what God has done and declared about the whole of human kind and the future of creation. All this discussion, in endless controversy, articles and even books about what really happened at the resurrection, and what must be really involved in order to make sure it really happened, and what proves 'it' – whatever 'it' is – all of this sounds and, I suspect and fear, is a form of Christian neurosis rather than an expression of Christian faith. And it arises, I believe, because all of us Christians, or at least most of us Christians most of the time, have lost sight of what the New Testament indicates that the resurrection is about.

I may say that I personally have become so bored with these controversies and discussions of which I have become, in some way, a focus or a substantial cause, that I have returned to searching the New Testament to try to be clear about what the resurrection meant to the first Christians – who, of course, were not known as Christians but *believers*: believers in the God who raised Jesus from the dead. I should add that I have never doubted the resurrection. It has always been abundantly clear to me that Christianity could never have arisen unless the first disciples had been turned into apostles by the discovery, conviction and assurance that God had raised Jesus from the dead. Ever since I have been a self-conscious and reflective Christian I have been absolutely clear that being a Christian means believing that the first disciples, become apostles, were right in their belief. God did indeed raise Jesus from the dead. The issue, therefore, is not 'Did the resurrection happen?'; the issue is: 'What does the resurrection mean?'

I should also make it clear to you that I am convinced that the missionary proclamation of the resurrection will not advance by attempts to produce evidence which proves that the resurrection must have *happened* but by being part of the conviction and practice of what the resurrection *means*. There can be no satisfactory and compelling proof that a happening must be attributed to God. People can always give other explanations. We may compare, for example, right back at the beginning of Christian things, the report in Matthew 23.11–15:

While the women were on their way, some of the guards went into the city and reported to the chief priests everything that had happened. When the chief priests had met with the elders and devised a plan, they gave the soldiers a large sum of money, telling them, 'You are to say: His disciples came during the night and stole him away while we were asleep. If this report gets to the Governor, we will satisfy him and keep you out of trouble.' So the soldiers took the money and did as they were instructed. And this story has been widely circulated among the Jews to this very day.

I am not convinced that this is an accurate report of what really happened. I suspect that, like much of the Gospels, it is an apologetic report about what might have happened and is directed to dealing with consequent rumours and arguments. All the Gospels are written well after the events on which they are commenting and no one could have detailed and accurate knowledge of what these events were. The authors of the Gospels were much more directly aware of arguments and problems in the second and third generations of the life of the church and its encounter with Jews and Gentiles. But the passage makes absolutely clear that from the earliest times in which the resurrection faith was preached, people could easily and plausibly produce alternative explanations for everything – including the empty tomb – which might be said to *prove* 'the resurrection', whatever 'the resurrection' was and was claimed to be. The *fact* of the resurrection is quite unprovable and unpersuasive – except to those who believe. What might persuade, catch-up and draw in non-believers is not the fact of resurrection but the meaning of the resurrection, the effect of the resurrection and the life or lives lived in the light of the resurrection. (This is *not* to say that the resurrection is not a fact. It is simply to make the obvious but frequently denied or deliberately ignored point that we are concerned in practice, not with how you prove a fact which is alleged to require faith, but with how you share a faith which includes a conviction about fact.)

So what does the resurrection of Jesus mean according to the New Testament? It means that God is about to make an end and

Jesus is the servant, centre and judge of that end. This may appear somewhat strange and disturbing to us, but I think there can be no doubt about it, although I have no time to do more than draw your attention to two more typical texts, over and above the one from our Easter epistle. First there is I Thessalonians 1.9–10, which is the earliest evidence we have of Christian preaching, for I Thessalonians is considerably earlier than any of the Gospels.

> They tell how you turn to God from idols to serve the living and true God, and to wait for his Son from heaven, whom he raised from the dead – Jesus, who rescues us from the coming wrath.

The resurrection identifies Jesus as the Son of God who will come from heaven to declare both the wrath and the rescuing of the true God. Then consider also an extract from the great resurrection chapter, I Corinthians 15.20–25:

> But Christ has indeed been raised from the dead, the first fruits of those who have fallen asleep. For since death came through a man, the resurrection of the dead comes also through a man. For as in Adam all die so in Christ all will be made alive. But each in his own turn; Christ, the first fruits; then, when he comes, those who belong to him. Then the end will come, when he hands over the kingdom to God the Father after he has destroyed all dominion, authority and power. For he must reign until he has put all his enemies under his feet.

The pattern is quite clear: God has raised Jesus; Jesus will therefore come to judge and make an end; we who believe in God through him will be those who 'belong to him' and therefore saved from the destruction of all who do not. (We may compare again from I Thessalonians 'Jesus, who rescues us from the coming wrath'.)

I do not think that there can be any doubt about it: in the New Testament, as distinct from very much thinking in the church and in sharp challenge to very much lack of thinking or imagination in the church, the resurrection is about God making an end. It therefore has universal significance for the sorting out of all things and the fulfilling of all things. Further, there is scarcely any doubt that the first Christians, certainly including St Paul, expected this final making of an end to occur either in their lifetimes or very shortly afterwards. (If you want to follow this up look at I Thessalonians 4.12– end.)

As we know, this end, in that catastrophic and terminating sense, did not occur. The world goes on; it goes on being a very mixed-up place, and those who continue to believe that God raised Jesus from the dead seem to see this resurrection as some sort of sign, evidence or promise that all men and women as individuals, or some selected men and women as individuals, have a chance of surviving death like Jesus survived death. This is a terribly weakened version of the original conviction that the love and the power, the judgment and the fulfilment of God, was manifested in the life, death *and resurrection* of Jesus so that to be in touch with the risen Lord, to have faith in the God who raised up Jesus and to be part of the body of Christ, was to be part of the judgment of all things and the fulfilment of all things.

I do not think I have time or resources this particular Easter Day to do more than to challenge all of us who believe in the resurrection of Jesus Christ from the dead to seek again a renewed sense of the urgency of the judgment of the resurrection, of the promise of the fulfilment of the resurrection and of the all-embracing universality of the resurrection. The resurrection means that there is a God who will make an end, that he makes the end by judging and destroying all that is contrary to his kingdom and purpose of love, that in so making the end he fulfils all his purposes of creation, holiness and love and that Jesus is the sign of this, the way to this and the means of this.

I am bound to say that I am not at all clear what this means in practice; but I am sure that it means much more than the present turned-in and self-preoccupied state of the church and of most Christian groups, sects and organizations. It means something to do with being so shocked, disturbed, judged and renewed by the power, vision and Spirit of the risen Christ of God that we become urgent on behalf of all men and women against the bitter injustices, destructive wastings and stupid trivialities of our present society. It means being so inspired by the power and the glory of God in the raising up of Christ that we are full of hope beyond all hope, of visions that go beyond all visions and of courage to renew ourselves and others in these hopes and these visions. And it must mean finding a readiness from the God who raised up Jesus, and a resonance in the God who raised up Jesus, which will take us beyond the bounds of the church into a pressing, urgent, hopeful and compassionate concern for a coming together of Christians with Jews, Muslims, Hindus, Sikhs, agnostic seekers, passionate atheists and the bewildered indifferent into a new quest for the universal kingdom of God, a new readiness to accept the judgment of a truly universal God of holiness and love, and a new concern that we may all share in the escape from the sin and death which is in Adam into the glory and light which is in Christ.

It can mean no less – and it must mean even more – for Christ is risen, he is risen indeed.

Part Three

Concerning being a Christian

1 · *How much Doctrine do we Need?*

(1964)

Questions – that is what we are faced with at every turn. Everything is under question. The word 'God', it seems, is either a meaningless noise or else describes simply one's attitude to the world. Morality, whether it be new, old or indifferent, is constantly under fire. Society is rapidly changing – yet in what direction and what, if anything, can or should be done about that direction is not at all clear. The church, the university, the educational system and well-nigh everything else is being questioned and questioning itself. Nothing is to be taken for granted. So much is this so that many people come by sheer exhaustion and bewilderment to the conclusion that there can never be any agreed or any reasonably assured answer to any question of any importance. Hence the only thing to do is to give up asking questions and make whatever you can of whatever section of comparatively ordered life that comes your way.

But there is one simple question which underlies and is relevant to all the questions and all this questioning. It is put to us in every question we now face and it is posed to us in the hour of our death. It is, 'Are we alone?'

Have we any resources beyond our own for dealing with our life and our living? What is the sum total of the environment in which we live? What is the last descriptive word about this universe? Are the possibilities and powers available to us, or acting upon us, exhausted by the sum total of the particles or of the quanta of energy which in a real, measurable and definable sense constitute the universe? Is there anything else, or are we, as far as our destiny and our possibilities go, on our own?

To this simple and perfectly understandable question Christians have always had an assured, confident and simple answer – *no*, we are not alone, for there is also God. Indeed first of all there is God, and he is for humankind. This is the Christian gospel, which is decisively good news. You are not alone. Over against you and yet wholly with you there is God – and he is for you. He takes your part. And the Christian gospel goes on to address itself to men and women in the very midst of their questionings, relativities, uncertainties. Therefore, says the Christian gospel, since there is God and since he takes the part of men and women, two things follow.

First, human maturity, human fulfilment, is built into the purpose of the universe. Questions – yes: putting to the most radical and disintegrating tests, bewilderment, despair in the face of meaningless evil. Hope, yes, hope destroyed, hope deferred. What can it all come to? How can we speak of 'all' at all? All these questions do rightly arise – radically arise – existentially arise. But since there is God and since he is for human beings, our making and fulfilment is built into the purpose of the universe.

Therefore all complacency is challenged. There is no excuse for accepting situations contrary to humanness. You may never say, 'This is the best we can do . . .'. Nor can anyone, in the end, get away with the cynical repudiation of humanness and humanity. Moreover, the challenge is not only to all complacency which accepts the situation, but also to all despair and indifference which is overwhelmed by the situation. So all despair and indifference is challenged. It is not true that there is no hope, that nothing can be done. Everything that makes for our true maturity and fulfilment can be done and will be done, and there is strength available and avenues open to start doing it. We are not alone; therefore no one dare be complacent, no one need despair, no one may excuse himself or herself with the escapism of indifference.

But the gospel has a greater challenge and a greater promise even than this. Since we are not alone, but there is God and he takes our part, this human maturity which is built into the purpose of the universe is an infinite possibility, the possibility of infiniteness. God is, and he is for us: therefore, we are offered the possibility of fulfilling all the matured possibilities of this universe in the infinite possibility of the life of God.

In practice, this means that the maturity which is offered to us is always open. There are always further possibilities to be grown into, further possibilities of love, of truth and of beauty. This is why this maturity is life indeed – true life – everlasting life – the life of infinite possibilities – not an achievement which reaches a static stage of fulfilment and then withers and dies. Since God is and God is for us, there is no end to our maturity – only more growth into the infinite possibilities of the divine life.

So, to the simple question, 'Are we alone?', the Christian gospel returns the simple answer *no*. There is God and he is for us. Therefore our maturity as human beings is both a real possibility and an infinite possibility.

But how do we know? How do we know that this is gospel? That this is gospel truth?

Our knowledge is the result of a three-stranded cord woven by the Spirit of God which binds the knowledge and assurance of the gospel to our hearts and minds. We know because we are told. We know because God finds us. We know because we find God.

We know because we are told. This is the whole *tradition* of the biblical and Christian faith. People believe in God because people believe in God. The Holy Spirit keeps alive a believing community who can meaningfully speak of their belief to others. There has been built up through long and varied experience of living, suffering and praying a way of talking about God which is to be found in the Bible and crystallized into the creeds, doctrines and prayers of the Christian church. This tradition is meaningfully handed on and speaks to us. So we are told about God and his ways and purposes. The gospel is spoken to us.

But this is not enough. We know also because God finds us. That is to say in some often more or less hidden, obscure and only occasionally remembered way we have experienced a presence, a power, a personality who is with us and for us, and if only that experience could be rekindled we know we should be sure that God is and he is for us. Maybe we cannot now pray. But we have truly prayed. Maybe now the inward but assured presence, like the still small voice of which the Elijah narrative speaks, is not very evident to us. But he has been evident. Therefore we know that God has found us and that he will find us again, and therefore we may know that the traditional Gospel of which we are told is about a present and living God. As the Holy Spirit has touched our hearts, we rightly believe others when they speak in the name of that Spirit.

But tradition and the experience of God finding us are bound together into living truth by the fact that not only does God find us but we also find God. We are called to live our lives on the policy which the tradition suggests to us and in the light of such vision as God has given to us. And as we seek to follow this Christian policy to be obedient to the Holy Spirit, in company with other Christians brought together by the Holy Spirit, we sufficiently find that life is enhanced in this living, experience is deepened and the tradition is illuminated. And we also find that tradition illuminates our experience and experience calls us to new policies of Christian living. So this three-fold cord (the tradition; our experience; the policy of common living) assures us that the gospel is indeed true. We are not alone. God is and he takes our part.

Since we have this assurance, we come finally and briefly to the needs of the church today. We come to this on the basis of the gospel and of our assurance concerning the gospel given to us by the Holy Spirit. The church does not need a gospel which is 'relevant'. The church is created by the gospel and continues to exist because the God of the gospel keeps her in existence. What the church needs is to be faithful to the gospel, to the God of the gospel. Christians are not called to be relevant. If you allow 'relevance' to determine you, you are being conformed to the world and you are heading once again for being alone. Christians are called to be faithful. What the church needs is faith and obedience to that which constitutes her. Out of this God will give saving relevance to, and encounter with, the world. But this faith and obedience certainly do demand involvement with the world.

Let me try to illustrate what I mean by referring to the need for dynamic doctrine. Out of the biblical and Christian experience of God, certain central doctrines have been crystallized in the tradition: concerning God (the Trinity); concerning God and his relation to the world (the Incarnation); concerning God taking man's part (the Atonement); concerning man (sin and grace); concerning the universe (the doctrine of creation). Now we are told that such doctrines as these are almost, if not entirely, mythological: pictures without any logical reference to reality. Therefore they are unthinkable and irrelevant.

That they have become unthinkable to many people and fossilized into irrelevance for most cannot be denied, or they would not be so lightly written off. But as they are truly part of the tradition which tells us of God and of his gospel, to write them off is to run the gravest danger of stopping the gospel being any sort of news, good, bad or indifferent, and of losing our grasp on the very existence of God. What we have to do is to work from the faith which the gospel gives us: that God is, that he is for us and that consequently his purpose of maturity for us is woven into the universe. On this basis we take the doctrines which the tradition which hands us the gospel has handed to us and we submit them to the questions which our speaking of the universe has raised for them, and we submit the current dogmas of our speaking of the universe to the questioning of the doctrines.

As examples of areas in which this might happen I would mention the following. The doctrine of the Trinity assures us that the ultimate reality of the universe (God) is truly personal, for God is rightly to be thought of (although not sufficiently to be thought of) as a really personal unity of an absolute oneness fulfilled in perfect relations and a perfect relationship which *is* oneness. We now have much evidence from psychological and sociological work and elsewhere that personality cannot be reduced either to an individual focus or to a set of social relationships, but must be understood in terms of both. There is clearly much room for dialogue here.

As psychology, psychiatry and the study of human social relationships give us more and more insight into the mechanism of blame and of guilt and of the part which self-acceptance and acceptance of others must play in developing mature and healthy persons, so we are provided with much that questions and much that illuminates the doctrines of the atonement and the role and purpose of the church as a community based on reconciliation which comes from the acceptance by God of men and women as they are. Also, the doctrines of the church and the atonement have much to say on these vital questions of human relationships and realities.

Since the doctrine of creation assures us that the world is related to the purpose and pattern of God, we cannot but welcome everything that a valid science validly discerns about that universe. We have to seek to bear witness to scientists that the universe as a whole demands a more worshipful consideration than they sometimes give it. But they have to remind us and, indeed, to inform us for the first time of much about the universe in many particulars.

So we are called to a faithful and fearless dialogue. Christians must not suffer faithlessly from an inferiority complex and let all the disciplines of science and the social sciences call the tune so much that all the given doctrines are dissolved away – and the gospel with them. But even more importantly, Christians are forbidden by the heart of their faith, their Lord, the Suffering Servant, to indulge in superiority complexes and think they may dictate to modern investigators what they shall think or what they shall discover. In quietness and confidence we are, in matters of doctrine and of understanding, to open ourselves wholeheartedly to all the questions which modern thought and science put to us or to our doctrines. Where the doctrines truly are part of what God has given us as part of his giving of the gospel they can only be re-established, re-invigorated and re-illuminated by this openness. And as they are so renewed to us and through us, so these great doctrines will shine afresh with a saving relevance to man in his aloneness. They will once again become the means under God of making it clear to the church and to the world that God is, that he is for us and that we are called to a maturity of infinite possibility in the very life of God himself.

2 · The Impossibility and the Necessity of the Church

(1974)

Christian social criticism has fastened on the fact that the church as an institution is part of that 'world' against which the Gospels warn. What is implied by an equally rigorous explanation of the biblical affirmation that the revelation of God requires a people, an institution which will receive and explore it? This article proposes ways in which the church can understand itself as both God-centred and world-directed – and hence ultimately of secondary importance.

Now that we know that pollution is seeping round us, population growth is threatening to overwhelm us, resources are running out on us and turbulence, uncertainty and violence are becoming more and more commonplace to us, what ought we to do about it? I should like to sketch out the suggestion that our distinctively Christian contribution to the affairs and future of our human race at this particular stage in history is to be concerned with, and to work at, the renewal of the church. In outlining this sketch I shall also try to show that being concerned for the renewal of the church implies almost the exact contrary of the most common manifestation of 'concern for the church' which we at present see or take part in at national, diocesan, ruridecanal or parochial level. I start from two assumptions which I believe to be theologically and practically valid. The first is that the church is of no importance. The second is that the church is essential until the end. As the first assumption is theologically derived from the second I shall take this first.

The church is essential until the end. The world is a highly ambiguous place as far as human existence goes, and human existence is highly ambiguous in its own terms. That is to say that it is scarcely possible to derive from the natural processes of the world assurance that the world as such has any concern for human fulfilment. Likewise we are quite as much problems to ourselves as obvious promoters of our own true happiness. If, therefore, we believe and maintain that there is a gospel and that, moreover, it is the gospel of God and of universal scope and concern, then we must have some other basis than the world on its own and natural human existence on its own for this knowledge, assurance and experience.

Further, the gospel is that the world is not on its own and that human existence is not defined by its limits and still less by its distortions. The gospel is that the world derives from, and is the arena of, the energies of God, and that to be human is to be open to collaboration with, and then to the fulfilment of, these divine energies. This gospel is both proclaimed and made credible by the historical presence and passion of the Jesus who is one with the Father and present by the Spirit. This glory and hope of glory is not a derivation, nor even an intuition. It is a revelation. A revelation requires people who will receive it, who will be sustained by it, who will respond to and explore it, and who will continue to be a conscious part of the revelatory process. It is quite clear to me that as a matter of history, of logic (where does the knowledge and language of revelation come from?) and of practical and psychological necessity Christian knowledge of the gospel and Christian identity comes from and through the church – and from nowhere else.

Moreover, how are we to be sustained and renewed in the knowledge and hope of the glory from which the gospel proceeds and to which it points? Unless we have a community whose very existence stems from the gospel and which is focussed on the worship of the God who is the giver and the life of the gospel, there will be no basis for Christian existence and no base from which we may go out to the authentication of Christian existence. And, last but not least, the more it becomes obvious once again that 'here we have no abiding city', that all is change, that change remains ambiguous and that every state of affairs has only a very limited future, the more we can see the necessity of a source of human identity which is related to an abiding God and an eschatological future.

Thus many considerations converge to make it clear that the church is essential until the end. That is to say that we are faced with the necessity of the church in history. Without the church there would not be the knowledge *in* history of this gospel of the glory of God and we should not have the possibility of the faith that *this* gospel speaks to and in *this* history of ours. And if the church is necessary in history, then the church as institution is inevitable in history, for continuing in history implies institutional existence.

The scandal of the church

But, on the face of it, this is intolerable. At least, it is intolerable if we do have any glimpse of the true glory of God and of the gospel in relation to the world and to history. For the recent history and existence of the institutional church, at least as manifested in the institutional churches of our part of the world (although, alas, they are not unique in this), contradict both gospel and glory. Our churches in their regular and institutional workings scarcely display much conscious awareness of the mystery of the glory of the transcendent God who trivializes our dogmas to the verge of agnosticism and relativizes our formulated knowledge of him so that we may break through to our deeper knowing. Nor does recent history or present practice show much freedom in the churches to be eager for, and at the disposal of, the future which God is offering to men and women. Rather, churches seem positively (! negatively) to be places of alienation from the realities of current human struggles. Again and again it has been necessary to defeat, or at least to ignore, the church if freedom, flexibility and openness for newness in human affairs and human development is to be advanced. The churches live not for the future of God and of men and women but from the religious past and for and from the social *status quo*. (It is not the Holy Spirit which sustains the Church of England but the Church Commissioners who maintain it.)

The arguments which are usually advanced to mitigate the sharpness of this type of criticism and to indicate that the institutional church, as necessarily a *corpus mixtum*, is not in contradiction to the gospel, fail to convince because of the very manner and purpose of their being put forward. Their purpose is to mitigate the judgment upon the church and upon ourselves, and the manner of urging them too often has something of self-righteousness or of self-pity. But the biblical presentation of and teaching about judgment does not encourage us in attempts to soften or deflect these judgments upon our falling short of the glory of God. Rather, we are encouraged to look for the strength of God to renew us when and as we accept the judgments and rely, in repentance, on God's resources rather than our own. It is thus that we shall be set free for creative change and collaborative exploration towards the one new man in Jesus Christ.

The condition of this freedom is, however, the grace to receive this recognition of our corporate and institutional contradiction of the gospel and the glory of God. Until we begin to do this our church will be less and less a place of, or base for, freedom and will be more and more obviously a place of bondage – to the 'weak and beggarly elements' (cf. Gal. 4.9) of our decaying Anglo-Saxon world. Thus the church is not primarily intolerable or impossible because our corporate manifestations and institutional activities fall short of the glory of God. The gospel is both real good news and truly credible precisely because it is concerned with salvation from sin for glory. And the Son of God was crucified in the flesh precisely by and for human shortcomings. The church is thus not the contradiction of the gospel simply because it is sinful. The blatant contradiction which constitutes the evident impossibility of the church arises because there is practically no recognition and acceptance of the reality of the historical, corporate and institutional acts and facts by which we have denied and do deny the gospel. Since our church so clearly ignores the judgment of the gospel, it equally clearly neither believes in nor seeks to live by that gospel. Thus the church which, in history, is necessary to the gospel is, in our present history, an impossibility for those who would or might receive the gospel.

Two symptoms of this impossibility which seem to me to be of particular significance, not least because they may also point to clues as to how we should handle the convergence of impossibility and necessity, can be briefly indicated as follows. First there is the way 'the church' approaches sin in society and the sins of a society. I am referring to the attitudes of church leaders and church pressure groups and to the expectations which people have of what these attitudes will be or ought to be. It seems to both expected and assumed (from within the church, that is) that 'the church' can and should identify and denounce sin and sins in society at large and that this can be done from some position over against society.

Now it is indeed the case that the biblical message and the Christian story, at its persistent heart, is focussed on an energy of love which is always at work to correct, absorb and overcome all the ways in which the gifts and possibilities of love are misunderstood, rejected and abused. There is an offer of salvation from sin for glory. So the gospel is certainly addressed to those who fall short. But it is surely addressed in the first place to those who fall short of the gospel which they say they hear and claim they proclaim. Thus the hearers of the gospel are not thereby authorized to denounce sin but rather to know and to acknowledge that they are sinners. From there it may be possible to set out on the process of universalization by which it shall become known that there are resources to deal with all that by which human beings fall short of what is and what might be involved in being human. That is to say, we may hope to move to a wider recognition of sin and a wider acceptance of salvation. But any attempt to denounce sin which is not associated with a deep and sensitive awareness of involvement in sinfulness makes the necessary witness a social and human impossibility. 'Self-righteousness' denouncing the sin of others is not a gospel witness but an institutional manoeuvre. ('The church ought to make its voice heard and so make clear its place in society'.)

The world: concern and arena of God

Thus while the church does have a necessary message about and concern with sin, the attitudes and expectations of members seem to force it into a position of impossibility with regard to freedom to live from and for the gospel in this respect. A second symptom of the impossibility of the church as an institution at present lies in its preoccupation with itself. So much time seems to be occupied with considering church re-organization, church activities and the view of the church on this and that. Questions of liturgy, of unity, of mission, and many others are discussed between different church parties or personalities. Campaigns, missions and series of activities seem to be launched more out of a felt need to perform, and to be seen to be performing, churchly activities than out of a deeply studied and sensitively considered response to the needs, problems and possibilities of the world. Thus the church does not receive the power of the gospel in the world because it concentrates on 'the gospel' and on 'the church' as if they were self-contained entities. It will not face up seriously to the world which is the concern and the arena of God, to which he sends the gospel, and in which he calls the church.

It is here that we return to my first theological assumption, which is that the church is of no importance. This is derived from the understanding of the historical necessity of the church as follows. The church is necessary until the end because it stems from the giving of God and so exists as a witness to the giving of God and as a place of receiving the giving of God, for the sake of the giving of God to and for the world. Thus the church is of no importance in itself. Its existence is derived from God and the world, from God in the world and from the world as to be offered to God and to be set free to enjoy God. Now God is so gracious, the world is so full of possibilities, and the gospel-offer of the fulfilment of these possibilities in this God is so glorious that the church must be set free from or, perhaps, even, in her impossibility for her derivative but necessary task.

This task, however, is not to strive to be God's principal agent in dealing with all the problems of the world, the problems I hinted at in my opening paragraph as now the context of our lives. The church's task is to be a principal agent for living with these problems, realistically, hopefully and with striving towards love out of the knowledge of love offered and available. At present the impossibility of the church is compounded, because as the self-centred church wakes up to the world, a growing neurosis about the problems of the world reinforces an already present neurosis about church organization. Thus we in the church are in grave danger of getting the worst of both worlds. We have neither whatever courage, expertise or indifference the world can muster about its own problems nor the peace which comes from a deep centring on God. Hence we betray the gospel before others and fail to enjoy it ourselves.

We can be set free from the impossibility of the church only as we come to have a clear view of the necessity of the church in so God-centred and world-directed a way that we also see the un-importance of the church. Then we can be enabled both to look for and respond to God in the world and also to let go every present institutional detail or expression which hinders us from God and the world.

To learn to live with resolution aligned on God and his purposes for the world and with tentativeness, and where neces-sary with abandonment, towards every institutional expression of human living, churchly expressions included, would be surely an immense contribution to living humanly with our problems. It could lead to a restoration and rediscovery of the sense of human life as an exploration, a pilgrimage and a response which are not frustrated by any failure, disaster or death and could set us free to discover what resolutions there are to present problems. It would also lead to the restoration and rediscovery of Christian doctrine and Christian spirituality. For both of these are fundamentally concerned with God and the world and with relating God and the world.

But for all this to happen the centre of our preoccupations and practices in the present church must be shifted. We must be aware that the church is inevitable until the end because and only because God cares for the world. Thus about everything we do or say we must resolutely ask and rigorously answer the question: 'What has this to do with God and with the world?' To introduce any question about the church before this has been answered and understood will be to return to impossibility, to the contradiction of the gospel and to the obscuring of glory.

3 · The Nature of Theology and Theological Education

(1966)

In view of what may be called the 'vast fluidity of the theological field' at the moment, it is perhaps desirable that I should outline in a somewhat rash way what my own position, as I understand it at the moment, is. My position is that theology is an entirely valid and, at its heart, distinctive area of study and of human enquiry. By saying 'at its heart distinctive', I mean 'has its own distinctive proper subject or object not in its entirety shared by any other area of study'. The difficulty, of course, is that the proper object of theology must be the proper subject of theology, to wit God, and this creates a quite exceptional number of difficulties. I am sure myself that the word 'God' is the proper name for the Existent and the Existence who wholly transcends all that is normally designated the universe and that in discussing theology I am discussing a proper area of study whose subject is God. I reject as theologically, philosophically and psychologically unsatisfactory all immanentism that cannot be distinguished from pantheism and all process philosophy that is not clear that the source and goal of the process is greater than the process itself. In other words, I believe that the word 'transcendent' in relation to God must have a continuing and unique use. I am further clear that the word 'God' in the use which I have here very crudely indicated and the phrase 'the God and Father of Jesus' designate one and the same Existence. I am not concerned to give any reasons for these positions, but only to indicate what some may call the basis, and others may call the prejudices, from which I approach the subject. Theology is ultimately a properly independent subject because it has ultimately a properly independent object.

But the proper procedure of theological education, as I understand it, needs to be guided by two factors. First, what I may be allowed to call my basis, which I have so crudely and roughly indicated, is extrinsically debatable. I need only touch on some of these areas of debate. We are all familiar with them. There are immense difficulties in the notion of transcendence, and it is a very proper question as to whether the notion of transcendence can be given a continuing and satisfactory content. There is also the question of the relation of this notion of transcendence to the worshipful. The very existence, indeed, of anything which can properly be called worshipful is quite rightly, in many ways, called in question. I myself believe that the atheistic existentialist has a very powerful case, a case which those people who welcome the arrival of atheism in Christianity would do well to examine. For, as Nietzsche knew, the death of God is a much greater tragedy than many of our latter-day atheists have yet discovered. But it may very well be the case that God is dead. There are immense difficulties in continuing the notion of God, in continuing even the notion of the fact that the universe as a whole may be considered as a whole. I see very strong grounds, often, against any sort of rational or idealistic assumption that 'the whole' makes sense. Some things may make some sense some of the time but that there is overall sense to be made seems to me very often to be highly debatable. Further, we know that there are very strong religious traditions other than the tradition of theism, and these are religious traditions that deal with the worshipful and with such matters as values. And then, again, there is the particular point which I put in the form that the word 'God' designates the same existence as the phrase, 'the God and Father of Jesus'. Here we come to the question of what I might be allowed to call the 'hypostatic centrality of Jesus', namely that the person who was designated Jesus is at the very centre of our understanding of God, human beings and the universe. We know, of course, that this is extrinsically debatable and that there are good grounds for wondering whether it is either nonsense or overweening arrogance. Therefore, the basis for theology, for Christian theology, for the sort of theology which I think it proper for us to be concerned with here, is extrinsically debatable. It is under challenge and it is challengeable. This does not mean that it is not true, but the question is at issue and properly at issue.

But not only is it the case that my basis is extrinsically debatable. I think it very important to observe that my basis is, if I may so put it, intrinsically explosive. Transcendence is transcendence; that is to say, it must pass beyond any account that one can give of it, any understanding one may have of it, and one is always committed as much to the *via negativa* as to positive utterance, and it is true that anything which is said about God, if it is truly said about God, must be untrue. Further, theism of the sort with which I believe we have to do in the biblical tradition and in its culmination in Jesus Christ and in its understanding in the Christian tradition – theism of this sort, transcendent as it is, precisely demands immanence and process. The God with whom I believe we have to do is a God who is very present in, and very concerned with, the whole process of the universe. It therefore follows that we are bound to be committed to a constant reconsideration of the meaning of our theological terms as the processes of the universe continue.

And there is a third reason why this basis is intrinsically explosive. That is, that the central figure in our understanding of this, humanly speaking, Jesus the Christ, has the form of the servant, and if we consider the form that he took, the life which he lived, we are bound to be confronted with the fact that the dimensions of love are constantly to be extended, that the dimensions of love are explored by the total self-giving of those who love, and therefore that every horizon which we believe defines what we understand about love, which is at the heart of our understanding of God through Jesus, must be a horizon that must always be extended.

Therefore not only is it the case that the basis of this theology is extrinsically debatable, challengeable by much in the universe and in our own lives and in our own experience, but it is also the case that any true understanding of a theology which is about such a God as I believe it to be about is always bound by its own understanding of this God, its own commitment to the involvement of this God in the world and its own following of the crucified Jesus to be constantly blown apart, to be constantly obliged to rethink and go further. Therefore, although theology is a proper subject, it cannot be an isolated subject. It cannot be a subject on its own, and at any given time and situation the very internal logic, if I may so put it, of this theology may require it to find its form, the form in which it expresses itself, the form, therefore, in which it is to be studied and taught, from other subjects. God is, as far as we can see, very much committed to and involved in all those things which are the proper areas of study of the other subjects.

Therefore, I would seem to be obliged to reformulate my original way of putting what I have to discuss, namely theological education. It is true we have to consider education in theology and ministerial education, but both of these things have to be considered in the light of the fact that the ultimate scope of theology, properly so called, must be universal and that therefore the particular theology which we can pursue is a proper subject only if it is properly related to other subjects. What sort of thing, then, would this or does this imply in practice?

First, by way of preface or introduction, it implies, I am clear, that in our theological education and in our concern for theological education we must always start from the particular place where we happen to be. One of the present tendencies which I find particularly tiresome is that persons suppose that because everything is in a state of flux one has to arrive at some firm ground before one can start going anywhere. Whereas, in fact, the essential theological principle of involvement requires that we should always have the confidence of knowing that we can start right from where we are. Not only can we not help starting from where we are, but above all we must not be afraid of it. The God and Father of Jesus and what we know about him both licenses and requires us to start from involvement right where we are, and to start hopefully and seriously from where we are. The God and Father of our Lord Jesus Christ licenses this hopeful starting, because the whole of the biblical revelation makes clear to us that in some real sense it is precisely out of historical particularity and situations, as men encounter them, that God makes himself known and works out his purpose. The God and Father of our Lord Jesus Christ requires us to start hopefully with this involvement, because the incarnation of Jesus makes it clear that God furthers his purpose by clothing himself, if I may so put it, in ordinary reality, in ordinary history, not in some specially significant history.

Here I might break off to observe that it seems to me that Bultmann's insistence on decisively separating historic *Historie* as 'one damned thing after another' from *Geschichte*, 'something which has meaning', is a fundamental gnostic error, and a destruction of the gospel. It is precisely because God is involved in one damned thing after another that we have the gospel. Therefore, we must be quite clear – and particularly clear at a time like this when everybody, even Oxford, is inventing new syllabuses – that this does not mean that we wait until we have the perfect syllabus before we do theology: we do theology by starting from even the impossible syllabus that we have now, and there must be no looking for theoretical starting places.

The fact that I have thought it necessary to draw attention to some intrinsic definitions about theology does not mean that I suggest for one moment that we have to do anything like start all over again. There must be no looking for theoretical starting places; rather, an attempt to be obedient right where we are, on the basis which we have, moving our obedience in a certain direction, the direction which is defined by facing the demands of the situation. The very questioning of syllabuses can be faithfully and not neurotically undertaken by seeking to look for the demands of God in Jesus Christ. And this must be done on the basis of where we are. Therefore, the theology which we are concerned to educate people in and the theological education which we are concerned to give must be strictly *emergent* theology. We must not get ourselves in any way into that very common and insidious and sapping error of adopting what I call an 'If only . . .' approach; if only we were able to have brighter pupils, if only we were able to have better teachers, if only we were able to understand better what the role of the clergy was, if only we knew better what we are up to, then . . . We do not answer any of those questions until we actually do something about it. Thus we need an emergent theology. We proceed from the confidence that it is related to the ultimate given of God's revelation of himself which climaxes in and through Jesus Christ, and yet which has to be opened to the future fulfilment of God's purposes for the universe.

Then, when we come to consider this emergent theology, we are confronted with the fact that the basis of our theology is extrinsically debatable, and that requires that our emergent theology should be *open* theology: a theology which takes care that it makes use of the given of all that has been passed on in the Bible, and in addition is open to all the questions put to it by the world. Doctrine cannot be taught without openness to philosophy, the Bible cannot be taught without openness to history, the doctrine of the church cannot be taught without openness to sociology, and much else in each case of course – these are examples only. The doctrines of man and of the atonement cannot be taught without openness to psychology. And openness must be *openness*, so that there may be a real encounter between the data of the tradition, the data which lie behind and give birth to the record of the Bible, the worship and understanding of the church and our present faith, and the data of the current world, the questions which are validly proposed by any valid discipline, as it is at present validly practised. Of course, taking current disciplines seriously does not necessarily mean taking them at their own evaluation. Each new advance in a particular field of human study tends to suffer for a while from *hybris*, a thing which theology permanently suffers from. So we can throw no stones. None the less, I think truth requires that one should be aware that there is no necessary need to take any particular development at the face value of the discoverers or developers. But they had better be given a hearing because they are likely to know better than us what they are up to. Therefore, there must be real openness. And I am much inclined to the view that in theological education the precise syllabus hardly matters. It must clearly fall within a certain area, but as long as the syllabus gives time for openness and the method of openness is applied – then, I suspect, theology will be done. What we have to be careful about is that there is no escape into mere theology, theology on its own, which is no theology at all because it is not about God, but is the biblical version of either classical or oriental studies or archaeology. There is a detached study about what some men thought in some way, at some time, about some being who might be called God. This may well be a perfectly proper study, but on its own it is not theology. Theology is about the actual relationship of God to actualities and the study of archaeology, history or other men's concepts is simply a means to that end, theologically speaking.

Further, not only do we require an emergent theology and an open theology, we have to take into account the fact that our basis is not only extrinsically debatable but also intrinsically explosive, as I have sought to indicate, and therefore our emergent theology, which must be open theology, must be *broken* theology. Perhaps this hardly needs illustrating in view of what I said earlier. But in view of the Godness of God, we have to be clear that in our doctrine we are concerned as much with an apophatic way, a way of denial, a way of having to warn ourselves that we must go beyond, as with a cataphatic way, a way of statement and affirmation. And in this connection we have to be quite clear that it is impossible to do theology apart from a spiritual discipline which is related to worship and prayer. If you want the cash value, if I may be allowed to use that term, of the word 'God', you can get nowhere near it without worship and prayer, and I cannot see how any theology can be done except by people who worship and pray. But even that means, or that means more than ever, that we are confronted with necessary brokenness. In this area of theology shading into worship and prayer, I think we are confronted with the same sort of problem as the scientist or any seeker after the truth has, when he comes into the area where he knows he is encountering his responsibility for truth, to the facts which build up into the truth. There is a commitment here without which there can be no real theology, and this demands brokenness, and because theology demands brokenness, there is no real tension between commitment to theology and open theology. That is the way forward, I am sure, in the matter of theology in a secular university or indeed in a secular world. If we are true to our theology, we must be so open that we cannot be accused of wrongly distorting the secular possibilities. That, any rate, is the goal; that, at any rate, is the ideal. In practice it is much more difficult. Since also, as I have said, we must be concerned with immanence and with process, it will always be the case that in our theology we shall never know in theory, only in practice, where to draw the line. Where *do* you draw the line? The answer is, 'you don't know until you try', and it is no excuse for holding back from such an inquiry that once you start you don't know where you're going to stop, because if there is a God and if he has made himself known in Jesus Christ and if the Holy Spirit is still the personal presence of such a God, then we shall not all go over the precipice. And if there is not a God then we should be thankful that we do go over the precipice. But we cannot suppose that in advance we may draw a line on mythology, on restatement of doctrine, on reconsideration of morals, though we must be clear that since there is a God we shall find a line to draw.

Thirdly, on this matter of broken theology: since we are concerned with the One who is in the form of the servant, we must be quite clear that our theological method involves quite as much listening as speaking. Theology cannot and must not claim an empire. She is not the queen of the sciences but the servant of all, at the service of other subjects in which we have to enable the terms of our service to emerge. For example, it is quite hopeless to suppose that we may dictate to psychology, psychiatry and so on the way in which we shall discuss human nature. On the other hand, when theology has listened to what these disciplines have to say, then it will be ready to make its contribution by maintaining that human nature cannot be discussed without the insights that lie behind, and are sometimes expressed in, such things as the doctrine of the atonement and the doctrine of original sin.

So theology is a proper subject, but to proceed properly it must be emergent, open and broken. What, then, of the actual practice of theology at the present time? There are signs of a concern to rebuild syllabuses and to construct departments which will be much more immediately related to the practical situation as we now have it than to the situation as we have inherited it. Thankfully, there is a good deal of looking for openness, a good deal of concern that the boundaries between theology and other subjects should be fully explored and, as far as possible, be integrated and opened up to one another. But I am not at all sure that many of us are really very ready for what I would call positive brokenness, that is to say a real readiness to reconsider our whole position which does not stem from a weak belief that the positions have been dissolved into other positions, but from positive belief that a very costly openness is required if we are to enter fully into our heritage. There is, I think, in many areas still a fear of commitment, still a tendency to retreat into scholarship in the name of keeping up standards, when it is not at all clear that this is really the issue. However, it ought to be noted here that there is a failure of nerve in very many subjects at the moment, and a refusal to venture outside any very small area of specializing in which certainty can reasonably be obtained. Here there is a great opportunity for theology to be bold. For theology, because she believes in God, must believe that there is still the possibility of building towards a synthesis, of getting something unified out of human studies. Theology, therefore, might very well play an important part in recovering the nerve of the studies in universities where people have withdrawn more and more into their own compartments. There are signs elsewhere that others are becoming aware that this compartmentalization must stop. The way in which theology responds to this opportunity constitutes a challenge, and could become a judgment.

If one turns to theological colleges, it is possible to see a considerable desire to emerge into openness and a readiness to take up subjects which clearly both bite into Christian tradition and bite into our present problems. Many of the demands and unrest and debates about what goes on in theological colleges arise out of the desire to be more open and to have the whole of our training much more directly related to the problems which God is pressing upon the church. It is also clear that there are very interesting experiments going on between particular theological colleges and groups of theological colleges and practical studies in such areas as mental hospitals, relations with social services and so on.

But while there are many hopeful signs of experimentation, there are a number of grounds for concern.

The first is that it still seems to be the case that over a large area of theological college thinking, 'theology' is itself a dirty word. I imagine that the blame for this must fall on persons like myself who are supposed to be academic theologians. We have not yet recovered our nerve about the proper role of theology within all our other concerns, so as to be aware that all our concerns have to be theologically aligned and orientated if they are to be true and proper concerns for the Christian church and the Christian ministry. And then there is, I suspect, no desire to emerge very far; there is too much readiness to fall back on the saying, 'Prepare me for the job' – the picture of the job being some image in people's heads rather than the rather alarming prospect that there is actually on the ground. It is not at all plain that people are really sufficiently confident in their faith to prepare for the openness, let alone for the brokenness, which real theology and valid ministerial training today requires. Further, it is to be questioned how colleges can face the rigours of responding to the situation at the present when their staffs are so clericalized. I am bound to say that I myself find much more interesting theology going on, though it is not always recognizable immediately, when I am mixed up with certain types of debate among psychologists, psychiatrists, economists, than when I am mixed up in most of the debates with my theological colleagues. Surely, until the laity are playing a full part in demanding theology and requiring theology and contributing to theology, we shall not get the open and broken theology which we require.

One fact remains. The practice of theology and the practices of theological education require a great deal of change. It often seems that the Church of England, along with many other churches, is in favour of change as long as it makes no difference. For making differences involves risking what you have. But failure to risk what one has for the sake of development shows lack of faith in the viability and validity of what we have. We have to recover our theological nerve sufficiently to put our theology really at risk. Until we risk theology as emergent, open and broken, theology will be neither educationally exciting nor excitingly educational.

4 · To whom do we pray?

(1967)

The situation with regard to prayer, the spiritual life, knowledge of God, is both far worse than people in the church think and far better. There is no danger of God being dead; the situation is far better than a lot of people seem to think in that respect – or have the courage at any rate to live up to in that respect. But it is far worse than, for instance, the gentlemen who sit on the Anglican Liturgical Commission think.

Most of the church's investigations into the liturgy and the like today are in the form still of escapist activities of persons who will not face up either to God or the world. The main reason people think God is dead is the poverty of the spirituality of the church at large, for spirituality is central to the whole business of belief in God. Therefore, the question to start from is, 'To whom do we pray?'; and the answer is, 'To the God and Father of Jesus Christ'. That is, the God of Abraham, the God of Isaac, the God of Jacob and, as Pascal would say, not the God of the philosophers.

This is the starting-point, because if you start from the God of the philosophers or the fact that the philosophers have now decided there is no God, you are back into the realm of mythology, for all metaphysics are mythology. They represent the tales that people have told about the world on the basis of what they have thought the world to be – or what they might think the world to be. Thus scientific metaphysics are also mythology. But Abraham is probably not mythology; Isaac and Jacob might be; Jesus Christ

162

certainly is not. The more I study these matters, the more it is clear to me that the question of starting-point, the question of that which is given, is fundamental, and I remain unrepentantly certain that the only religion which is finally based on anything other than mythology is Christianity. Science in its proper sphere has something to go on; Christianity has something ultimately given to go on; everything else is mythology in the end.

So we begin with the God and Father of Jesus Christ; and this is the God of Abraham, Isaac and Jacob. There are really only two possible foci for the spiritual life: one is God himself and the other is me now in the presence of God.

There is no answer to the question, 'To what do we pray?' This is always the mistake of any sort of substitute-talk like 'ground of being' and so on; you cannot pray to a 'what'. In an address which Paul Tillich gave in the synagogue in New York on the death of Martin Buber, he said that one of the things that Buber taught him was that the term 'God' is a primary term and there is no substitute for it.

I stand by what I understand to be the Augustinian and Anselmian, and I would indeed say Barthian, tradition of spirituality. Unless there is a discovering in encounter of God, then I see no possibility of putting meaning into the symbols of the church, because the symbols of the church are ultimately concerned with response to God, who can be described and defined in no other terms than that he is God. Therefore, unless there is direct encounter with the Reality who is God, there is no evidence for this Reality. And that is why prayer, in its fullest sense of the term, which in the end has got to become living, is at the heart of the matter. Tinkering with symbols is neither here nor there. When you see the problem properly, however, you may well have to do a lot of things with symbols, because any symbols which get in the way of this directness or do not facilitate our opening up to God are a menace.

So we pray to the God and Father of our Lord Jesus Christ, the God who is discovered in encounter, who is vindicated in Jesus, and whose discovery is renewed in experience. To put it bluntly: people believe in God because people believe in God, and if God does not keep people believing in himself, that will be the end of the matter.

This is why I find the focus of prayer – or I should say the foci of prayer, which are in the end the same thing as the foci of life – in the two areas which I would for convenience call worship and grace. Worship stands for the response to the supremely valuable, ultimately transcendent personalness, who is God. Worship directs us to the reality and worthwhileness of God as God. If you say, 'We can only worship now through working', and so on, you have at once made sure that you will not have a proper use for the word 'God'. I am not saying for a minute that the worship of God does not demand work – that is another matter; but one focus of prayer is worship, which in this context stands for the fact that God is God. There is this indefinable 'other' who is God, who is best described as the Father – the God and Father of Jesus Christ – and to whom we are making response; and the end of the response is God, just as the beginning is, I am increasingly convinced, philosophically and practically, that either this is true or everything is nonsense. In the end language will not hold together, science will not hold together, certainly psychology will not hold together, community will not hold together, people will not hold together, humanity will not hold together if everything has to be described in terms of something else which requires something else to describe it in terms of.

It occurred to me the other day as I was gazing in a tube train at a poster which said 'There is no substitute for wool', that if you go carefully into the development of intellectual thought in the nineteenth century, if you go to meetings of psychiatrists, psychologists and sociologists, if you listen carefully to individual secular people who cannot in truth accept a process that simply goes on and on and on, then the other slogan to put beside it is 'There is no substitute for God'. Indeed, to know what truly prayer might mean in a secular age, we should read Sartre and see if we can do better than he. For if we can do better than he, then, providing the human situation is being faced as clearly as he faces it, we have already got on to praying. Of course, many people look as though they are doing better than he because they have not analysed it as he has. Sartre is the man who knows what it is to be a human being in a secular age in the sense of 'there is no God'. Many of the Americans who speak of the 'death of God' do not seem to know what this is at all. They seem to be people who go around treating the death of God as if it were a farce or perhaps a comedy. Nietzsche knew it was a tragedy and went mad, and now Sartre knows it is a tragedy but has not gone mad.

The other focus of prayer is grace: the awareness, or the occasional possibility of awareness, or living in the hope that there might be this awareness, of the presence of an otherness which gives resources beyond one's own. This is the experience of worthwhileness actually here and now. It is an experience of the immanence of the transcendent. Our spirituality must be concerned with evoking and developing and following up this awareness, this awareness of an otherness which is closer than ourselves. Indeed, the ultimate basis for prayer must be trinitarian. That is to say, we are concerned with the God who is wholly God and therefore wholly other, who is wholly incarnate in Jesus Christ without in any way diminishing or detracting from his utter otherness, and who is also present in personalities and through personalities as the Holy Spirit. And it is this being taken up by God for God which saves the whole of life from absurdity.

Prayer, then, is to the God and Father of our Lord Jesus Christ, who is discovered in encounter, vindicated in Jesus, and renewed in experience; and this experience has two loci, worship and grace, in which God the Holy Spirit is immanently at work. Once we have understood this, we may turn to the question of what prayer means in a secular age. We then get on to all the difficulties that arise over what is the really distinctive thing about our secular age, which is its flatness. We have produced a manner of thinking, which affects many more people than reflect upon it, that is very largely 'flat'. It has no room for the notion of transcendence in any way, and has fallen into the habit of believing that the only way language works satisfactorily is when it is literal. The model of meaningful language is the instructions which you can understand on the back of a television set or the instructions which you could understand if you had the proper instruction in television mechanism and so on. This is where the whole Christian situation is so much up against it that it has caused people to panic and think that the thing to do is to throw over transcendence instead of to renew spirituality, so that Christians can live so authentically that people will want to learn the language.

It is true that the *Zeitgeist* is against even our authentic symbolism working. For example, people are overwhelmed by arguments like those based on size. Are you going to say that there is a possibility of personal response when the universe is so macroscopically and microscopically vast? But this sort of argument is simply a logical muddle which gains added force from our own psychology. Who has discovered that the universe is so macroscopically vast and so microscopically vast? Human beings. And there is no logical reason for deciding that what reason has told us obliterates our reason. I know that logical reasons often carry little psychological weight, but they are important with regard to truth, even if less so with regard to persuading people of truth. At any rate, we can be clear that arguments from size ought really to carry no weight. But one of the reasons why they have such an impact on the whole area of prayer is precisely because our spirituality has been so poor and people have largely lost the living awareness of absoluteness, infiniteness, the otherness of God. The spiritual poverty of the church makes it look as if God was the being who existed to keep in order a measurable universe, and now that we know that the universe is immeasurable, we know also that we have no one keeping it in order. Logically this is all wrong, but that does not mean that it is not a problem. It is a matter of authenticity, in the spiritual life as elsewhere. People learn or know that other people can learn about nuclear physics. They realize that beyond a certain stage even most educated people cannot go because only a few people can cope with certain types of mathematics, but they will still believe that those people are on to something because the whole operation is one of authenticity. Similarly, people will learn how to pray – or be prepared to learn how to pray – if it looks as though people who are praying are doing something authentic.

I already referred to how, in the history of thought and in the present situation with regard to science and psychology, there is the possibility of awareness of mystery when I coined the phrase

'There is no substitute for God.' People in the church at large ought to be clear that there are no decisive reasons for holding that you cannot believe in God and that if we analyse, say, the biological sciences or the philosophical scene or the problems that doctors, social workers, psychiatrists and so on are up against in the community, there is quite as much evidence that no framework will satisfactorily include, explain and satisfy the human as there is evidence that any framework will. Indeed, this is to put the case at its least favourable. I stress this in relation to praying because it seems to me we have to have the nerve to pray, and one of the things which is related to praying in a secular age is the recovery of nerve. It is a pathetic fact, although I think there are understandable psychological reasons for this, but a large number of people are put off doing things or trying things by the sort of general feeling that they would be absurd or nonsensical. We may compare, for example, the frequent current use of the adjective 'thinkable'. I think that the only thing to do when we are told that nowadays we cannot think so and so is to get up and say, 'Oh, can't I? I can'; and if somebody says, 'How can a rational man be a Christian?', the answer is, 'I am a rational man and I am a Christian, therefore a rational man can be a Christian.' I may be no more rational than most and I'm a bad Christian, but there it is.

So there is no substitute for God. But it might be, of course, that although there is no substitute for God there is no God. My present argument is not an argument for the existence of God. I am only pointing out that the existence of God is as much a possibility as atheism. It is here that we see the central importance of praying. The really clinching business about the existence of God is the spiritual life, and you will not find the decisive evidence anywhere else.

Now the problems that arise over the possibility of believing in God in so vast a universe and of 'How can we talk about personal purpose responding to personal purpose in so vast a field?' are, I believe, to be tackled with the help of the unique Christian discovery of the relation between transcendence and immanence, or, if you like, between detachment and involvement, which I was referring to when I touched on the doctrine of the Trinity. If we study how it arose, we see that this doctrine reflects the Christian understanding of what seems to have been the last thing that men wanted to think. Therefore we may be clear that it has been experimentally discovered and is open to experimental vindication. In fact, the doctrine of the Trinity is an experimental doctrine which is related precisely to the question of transcendence and immanence. What those who have popularized the 'death of God' say is absolutely true: God, in his Godness, is to be encountered in the here and now, and God is as fully God when he is in the here and now as when he is God in his 'thereness'. The point about most ecclesiastical spirituality, most ecclesiastical use of the Bible, most ecclesiastical activity is that it is neither here nor there. That is, it does not key in with the actual concerns of living men and women, so it is not here, which is where God is; and it is not there, as it does not really have spiritual depth. To be out of touch with the 'here' is fatal for godly living. The spirituality of Christianity is precisely concerned with the 'here' which has the 'there' in it, and the 'there' which draws us out of the 'here', but not with a 'neither here nor there' in the 'betwixt and between'.

But it might be said, 'Well, in that case, how do you pray?' The first point to be considered is that contained in the oft-repeated and much-abused slogan of Dom Chapman, 'Pray as you can and don't pray as you can't.' This is not to be interpreted in such a way as to lead to the expectation of 'cheap grace', as seems to happen with many who use the last few pages of Bonhoeffer and do not seem to know about his life. We need to be liberated from the inhibiting burdens of past patterns of prayer still imposed upon us as if they were *the* ways to pray, so that we feel guilty when they do not help us. But prayer remains an activity which requires attention, effort and organization, however much this must be combined with tentativeness and sensibility. We can get a great deal of help from psychological insights into the way in which personalness is liberated. One of the things to be investigated carefully is what can we now learn from psychology about such things as regularity, patterns of praying and so on, in order that people may be liberated and not fettered in realizing the awareness of God in the midst. Everyone who lays down, or who is concerned with helping in, a pattern of prayer knows it is not the pattern that matters; it is whether the pattern will help us get on to something. But even I, in only twelve years of being a priest, have come up against people to whom I have had to say, 'Stop listening to your spiritual director, because until you stop, and stop trying harder and stop trying to fulfil his pattern, there will be no liberation towards the true end – God in you.' We must be set free, and set others free for, flexibility and openness.

One of the things we have to do is to get people to recognize what in their lives is really either praying or very nearly praying anyway. A phrase which helps me in this area is that of 'focussed awareness'. 'Focused awareness': helping people to have time or to think it worthwhile to be quiet, to attend to whatever there is to attend to, in the belief that in the end this may lead them to discover that there is one sense in which they have been praying on and off all their lives. The whole question of attention, contemplation, focussed awareness is very relevant to spirituality today. Of course, one knows from the history of Christian and general spirituality that this can go either way. Contemplation and awareness are not necessarily personal. We have nature mysticism, oriental mysticism and so on. But this is where the Christian tradition and the authentic living Christian fellowship comes in. I have actually seen, although admittedly on rare occasions, a man who has been set free to attend to what he was nearly attending to anyway, so that he has thereby become aware of what is really the dimension of God and then been able to recognize that this is really also what Christians are trying to be concerned with. But, of course, if there is no focussed awareness or its equivalent in the particular Christian community he happens to be connected with or ever sees, there never will be a tie-up.

Another aspect of all this is what I would call 'corporate attention' in the sense of dedication to a common worthwhile end. This seems to be a way in which many people – especially young people – have a chance of getting on to the dimension of God. They are concerned with 'What shall we do about Vietnam?', 'What shall we do about mental health?', and so on. And the coming together to work together is another form of concentration, a form of concentration which is much more corporate, which is much more a matter of the will and the emotions and the desire to work something out. This ties in with the fact that in many ways prayer should be understood as a form of action rather than as a form of thought.

The sketchy suggestions touched on here are related to the earlier part of what has been said by the fact that the initial assumption was that either God is there and is concerned to make himself known or there is nothing one can do about it. The question is, how to develop an awareness of the fact that God is there. My first way was the individual matter of focussed attention, and the second one was the more active, corporate attention to a worthwhile end. But we must be aware that there is no reason why at any given time a particular person should know that what he is engaged on is the beginning of a response to a transcendent personality or personalness. We have to be ready to allow this sort of thing to go on for a long time in certain cases, and not try at once to drag it into the church, where it will be killed off. There will be many 'fringe activities' (on the fringe of the church, that is) which are true spirituality and which will mean in the end that those involved will be led into the fullness of their ultimate meaning through the authenticity of the Christian fellowship and the interpretation of the Christian tradition; but at any given stage this will not necessarily be the case. We must reckon with those people who use all their energy in campaigning for nuclear disarmament, social work and the like. This is the way their whole energies go, and they have no time for the church. But the energy they are developing is spiritual energy. And we have to be sensitive to the ways in which this sort of energy leads on to the dimensions which raise questions of grace and worship and the whole matter of transcendence, mystery and the dimension of God.

Then, more within the Christian tradition, we need to have much more training at all levels than we have tended to do in what might be called, for the sake of brevity, 'openness to inspiration'. People must be trained to know that prayer is a form of action rather than a form of thought in the sense that it requires effort. Further, we ought now to be beyond the stage of saying, 'Well, the Bible is thoroughly undermined and archaic.' We ought to have understood that the Bible has no use so long as it is just treated as 'the Holy Bible'. We have to go beyond that and teach people to concentrate on it, not listen to it as if it was a 'holy book', but just listen to it. Similarly, we need to tell people just to look at and reflect on the record of Jesus. It is of interest that among some agnostic students of ancient history there is a revival of interest in the whole history of Christianity as part of culture. And after a detailed study of the New Testament they may say, 'Well, the Book of Acts is an extremely good piece of evidence about what the world was like in those days;' and then they go on and say, 'If you actually read the Gospels, Jesus makes quite an impression.' They feel free to say that so long as they do not have to fear the Christians are going to 'get at them' about it. We are, I believe, nearly at the stage when it will be possible to let the Bible speak for itself again because it no longer looks as if we are trying to bludgeon people over the head with it. If a man can attend to the Gospels in an unprejudiced manner, not supposing them to be holy books to be treated with caution and care, then it may well strike him how extraordinary Jesus truly is. But there must be unprejudiced openness to what is really there.

So openness to inspiration by concentration on what actually is in the Bible and to the patterns of Jesus is another way of rediscovering the possibility of transcendence wherein may be found the response to personalness. Finally, this may lead eventually to the position – and this seems to me to come last – where once again we may actually be able to enter into intercessory and petitionary prayer, because as we are alerted to this personal response to personalness we may gradually be aware once again of what simple people have always known, which is that you cannot really put anything past God, that the transcendence-immanence situation is such that even a miracle is not beyond the bounds of possibility. It is very right and important to put it this way round, because it is belief in and experience of the possibility of a personal presence which is essential before anything which 'miracle' in the biblical sense stands for can be in any way thinkable today. Hence 'praying for', in any powerfully individual sense of interceding and petitioning, seems in the present climate of opinion the last thing that people can be expected to do. But 'last' here should be used in the teleological sense. I suspect that if one goes far enough along this way of the knowledge of the response to personal presence and purpose it will be possible to intercede without any sense of embarrassment, which I, as still a 'secular' man, continue to feel acutely.

5 · The Sacraments in the Church in Relation to Healing

(1967)

Our concern is with that joyful response to the givenness of Jesus Christ in his church which liberates the power of the gospel and enables true health. Jesus Christ himself is *the* sacrament because in his incarnation he embodied the union of God and his creation which fulfils the possibilities of the world in the personal fullness of God. Our entering into the fullness of this possibility, discovering even that it is a possibility and what the possibility means is a process. The sacraments of baptism and eucharist focus the universal givenness of Jesus Christ in the action of the church located in the particularity of the local church and congregation. So the universal reality of Jesus Christ is related to us within the particular, local and limited processes of which we are a part.

I suggest that this means that we have to understand baptism into Jesus Christ in relation to health along the following lines. If we are baptized, we are made part of the community of Jesus Christ and of the pattern of the life of Jesus. This is a life of being plunged into living through dying so that we may experience creative living. In practice, this is not to be understood romantically, but realistically. It means that there is strength available (the strength of Jesus Christ) to face hopefully and openly all the demands our living makes upon us. Situations in our lives are constantly, in small ways and great, making demands upon us to be altered. As we are baptized into Jesus Christ, we have the strength, if we wish, to face these demands and be altered into deeper and truer selves instead of being obliged to defend ourselves against life and to become more and more closed and defenceless. This strength is available to the individual through the community and to the community through the individual. Baptism in Christ means that all plunging into life can be hopeful, and what we learn in the little crises of our lives can be built up into the strength to see and know that our greater crises of suffering and doubt and our ultimate crisis of death are all likewise part of the pattern of the life of Jesus and therefore part of created living into the true, full and eternal life in which Jesus Christ unites God and man.

The eucharist, the Lord's supper, the holy communion stands in a similar way for the givenness of Jesus Christ in relation to the processes of our lives. The sacrament understood as eucharist is given to make real the fact that all life may be thankfully received and responded to as an opportunity to receive, whether through brokenness or through a new wholeness, the pattern and process of living into divine fullness. Understood as the Lord's supper, the sacrament is given to make real the fact that all people have a hopeful history within the history of the people of God. Fragmentation and hopelessness is not the dominating fact of our lives. God makes a pattern for his people, and each man and woman can receive the reality of this pattern and be given direction, life and hope. Understood as communion, the sacrament is given to make real the fellowship and family of God to which all men and women are called to belong and so be at home and be sustained in their journeying through the process of life to the realized fellowship of love which is the kingdom of God. The sacrament of the altar is given to make real the good news that any and every life in any situation can be thankfully received, hopefully directed, sustained through fellowship and developed through sacrifice.

Because we are given the eucharist, we are to be enabled to receive the demands of life, of our neighbour, of the world as opportunities to receive more of the life of Christ. To give ourselves to our neighbour and to the world is to receive Christ in and through our neighbour and the world. It is by giving out life that we receive back life. Sacrifice is not the mutilation of life in ourselves, but the finding of life in our neighbour. Such creative giving and receiving is the fruit and the proclamation of that victory of Christ of which the eucharist is the given symbol with creative power.

But this given reality of the sacrament will not be realized by us, we shall not show the fruits of sacramental living if we withdraw to the sacrament of the altar and Lord's table as if it was a private medical or even magical thing given to privileged Christians to enable them to be sustained against the world and away from its pressures and threats. For example, to have ecclesiastically authorized ministers slipping into hospitals to dole out the sacraments to the privileged few who are marked out for this privileged and 'spiritual' medication is not to respond to and speak of the universal gospel of God, but is to perpetuate churchly selfishness and defensiveness. In such peddling of 'the medicine of immortality', the church too often makes it look as if it has no water of life even for its members, still less for all people. We all have to learn – every congregation of Christians and every ordained minister of the church – that eucharistic and sacramental living in the world is not achieved by the performing of the rite of the eucharistic sacrament as such and in isolation. In too many congregations the celebration of the sacrament is a mere rite. This rite has to have its reality kindled in the lives of the members of the congregation, laity and minister alike, by a eucharistic and sacrificial readiness for living in community. There will be no reality experienced in and through the sacrament in the midst of the congregation gathered if there is no sacramental living in the midst of the world by the congregation dispersed. The eucharist offers strength for thankful living to those who bring to it the desire and attempt to practise a thankful receiving of the demands of their neighbours and their world. The holy communion offers the strength of sustaining fellowship to those who are open to the demands of being a sustaining neighbour, member of a family, part of a professional, industrial or educational team. The Lord's supper offers the strength of direction and purpose to those who are concerned to give purposeful hope to those by their side who live in apathy, indifference or despair. If there is no reality of encounter with the life of Christ in the world, then there will be no reality of encounter with the life of Christ in the sacrament. It is the demands of sacramental living, of drawing health from sickness, living from dying, believing from doubting, response to the love of God from the indifference and cruelty of human beings, which will send members of the Christian congregation thankfully and hopefully to the eucharist. There they may receive the power to offer what they have so far discovered of sacramentality, of the reality of God in the realities of the world. And as they receive this power to offer, so they will receive the power to be directed and the power to be renewed for further and deeper creative living – but living not at the eucharist but in the world. The ineffectiveness, either by way of power of creative living or of faith-kindling proclamation of the Gospel, of the formal presence of the sacraments in so many situations of sickness and of healing, shows us that we are being called to receive a renewal and a reform of our understanding and practice of the sacraments by a faithful facing up to the opportunities and possibilities of sacramental living in the world and for the world.

In this connection, I would also suggest a wider consideration of the celebratory aspects of mankind's life in various cultures. The actual liturgical 'doing' of the sacraments needs to be given a celebratory aspect which is clearly so in terms of the way of life as lived in the society, institution or neighbourhood where the sacrament is being performed. And, conversely, we need to be able to see and heighten the sacramental aspects of the human celebrations of the rhythms of personal and natural life. The gospel declares that Jesus Christ is life that men may have abundant life. Every affirmation of life and of its abundance, birthday, anniversary, turn of the year, gathering of the harvest and so on, needs to be considered for what help and clue it can give us to living life in a celebratory way which is thankful and truly life-affirming. Thus celebration, sacramentality and sacrament may become a chain through which a cleansing, uniting and fulfilling power of the life of Jesus Christ may be received, realized and expressed.

6 · *Worship and Doctrine*

(1964)

I wish to investigate the meaning of the often quoted statement, '*Lex orandi, lex credendi*', that the law of our praying is the law of our believing. This presumably means that worship is relevant to doctrine. I would suggest, however, that it must also mean that doctrine is relevant to worship, and that we have two points here and not one: what you do affects your understanding of what you know, and what you know affects your understanding of what you do. It is worth dwelling upon this point, although it is so obvious, because, with regard to the whole notion of belief in God, we are in some ways in something of a crisis, which could be called a crisis of epistemology, a crisis about our knowing. In this situation, it is important to see that what you know is relevant to what you do, and what you do is relevant to what you know, and that what you know and what you do are not one and the same thing. As yet. I take it that one of *the* points about the Beatific Vision, as it is one of the points about the Being of God himself, is that with it there is a perfect coincidence between – not a coincidence between, but an actual equivalence of – knowing and doing. But here knowing and doing are different things; and when I am talking about knowing, I am talking about knowing in the doctrinal sense: knowing looked at primarily from the end of intellectual formulations, rather than existential impact, if I may put it in such a way.

That this is not merely an academic point, but a perfectly practical point can, I think, be illustrated like this: there are a good many people who say that they believe in the creeds, but it seems that very many people who say this do not really mean it in any sense which involves much of an existential impact. 'I believe in the creed' seems to mean in practice: 'I am worried when people tinker with clauses of the creed. It upsets me. I do not like people to suggest that there are difficulties about the virgin birth. I do not like people to suggest that the notion of ascension is a difficult notion, and so on.' But in practice their belief in the creed makes absolutely no difference. That is to say, they do not seem to have any real understanding which informs the whole of their life and their activity and their commitment to their fellow men and women. Nor do they appear to see what it means to say that in Jesus Christ there is a fresh start, such a fresh start that something like the virgin birth is appropriate to the beginning of it. They do not seem to understand anything about the nature of the ascension in the sense of the life of man being taken up into the life of God, and there being a transfusion between the two.

It therefore emerges that in practice, for a very great number of persons, doctrinal formulations are really fragile shells, or magic symbols. They are something to do with an entity that is very difficult to get at, called 'my faith'. 'My faith' is enclosed in a fragile shell of doctrinal formulations to which no content can be given; but taking one piece out can cause a great deal of worry. Or it is a magic symbol – 'This is untamperable with: that's how I know that God exists.' Thus knowing can very easily become, and it seems to me, pastorally speaking, that it has become in very many cases to very many people, what I might call flatly propositional. It is just a question of sentences which people are prepared to recite. And there is no connection between this type of knowing when it has become this absurdly flat propositional sort, and acting.

On the other hand, there are plenty of people who want to concentrate very much on things like sincerity, warmth, depth of feeling, who would say, 'The great thing about being a Christian is that I am committed,' full stop; 'The great thing about worship is that it comforts me,' full stop; 'The great thing about ethics is that I feel it right to do so and so.' Now it is perfectly true, as no less a person than Pascal has taught us, that the heart has its reasons; but it is also perfectly true that the heart is deceitful and desperately wicked – at least there are reasons for believing this. And it is therefore clear enough that doing, acting, committing oneself, can become concentratedly self-centred. We are confronted at the present time with a large quantity of so-called philosophical and theological understanding which turns the sentence 'This has meaning' into something like 'This sends me', or words to that effect. And to ask the question 'Where to?' is improper.

It is therefore obvious enough that doing and knowing are not necessarily related at the present, and that there are people who put far too much weight on knowing, in the sense of being committed to propositional statements, and there are people who put far too much weight on doing, in the sense of existential impact pure and simple. But I think it is further necessary to declare, and that was the point of my reference earlier on to the Beatific Vision, that here and now there will never be a perfect coincidence between knowing and doing. This is part of the dichotomy of our fallen state, it is part of the fact that it does not yet appear what we shall be. There will always be a tension between knowing and doing, there will always be the danger of over-emphasis in one direction or the other. And it is therefore very necessary, and particularly necessary in view of what may be called the crisis of belief, today, that one should investigate this notion of what is meant by, what is involved in, *lex orandi, lex credendi*. It seems that it must work both ways: that worship affects doctrine, that doctrine affects worship. And there are two particular ways in which the interaction between worship and doctrine is of particular importance at present.

There is, first, a very direct connection between the poverty of much worship, in both its practice and its shape, and the danger of losing grasp of the objectivity, of the otherness, of God. Misunderstanding of the inwardness and the nature and purpose of worship deprives us of the awareness that God is both transcendent and yet, although other than us, none the less real to us. For we must realize that worship is primarily *attending to God as God*. As a matter of fact it is only possible to do this in Christ, through the Spirit, but that is a doctrinal point which I shall come to in a minute. Worship is attending to God as God, and the church at worship is the church concentrating upon the purpose of its existence: that is to say, God. And when the church is concentrating upon the purpose of its existence, the church is in fact concentrating upon the purpose of all men and women, that is to say, God. For to attend to God, to be focussed upon God, to give that attention to God which is worthy of God, which is only possible in Christ through the Spirit, is life. To attend to God is life in at least two senses: first, it is the source of life, for unless one is in relationship to God there can be no real life, no everlasting life; there can in fact be no life, there can only be existing until you die. To attend to God is life both in this sense of giving life, and also in the sense of making life worth living: there is no point in life ultimately, there is no fulfilment in being a human being, except and unless there is fulfilment in all the riches of God, in the perfection of God: so to attend to God is to be concerned with the purpose of life both in the sense of being concerned in the possibility of life, and in the sense of being concerned in the fulfilment of life.

It needs to be made as plain as possible to people who are struggling to believe, to people who would believe but think it is not possible, that it is attending to God with which the church is concerned, and that worship is the very heart and centre of this attending to God. To join in worship is to join in the church's attending to God, in the continuing tradition of what the church has learned through all the ages of how to attend to God. The liturgy brings to bear, crystallizes, focuses upon our daily concerns the whole living understanding which the church has had, and which the church has inherited from Israel, of encounter with the living God. Worship is thus the focus of the prayers of the faithful, both in the sense of distilling and carrying on the essence of the prayers of the faithful all through the ages, and in the sense of drawing together the prayers of the faithful as they are praying at this very time.

In this way, to attend to worship cannot fail to root those who take part in it in the objectivity of God. It is clear in the worship of the church, when it is a true expression of the continuing life of the faithful people of God, that here we are attending to God: not that we are contemplating, full stop, whether it be contemplating our navel, or just contemplating, but that here we are in the presence, that here we are being confronted with a Presence. It is above all in worship that it is made clear beyond a peradventure, as a matter of fact, in the reality of our own lives, and yet a reality which takes us beyond our own lives, that we are indeed responding to God, that grace is not a question of 'You are accepted', but that it is a question of 'You are accepted *by God*'.

Unless this objective worship is at the very centre of the church's life, and conducted in a manner which takes the whole notion of objectivity into full account, it is no wonder that people lose their grasp of the fact that grace is being accepted by *God*, that worship is facing up to *God*, that the response of the Christian is response to *God*. And therefore there is an urgent necessity, in view of the need of making the knowledge of God something real to our contemporaries, to wrestle precisely with the question of the *lex orandi, lex credendi*, of the connection between the objectivity of worship and the assurance of faith that God *is*, and that it is not a question of a theistic attitude, but a question of a response to the living God, the Father of our Lord Jesus Christ. Thus the practice of worship is essentially connected with the continuing grasp on the objectivity of God, and this is a vital matter with regard to belief in the world today.

But it is necessary to see that, when one talks about the objectivity of God, one is talking about the otherness of God, and not about the object-likeness of God. It does not mean that God is an object like ourselves. That would be worship, but it would be idolatrous worship, worship concerned with an object. And this is the point at which it is necessary to change direction and to speak about doctrine in its effect upon worship, instead of worship in its effect upon doctrine. The shape of worship and the understanding of worship must be trinitarian. All of us who have any concern with, or responsibility for liturgical reform, or make any contribution to it, must be clear that we are concerned in the shape of our worship with the worship of God the Father. This point is necessary both doctrinally and practically. Indeed, there is a complete connection between the two.

Worship of God the Father is what the whole Christian tradition both represents and requires. The whole biblical picture and presentation is consummated in response to and worship of the

Father, and it is this presentation of God as God and Father which is sealed by Jesus Christ and presented to us through Jesus Christ. It is, moreover, this worship of the God who is above us, beyond us, transcends us, which is absolutely necessary to our fulfilment in our humanness. It is not possible to have the fulfilment of our humanness except in relation to God: the living God of the Bible, the God of the tradition of the church, the God who is the true and living God. For us to be fulfilled, we must be taken out of ourselves into God. It is no good allowing ourselves to drop back into our ultimate concern, to drop back into our depth; we have to be taken out of the depth into the height of God. It is perfectly true that there are plenty of uses for depth imagery, and that they are very important, but I think the point is made clear to us by trinitarian doctrine, by the worship of the church – and I suspect the psychologists will get on to it in due course – that it is only as we are taken out of ourselves and beyond ourselves, that we are able to be fulfilled as ourselves in God. To put it another way would be to say that there is no point in salvation *from*, unless there is salvation *for*, and that the worship which is of God the Father, of the transcendent God, the overall and beyond, is the essential point of being saved because it is what we are saved *for*.

We worship God the Father, who is the source of Godhead and the fount of all things, and we worship through the Son. The proper place for our understanding of Jesus Christ is in relation to the Father and in relation to us. There must be no Jesus-cult: we worship through the Son, Jesus Christ, the Word of God, who is also the last Adam, Jesus Christ the Mediator between God and man because he is both the very expression (of one substance with the Father) of who and what God is, and also the embodiment of perfect humanity; Jesus Christ who shows us that God is for us, and therefore we dare to worship God, therefore we have a standing-ground in which to worship God; Jesus Christ who is the first true man, and the source of all real humanity. It is in Jesus Christ that the gap – the gap that so worries people who want to fall back purely into subjectivity – the gap between God and man, God who is truly other, and yet God who is infinitely concerned with us, is finally and decisively closed. It is Jesus Christ who is the at-one-ness, who is the union between God and man, and the source therefore of the possibility of our daring to stand before God, and daring to hope to receive the life of God in the mode proper to a creature. And in the present controversies and discussions it seems very clear that we need this balance between otherness and transcendence, and immanence and presence. We need also the union between these two things, the union and communion between God and man, which is established in reality in Jesus Christ, and made possible through Jesus Christ. And therefore we worship God the Father, but we worship through the Son.

And then we worship in the Spirit. God himself is present in his own self both in us and among us, and above all when the church is at worship. That is how the worship is made real, that is how there is the possibility of knowing God and responding to God, that is how it is possible that Jesus Christ himself should be present among us. He is not present among us by an exercise of the historical imagination, by an attitude of mind towards Jesus Christ which puts him in the position of authentic existence; he is present among us because God himself the Holy Spirit dwells both among us and in us, realizing in us the very same reality of presence as is the reality of the presence of God and man in Jesus Christ, as is the reality of the presence of the Father in heaven: it is all one reality, Father, Son and Holy Spirit. We worship God the Father, we worship through the Son, and we worship in the Spirit, and that is the way in which what you might call our doctrinal understanding and the existential impact in fact come together, by one and the same *physis* and *energeia*, by one and the same activity of God in accordance with his essential nature. We are not struggling, we are responding: indeed God is responding in us, and it is on grounds such as this that it seems quite clear that the only practicable shape of worship, the only shape of worship which really makes sense, the only shape of worship which enables worship to be worship, is the pattern of 'Glory be to the Father in the Son through the Holy Spirit,' in the Son because we are Christians, through the Spirit which is the spirit of fellowship.

I have one more point: worship is *the* activity of the church because doctrinally we know that the whole concern of the church, which is the concern of man, is God. But as things are, worship is a separate activity of the church: the church has to have occasions of worship, foci of worship. This is necessary because of sin. We are not yet in the presence of God as we will be, and therefore it is not the case that the whole of our lives are automatically worship; and it is necessary also that the church should come apart to worship, simply because of the distinction which exists between Christians and the world: there are those who respond to God, and there are those who do not as yet consciously respond to God. And therefore there must be this separation and this separateness of the church in worship. But – and this is my last doctrinal point – such worship must not be an isolated activity. Worship is *the* activity of the church, worship has to be a separate activity of the church, but it must not be an isolated activity of the church. If the doctrine of God requires worship to be *the* activity, and the doctrine of sin requires worship to be a separate activity, the doctrine of the incarnation requires that worship should not be an isolated activity. The form of Christ is the form of the church; the body of Christ exists for God and for the world, and the church does not exist for herself. Detachment, separateness, is for the sake of involvement, and I would suggest that the grave danger in the practice of worship in the Catholic tradition is really monophysitism. I know it is clean contrary to the intention, but in practice I believe it to be true.

Let me give two examples as to why I think this is so. Attending to God in practice very often would seem to have been worked out in a way which has forgotten that he is the God who became man. This can be seen in discussions about liturgical reform where, for instance, it is said that worship is the church's activity: what people must do is learn the forms which have been hallowed by tradition. We must not water down anything, we must not pander to *hoi polloi*: we must not be concerned with people who cannot understand: they must be instructed: we have failed to instruct them through the ages, but they must be instructed. We must in no circumstances reform in such a way as to leave anything out: we must do archaeological research: we must go into the whole tradition of things, and make sure that everything is included. There is a great *hybris* here which is particularly given to the priest and those people who think they understand, and in thinking they understand show that they do not. We forget that the God who is attended to in worship is the God who for the purposes of salvation became man. And the notion of there being some virtue in the liturgy being incomprehensible is to my mind perilously near to a blasphemy.

Finally, a point about worship as the *opus Dei*. Here I would suggest that we consider whether worship really is the *opus Dei*, the work of God, any more than mission to mankind and service of mankind, in the involved sense of those terms. We know that one element of meaning in the doctrine of the church as the body of Christ is to show that some concentrate on this function of the church and some on that: the theory is all right, but what about the practice? Without a continual concern for involvement, not merely in God (as it seems to us) but in the concerns and affairs of men and women, of mission and service, there is very grave danger that the *opus Dei* becomes heretical, monophysite. And so it could cease to be *opus Dei*? To suggest such a thing would be over-Protestant? But the question which Protestants in fact put to this whole tradition is that a concentration upon attending to God, if you forget the total involvement of God in the world as it is seen in Jesus Christ, and the necessary response to that, in mission to men and service for men, can be in real danger of betraying the God who is revealed in Jesus Christ. I believe that the whole Catholic tradition is much under judgment here, of course, for being false to itself; not for being untrue in itself, but for being untrue to itself. A much deeper penitence and repentance will be required of the Catholic tradition before we shall find the one fullness which is in the will of God. If we have been priding ourselves at all on preserving objectivity, let us wonder how far in preserving this we have in fact been obedient to the God who is involved, to the incarnate God; for we have to remember that the *doxa*, that the glory of God, the Shekhinah which is the presence of God, according to St John, is seen on the cross, in the suffering man who is wholly identified with the world.

We must attend to God in worship: that is the only way of objectivity, of reality, of truth, and this worship must be trinitarian: 'Glory to the Father, through the Son, in the Spirit'. But we need to remember that on earth the glory is manifested in

Jesus Christ, and that worship is under the judgment of involvement, and that there is the necessity of making sense of worship to all the faithful, and there is the necessity of seeing that worship is united in the one hypostatic reality of the body of Jesus Christ with mission and service to all.

The Authority of Faith

(1969)

In this Christian living with questions, is it possible, despite the fluidity and provisionality of the situation, to state where one *stands*? What account can be given of the basis, rather than the procedure, of the Christian position? The thesis I would put forward is that it is faith which is the only ultimate basis *from the human end* of the Christian gospel and of the authority which church and Bible carry. For the knowledge of the truth of the Christian affirmations about God, the world and self is likewise arrived at by and ultimately rests upon faith. This does not mean that faith is to be opposed to either reason or knowledge, nor does it mean that the authority that is to be encountered in connection with the declaring of the Christian gospel is either unreasoning or unreasonable. Still less does it mean that such authority is absent or is a mere matter of a subjective attitude of those who happen to be believers. But what needs to be exposed and spelled out is the true nature of the situation with regard to the basis of Christian truth and Christian authority. Until this is radically faced-up to, the Christian church will continue to fail to live and to witness with the authority and power to be expected and required of a body sent out and sustained by God.

Faith, then, is, from the human end, the ultimate basis and, ultimately, there is no basis for faith – from the human end. Before we attempt to clarify the concept of faith it is necessary to be clear about 'ultimately' and 'from the human end'.

'Ultimately' is not intended to be taken in, say, a chronological or a psychological sense, but in a logical sense. We must make a distinction here. There is the type of answer one would give to particular questions like, 'Why does my faith exist now?' – or better, as we shall see later, 'Why am I now a believer?', 'Why do I go on believing?', 'How does this unbeliever pass from not having faith to having faith?' These questions can have perfectly good answers which contain elements of psychology and chronology (an account of a series of events and experiences) which are relevant to the particular cases. 'I am now a believer because I was brought up as one and my subsequent experiences have confirmed rather than undermined my faith'; 'X became a believer because Y, an authorized minister of the church, so authoritatively expounded certain passages of the Bible that X felt obliged to make a serious response to that which was so expounded and this has led him into a way of life in which he takes it for granted that the Bible is or can be a source of authoritative insight into God and his purposes.' In this whole range of particular questions and instances it would not be true to say, for instance, that *my* faith has no other basis than my *faith*. My faith can clearly be said to be in some sense based on the faith of those who brought me up and on my own subsequent experience. Similarly, it would be true to say that X's faith is based on the Bible and the church or on the Bible set forth by the church, or on the church expounding the Bible and so on. At any rate, that X is a believer does not depend upon, is not based upon, the fact that X is a believer. I am not therefore arguing that particular cases of faith are based on nothing but the faith of the particular believer or believers concerned. Indeed, it will be a later stage of the argument that faith is neither unreasoning nor unreasonable, precisely because grounds can and should be given for holding particular beliefs or for taking particular decisions which commit one to 'faithful' ways of living and acting.

The question at issue is not a generalized form of questions about why particular believers believe or why particular beliefs should or should not be part of the mental furniture of those who are believers. These questions are, of course, related to the present inquiry and come later. The question at present is about the ultimate validity of faith as such. The church may persuade me to faith. The Bible, through expositors or through my own reading, may compel me to faith. My own experience, as I seek to face life 'faithfully' and to live as a member of the community of believers, may cause me to grow in faith. But supposing I ask myself or I am asked the question whether this faith is an ultimately valid response to 'reality as it really is' or, 'What are the grounds for holding that this faith is somehow or other true, laying hold of truth, related to truth . . ?'? It is an accurate description of present facts that I am encouraged in a faithful attitude by church, Bible, fellow believers and experience, and, indeed, the faithful attitudes 'work', i.e. are 'life-enhancing', in a way which believers and unbelievers might agree to recognize. But are they grounded in objective truth? To put it crudely and bluntly, 'What is the basis for maintaining that faith is true?'

It is in connection with this type of logical question that faith is, from the human end, the ultimate basis, and, ultimately, there is no basis for faith – from the human end. There are many what might be called 'mediate' arguments for faith. That is to say, there are many reasons (as I shall maintain, validly and reasonably called 'reasons') which persuade people to commit themselves to belief and which justify the holding of particular beliefs. Moreover, it may very well be the case that it is right and proper that most believers for most of the time should be convinced by and remain contented with the 'mediate' arguments only. But when and where the ultimate question of faith is raised it is necessary to be clear that there is no 'final' argument. To appeal to church or Bible as ultimate logical *guarantees* of the truth of the faith which is proclaimed is patently circular. This patent circularity could be ignored as long as church or Bible enjoyed an unquestioned prestige. But once external changes and internal divisions and questionings remove this prestige, then the question of what is the *final* authority, the *ultimate* argument has to be faced in its starkness. The present thesis is that there is no ultimate *argument*, only mediate arguments, and the final authority comes from faith – but it is none the less authoritative faith, nor any the less connected with truth. From the human end there is only one way out of the logical circle which arises whenever an attempt is made to find a *basis* for Christian faith, e.g. 'Why do you believe so and so? Because it is true. How do you know it is true? Because the church teaches it. How does the church know it is true? Because she believes it and has always believed it.' The only way out of this circle is not the authority of the church and the authority of the Bible refurbished by either being brought up to date or being restored to its old weightiness. The only way out is the authority of faith.

To clarify and support this thesis further and as a step towards the clarification of the concept of faith to which we must eventually come, we must now pass from the consideration of 'ultimate' to the consideration of 'from the human end' in the thesis 'faith is, from the human end, the ultimate basis'. It is necessary to insert a phrase of this nature to draw attention to the fact that all who have faith would presumably admit that the decisive and absolute basis of their faith does not lie in the human end at all but in God. Since God is the 'object' of faith, since the truth to which faith is related is God, it follows that God and God alone is the ground of faith. The only adequate, decisive and irrefutable establishing of faith beyond all denial is God. But the only 'verification' of God is God. This is so because even if we allow God to be spoken of as an 'object' of thought at all, God will by definition be greater than and not commensurable with any other objects of thought whatever. Hence God cannot be established by means of arguments using other objects of thought. (It might be that such arguments tend to show that God probably exists or do persuade some people that God does exist or raise questions which appear to demand an answer which 'goes beyond' the other objects of thought, but the God who is the 'object' of faith is not a hypothesis, a probability or the answer possibly required by a dimly conceived cosmic question.) 'From the human end', therefore, the position is that either there is no God or God cannot be known or God makes himself known. This last is, of course, the assertion of the biblical and Christian tradition, and it is that tradition's 'faith' that we are discussing.

It might be thought unnecessary to draw attention to so obvious a point and absurd to attempt to traverse so vast a field as proofs of the existence of God and questions concerning our knowledge of God in a paragraph. But the necessity of at least stating a position in that field cannot be avoided because the authority of faith is clearly related to the connection of faith with truth; furthermore, since faith is faith in God, faith's connection with truth is equally clearly related to knowledge of God. Faith may happen to be truth, but if it is not assuredly known as such it cannot be validly authoritative. Hence we must face the fact that the ultimate and decisive assurance about God cannot be based on any 'mediate' authorities like church or Bible, nor in any 'mediate' arguments drawn from the language and tradition of the community of believers or the experience of oneself, but can rest firmly and finally only on God himself. If God is and if God is God, God cannot 'be established'. God can only 'establish himself'.

Indeed, in this matter of seeking to 'establish God' and to state a basis for faith on which men and women may rely for the truth and authority of the believing which is demanded, there would seem in both Catholic and Protestant circles to be some grave forgetfulness of the doctrine of justification by faith. It might be proper and salutary to see parallels between an attempted relationship with God which relies upon 'faith' expressed in accepting certain propositions guaranteed by the church or by the Bible and also expressed in performing certain activities required by the church or the Bible on the one hand, and, on the other, an attempted relationship with God which relies on acceptance of the Law of Moses as the very Word of God and an attempt to live according to this Law. It might be argued that in both cases the real object of faith or ground of the believer's life was not God but religion, that the believing practitioner really relied on his orthodoxy and orthopraxy to 'keep him right' with God and that consequently the possibility of his or her being truly and totally centred upon God and upon God alone was gravely imperilled. Such a line of thought would further suggest that the God who does not abandon his people, however often they may turn back from him to their own ways, is even now thrusting upon his church the further reformation which is needed by removing further and further from us the possibility of once again finding plausible any out-and-out reliance upon an infallible church or an infallible Bible and by leaving open only the possibility of reliance upon and faith in him. Certainly the near-panic which seems to develop in many quarters in the church when old authorities seem to be resolutely questioned does suggest that faith *in God* is not a very dominating element in the life of the church. It seems to be feared, and very strongly feared, that doubts about historicity in the Gospels, or compromising the inerrancy of Scripture, or the possible undermining of the whole concept of the validity of orders, if worked out to the end, may well destroy our faith in God. This sort of thing would seem to evidence not faith but faithlessness. Indeed, it is the argument, explicit or implicit, of this whole book, that from a proper understanding of the nature of faith there arises a demand for the constant questioning of mediate authorities and that it is in such questioning that faith lives and again and again renews its authoritativeness.

To place the basis and validation of faith anywhere else than in God himself is to attempt to go back to a non-Christian position wherein it is implied that men and women have some standing-ground of their own from which they can control and validate their knowledge of God, independently of God. They think that they can accept the authority of the church and *thus* be sure of God or that they can be satisfied that the Bible is a guaranteed source of guaranteed truth and *thus* be sure of God. But to be sure of God on any other grounds than God himself is to set those grounds above God and oneself above both the grounds and God. So it is that the only ultimate basis of faith is God. And so it is therefore that *from the human end* there is, ultimately, no basis for faith. For faith is precisely that activity or response of the human being wherein God is sought and known. The core of faith *is* being sure of God. So to look for any basis for faith is to display faithlessness, and to require an authority which guarantees faith is to border on the verge of blasphemy, for it is requiring guarantees for God.

We have therefore come to the point where we have started on the clarification of the concept of faith and this we must now pursue further. When we are talking about faith, *what* are we talking about? There is no specific 'what' that we are talking about, for faith is an abstraction; it is an abstraction from the life and experience of believers, believers, that is, who stand in the biblical and Christian tradition. We are not concerned with all and every sort of belief and believing. Faith, then, is an abstraction from the life of believers and refers to the quality or activity or response which is found in each and every believer and which constitutes him or her as a believer. Faith cannot be pointed to, but believers can, and they are recognizable by their being disposed to do and say certain things and so on. Faith is what lies behind or what is expressed in these doings and sayings. When I speak of 'my faith', the primary reference is not to *what* I believe, but to the fact *that* I believe; although what I believe is certainly bound up with, related to and derived from the fact that I believe.

But when I 'believe', what am I doing? It will seem to the 'outsider', i.e. to the non-believer, that I am taking up or expressing an *attitude*. I am looking at the world in a certain way. I am understanding things or making decisions (or think I am) in a certain context, and so on. 'Believing' is being in a certain state of mind which I have either grown into for reasons of environment and upbringing and never cast off, or else which I have chosen to adopt. Hence faith is a matter of 'mere' belief. It is 'just an' attitude. So faith will seem to the unbeliever (and so it *must* appear). But this is not what faith is.

It certainly involves an attitude, a way of looking at the world, the understanding of a context within which decisions are or ought to be made and the constant reiterating of choices to remain faithful and to adopt faithful responses to and interpretations of situations. But the believer knows that all this arises from the fact that faith is at its heart a response, an awareness of and an enjoyment of a relationship – a relationship with God, a response to God. However we formulate this point, we must be careful. We may be allowed to say (it *is* said!) that we are related to God *by* faith, we respond to God in faith. But faith is not something different from the awareness of the relationship or the making of the response. Faith *is* awareness of God, this responding to God. This is most important, for it is the crucial point about knowledge of God and the truth or validity of faith.

For faith is the normal mode of human knowledge of God. (I say 'normal' because I do not wish either to discuss or exclude the question of a peculiar mystical way of knowing God.) And it is a knowledge of God, not in the sense of a descriptive knowledge of objects but in the sense of a responsive knowledge of another person. A great deal of descriptive knowledge about God has been built up, can be discussed, assessed and conveyed, and is of use in helping individuals towards the knowing of God himself. But the authoritative pivot of all knowledge about God is that faith in God which is, at heart, awareness of God. There is some 'point' or 'focus' in believers' range of experiences and assembly of dispositions at which they do not *claim* that in faith they have knowledge of God and do not *believe* that in faith they are responding to God. At this 'point' they *are* knowing God, they *are* responding to God. They may translate their personal knowledge of God into all sorts of confusing and conflicting propositions, most (or even all) of which they may eventually hold to be incorrect. (We shall discuss this matter of 'propositional translation' later.) They may conclude later that the modes and methods of their responses may very well have been misconceived – certainly imperfect. Moreover, this 'point' or 'focus' may be a very dim or elusive one, not to be chronologically pinned down and almost certainly never to be self-consciously apprehended at any given *present* moment. But if they attend carefully to their position as believers they will find that it is not sufficient to say that the sum total of their position taken in its history of experiences and its present deposit of dispositions and character is covered by a claim to know God or a belief that they respond to God. There is some core of faith which does not have either this affective tone or the sort of epistemological consequences which flow from mere claims and beliefs. The core of faith is neither affectively nor epistemologically hypothetical. It is, in whatever fear and trembling, and with however much unsureness in application and action, unquestionably *indicative*. God is here and here God is known. Because God is God, in the moment in which I dare to say 'here' I know also that I must say not 'here' but 'there', for no 'here' can contain God. None the less, I must say at least that God was 'there', which was a 'here' in which I then was, and I cannot now deny that I have known God. To accept this as just a claim or as merely a belief would simply be to perpetuate a falsehood. I knew and I know I knew and the *truth* is that God is and can be known.

What is being pointed to here is surely what is also being pointed to, although in a form which has much greater vividness and also much more content, by all the great encounter narratives of the

Bible: Moses and the Burning Bush, Elijah and the 'still small voice', Isaiah in the Temple, Paul on the Damascus road. Or perhaps such narratives as these highlight in a peculiar way the more 'routine' (!) encounter with God which after a 'call' sustained and informed a Jeremiah or a Paul in their respective missions. And surely one is also referring to pathetically dim and sporadic examples of that awareness of God which seems to have been so strong (and – at any rate up to the cry of dereliction on the cross? – so unbroken) a feature of the life of Jesus.

I rather hesitatingly thus compare small things with great because I wish to point out that the whole of the biblical tradition concerning God and the truth of God finds its ultimate authoritative anchorage and guarantee in this type of personal encounter and awareness. We have therefore, as Christians, neither any right nor any grounds for looking elsewhere for the ultimate basis of our authority. Moreover, we have no reason at all for any panic or despondency when we are thrust back on this type of ultimate authority. That we are so upset shows simply that we have forgotten or misunderstood the tradition in which we stand and the faith in which we live. God never has been verifiable. God has always taken steps to make himself known, and those who have encountered God have known this. They have not 'just believed'.

I am saying that knowledge of God normally comes by faith and that faith is the normal mode of human knowledge of God. It would seem, therefore, that I have neither explained nor explicited anything and that we are back in that circle from which it was alleged that the only way out was the authority of faith! It is to be hoped that this is not so, but that rather attention has been drawn to the fact that the ultimate authority for and validity of knowledge of God and statements about God must lie in the realm of personal relations. If anyone is asked 'How do you know you know God?', the answer must, by however devious a route, finally end up in the reply 'Because I know God'. This is so because the God with whom we have to do (as the Christian must say) or the God with whom we claim to have to do (as the non-believer must say) is a personal God – that is to say, a God who is known *as* a God who takes the initiative in evoking personal responses from human persons and who is known *because* he is such a God. Thus it is not only reasonable but inevitable that the decisive answer to the question 'How do you know you know God?' should be 'Because I know God', for this is very similar to answering the question 'How do you know you know your wife?' by answering in the end 'Because I know my wife'. In a relationship between persons, awareness of that relationship is ultimate and not to be established on any other grounds. And this is not affected by the philosophical difficulties over knowledge of other selves nor by such possibilities as that if my wife dies before me I may in my dotage have hallucinations about my wife's presence. Personal knowledge of persons is an ultimate epistemological category, and no person can possibly get outside it or 'do better' than it.

Such knowledge may be said to be self-authenticating and to carry its own intrinsic and decisive authority. It is true, as has been indicated, that it is possible for individuals to be mistaken or deluded about particular experiences which are taken to be encounters with another person (e.g. the hallucination concerning a dead wife), but the knowledge of another person of which I am speaking is a matter of reciprocal relationships built up over a period and such knowledge is its own direct authentication. I know this other person because of the relationship I have established and enjoy. The other person establishes his or her existence by 'being there' to be related to. In a similar way, God 'establishes' himself by 'being there' and those who have encountered God can neither doubt God's existence nor doubt that they have *knowledge* of this existent God. Consequently they are bound to maintain and are entitled to maintain that their knowledge has connections with truth, validity, reality (which is the same thing as maintaining that it *is* knowledge).

All the complications arise because, although God is known, God is not known as objects are known. God does not share in an object-like nature as human persons do, and therefore God is not 'there' to be pointed at. Consequently, I cannot have any simple 'drill' or assured technique whereby I can put you assuredly and rapidly in a position where it can be practically guaranteed that you will enter on a personal relationship of knowledge which will straightway persuade *you* that the personal God is indeed available and knowable. Indeed, I cannot do it for myself. Therefore we are obliged to speak of knowing God by faith. And therefore, also, the non-believer quite understandably and inevitably says that we are simply making a subjective claim and we are concerned *not* with knowledge *but* with faith ('mere belief'). But it may now, perhaps, be clear why believers must both understand that the demand of the non-believer will be 'Establish your claim' and also be aware that they cannot, and indeed must not, attempt to meet that demand directly. (The way in which this understandable, and from the standpoint of the questioner, reasonable demand can be reasonably met will, it is hoped, appear in due course.) For the demand amounts to requiring us to 'establish' or 'point to' God, and God must be left to establish and reveal himself. And this occurs only in faith. Hence it is that faith is the only ultimate basis for authoritatively establishing the relationship of Christian affirmations about God, the world and the self to truth and reality. Faith, in fact, is the only ultimate human ground for asserting that there is objective truth and reality involved at all.

I have thus far sought to show why it is that any attempt to find the ultimate basis of authority in Christianity is bound to be thrust back upon faith, and that this means being thrust back upon the biographies of particular believers and also upon the autobiography of oneself as a believer. The reason lies in the being and personal nature of God. If God is as God is understood to be in the biblical and Christian tradition, then no other position with regard to authority could reasonably be looked for or sustained.

It is now necessary to go on to attempt two things. First, to show how this recent argument getting back to individual biographies and an individual autobiography is to be related to the earlier contention that we were not 'arguing that particular cases of faith are based on nothing but the faith of the particular believer or believers concerned'. That is to say, there must be a consideration of the interaction between the individual impact of faith and the corporate context of faith. This will provide us with material for the second attempt. This must be to sketch out the lines along which the basic authoritativeness of faith, as I have attempted to describe it, is to be related to and, up to a point, transferred to, the vast complex of propositions in the forms of theological statements, ecclesiastical instructions, pastoral advice and so on in which and about which so much debate and controversy rage. For it is in these fields that the problem of authority is so acutely and practically felt.

First, therefore, some thoughts concerning the authenticating faith of individuals and the corporate context of faith. All individuals come to faith, or faith develops in them, in the context of a community. The direct encounters which constitute the ultimate authentication of faith (i.e. which provide the authentication which faith gives) occur in connection with the individual's relationship to the (up-to-a-point) believing community and take the form either in which they are experienced, or at least in which the experience is remembered and conveyed, from symbols, images and sentences which are 'current coin' in the life of that community. Moses is portrayed as receiving the revelation of the 'new name' of God in the incident of the Burning Bush, but it is the God of the fathers, the God of Abraham, the God of Isaac and the God of Jacob who reveals himself. Isaiah's vision is actually in the Temple and is clothed in images of Temple liturgy and Temple sculpture. Saul was actually engaged in persecuting the community whose Lord he was sure he had encountered. And lesser believers have their (not always lesser?) assurances in connection with praying or worshipping or reading the Bible or the fitting together of ideas drawn from such sources in connection with some problem or excitement with which their lives present them. Faith is thus neither absolutely arbitrary nor completely incoherent but related to an already existing pattern of community belief and life which may be said to be, from the human end, the *causal* ground, although not, as has been argued above, the ultimately *justifying* ground of faith itself.

Further, as I have also tried to indicate above, very many believers cannot point back to actual identifiable 'moments' of authenticating encounter. It is only that a survey of the total position of believers arising out of their history of experiences and present disposition and character leaves them with an impression equivalent to or parallel to the highlighted impact of such an encounter. They are able to recognize and unable to deny that in their dim way they are really related to this same Reality of which the tradition speaks with so much more confidence and (symbolic) clarity. Thus it is in all probability the case for many believers most of the time (and surely all believers some of the time) that not only would there be no question of their ever having come to faith without the believing community, its tradition and its life, but that further they would scarcely recognize that they had faith at all if it were not for their part in the life of that community. The vivid and convincing personal encounter clearly enjoyed by some believers and able to be recognized by all has an essential role in the understanding and justification of faith, but it is not sufficient of itself psychologically and in actual practice to sustain faithful living.

Moreover, the isolated and individual personal encounter would not be 'sufficient of itself' to allow one reasonably to assert for faith the objectivity and authority which is the burden of the first part of this essay. It remains true (how can it be otherwise?) that only God can establish the reality of himself, that he does this in personal encounter, and that consequently the ultimate assurance of the reality of God can be based only upon the encountering of him by persons. Such encounter will necessarily be inter-personal and, therefore, from the human end by human individuals. Consequently, the absolute and ultimate basis for our understanding of God and for our assertions about him must lie in the faith-experience of individuals. Further, *any* individual who really does encounter God could neither doubt nor argue with such an encounter. He or she will be absolutely sure of his or her objective knowledge and believers will be right to be sure about it. But taken as isolated individuals they may as reasonably be taken for completely deluded men and women as for witnesses to the one true God. Strength of conviction may be reasonably persuasive grounds for investigating that conviction and sharing it. But the situation is worse than this.

As every believer must be painfully aware, the strength of one's convictions notoriously fluctuates. Any reader who has got thus far must have asked again and again what right I had to talk with such reiterated assurance of the assurance of faith, of 'knowing' and 'knowing that one knew' and so on. Certainly, if I were talking of isolated and individual encounters I would have no such right. For just as the isolated individual may as reasonably be concluded to be deceived as inspired, so the reflective individual may subsequently conclude that any isolated and individual experience of assurance or knowledge he or she had was at least as likely to be a mere subjective disturbance as an actual objective encounter. Yet both our present difficulties and our previous assertions arise out of an attempt to describe *all* the aspects of the 'faith-situation' from the inside. The excuse for so temerarious an attempt is that nothing else can be done. Belief in God is something abstracted from believers' believing. And whatever may be the role of the community of believers (it is surely immense), descriptive analysis is bound to fix on where belief 'resides', i.e. the individual believer. And since belief in God is a personal relationship with a personal Being, one is forced back upon the only person of whom one has 'inside' knowledge, viz. oneself.

I am obliged, therefore, to hazard an attempt both to describe the epistemological assurance perceived in faith (faith is not the *grounds* for 'being sure' but *is* being sure – of God) and at the same time to do justice to the fact that faith is no guaranteed disposition to enjoy constant assurance at the forefront of one's thinking and experiencing. I wish, at this stage in the argument, first to give some account of why faith should have this double, even ambiguous, nature and then to indicate what grounds there are (beyond the fact that no other procedure is possible!) which justify the offering of an account of faith based on a particular believer's experience of faith (viz. my own) as a general account of the nature of the faith which can be reasonably offered for general acceptance and illumination.

Faith has this ambiguous nature of assurance and diffidence because it is a relationship between a human being such as myself and God. All inter-personal relationships clearly take their quality from the characters and natures of the persons in relationship. As has already been pointed out, human beings do partake of the nature of 'objects', i.e. they have a recognizable purely physical existence which can be pointed to – although it is perfectly possible to know 'who X is' without 'really knowing X' at all. Only by entering into some reciprocal personal relation with X can this latter knowing begin. But God is a personal being who is not object-like at all. This is a consequence of his transcendence and sovereignty. God cannot be observed impersonally like an object wherein the knower has the initiative and the 'object' is purely passive. God can be known only as the supremely personal, and in this knowing, the initiative and the primary activity is always and inevitably God's. Consequently, knowledge of God can never be a taken-for-granted 'possession' of the knower over which the knower has more or less complete control. It must always be 'there' and 'not there' – until God pleases 'in the End' to give us the blessed vision of himself which is the completed enjoyment of his eternal life.

But there is not only this, as one may say, 'good' reason why faith must also involve diffidence. The quality of the relationship is contributed to not only by God but also by us, and we are both naturally underdeveloped beings and also sinfully misdeveloped beings. We have yet to grow to the stature of beings who can fully enter into the enjoyment of relationship with God, and we also perversely pursue projects and developments of our own which stunt our true development and take away even from the capacity we might have to respond to God as he makes himself known to us. We do not enjoy the awareness of, or respond to, the relationship with God as we might and could and should. Thus the diffidence which arises from the very being of God who must always remain supreme and transcendent is heavily interlaced by the fitfulness and even forgetfulness of our own imperfections and disobediences. Not only is God never our own, even intellectual and moral, 'possession', but we do not even respond to or enjoy as we might God's possession of us. Faith is therefore complicated not only by diffidence but also by faithlessness.

Thus this ambiguous nature of faith is in the nature of the case. It is both our only ultimate access to an assurance of God which, being a true relationship with him, is a guarantee of objectivity and therefore is entitled to be called knowledge, and yet it operates so differently from our other knowledge that we do need this distinct word (i.e. 'faith') and we may well understand the logicians' refusal to admit that faith is in any sense knowledge. (It might be better to drop all attempts to use the word 'knowledge', provided that such a giving up of the word was not taken to be an admission that faith *is* purely subjective and not a matter in which legitimate claims to truth can be involved.)

And yet, whatever the difficulties, it *is* the nature of faith to be not hypothetical but indicative, and the believer is bound to say at the 'intense' end of the scale of his faith 'I *do* know'. Even at the 'attenuated' end believers will still find themselves obliged to say 'I cannot deny that I know.' And yet, again, it must be admitted that this 'cannot' is not the obligation of logic but the obligation of will. God is a personal being known to me whom I cannot deny (although under temptation or persecution my will may fail), not a fact which my intellectual integrity and understanding obliges me to underline on the page of life. But this again is in the nature of the case, the case of the relation between the supreme personal being and his personal creatures. And the fact that there is in faith an element of decision (always, therefore, a decision of me and other individuals, for only individuals actually decide – whatever 'makes' them) does not rob it of its authoritativeness. Nor is the decision – or rather nor are the decisions – of faith to 'keep faith' unreasonable, although this reasonableness does not itself justify the *absoluteness* of both the commitment and the authority of faith.

We must, however, move towards an explanation of these last statements by going back to the question of why it is reasonable to offer a general account of faith based on the individual evaluation of an individual autobiography. In doing this we shall be moving back to the main stream of the argument, which is concerned with the authenticating faith of individuals and the corporate context of faith.

I endeavour to explicate and evaluate faith from my own understanding and experience of faith. This is inevitable because faith is a personal matter; to get to the heart of it, personal experience is required, and the only personal experience to which I have direct access is my own. But how dare I do this? Do I set myself up as a 'hero' of faith worthy to be inserted in an appendix to the eleventh chapter of the Epistle to the Hebrews? And, in any case, what is the use of such a procedure? To be so utterly and openly subjective when the whole argument is supposed to be directed to the expounding of the authoritative objectivity of faith is surely to make certain of either pity, ridicule or contempt. It might be hoped that at least some hints to the answers to these questions could be filtered out by the well-intentioned reader from what has gone before, but the argument requires a specific facing up to them.

The answer lies in the fact that I recognize in my own experience some faint echo, indeed some faint realization, of what the biblical 'heroes of faith' are exemplifying and of what believers since biblical times, including believers alive now, some known to me in person, are likewise speaking of and exemplifying. I am persuaded, therefore, that I am seeing, however dimly, what they saw or see with whatever clarity and force. *They* 'endured as seeing him who is invisible' (cf. Heb. 11.27), and they endure. Furthermore, although the AV translation of the Greek verb *karterein* certainly suggests too heroic a tone for my faith, I do none the less share in something of the 'resoluteness' or 'steadfastness' of the conviction, knowledge and commitment which was and is theirs. Moreover, this commitment of mine is both epistemologically reasonable and morally compelling.

The whole thing arises accidentally, empirically, as a sheer matter of fact, for no theoretical or *a priori* reasons, but just out of the 'givenness'. (I am ignoring theological complications about prevenient grace, the Holy Spirit and the like!) I am faced with examples of the class of believers. They are not people of any sort of belief or faith or credulity, but they are believers in this biblical and Christian tradition. (I.e. they 'stand in' their tradition; not 'they all hold as the content of their belief the same set of propositions called "the Christian tradition"'. We shall come to propositional truths shortly as the last stage in the essay.) It may be that I am confronted with them from within their number (e.g. baptized and brought up as a member of the church) or I may be confronted with them from without (e.g. 'Why do not those hypocrites who talk about a God of love make a consistent stand against the H-bomb?', or, 'What right has *he* to preach at me?', or, 'Can there be anything in this business of "God"?', and so on). This 'being confronted with' is purely arbitrary, i.e. there was no theoretical necessity for it to have happened this way or for it to have happened at all – it would not have happened to me in this way if I had not happened to be me. In this it is like all other experiential data which come to us. I find myself attending to these data. The form of this attention, at any rate to start with, may not be reasoning (i.e. the attention has nothing analytic or self-conscious about it) but it is not unreasonable. It is presumably never initially unreasonable to attend to something which engages our attention. I find (causal) reasons for continuing with this attention which may take a wide variety of forms – attacking believers, debating with them, seeking instruction from them, joining in (or at least being present at) some of their characteristic activities like a service of worship or a prayer meeting. My 'reasons' for continuing with this attention or participation at any stage will be very various; some of them would not seem even to myself to be really justifying reasons if they were coolly and openly examined and quite possibly none of them would seem sufficient to some persons. But I can talk about and support my giving of attention. It is certainly not a totally unreasonable and unreasoning procedure. (There is probably a very widespread and implicitly accepted myth current as to what are 'really reasonable' reasons for various forms of procedure which makes people suppose, erroneously, that 'religious' behaviour is very much more unreasonable than other sorts of behaviour. But we cannot go into that now.)

As I proceed in my attending to and participating with believers, I find that despite bewilderment, disagreement, lack of clarity and inconsistency both in behaviour and argument among believers themselves, they do have a discernible pattern both of thought and of life which is meaningful to them and shows signs of being meaningful to me. That is to say, I begin to perceive and appreciate connections and coherences between bits of their 'doctrines' or between these and things said and done in their services, and I find that the sense and coherence I am beginning to perceive also occasionally makes sense of and makes sense in the conduct of my life and in facing up to and dealing with the situations that I find myself in. (The order of the discovery of 'meaningfulness' may very well more often be from the practical to the intellectual than the order which I have just given.) Since I have 'seen for myself' something of what believers say the tradition of belief and the life of believing is about, it is perfectly reasonable for me to suppose that they are 'on to something' and that it is not all mere talk and attitudes.

The artificially abstracted and intellectualized 'I' who is being used as the stalking-horse for this exposition does not yet *know* that believers are 'on to something' (viz. in touch with God), but my supposition that they might very well be is perfectly reasonable and supported by reasoning. In actual practice, if I attended to my attending, I should doubtless find that I had imperceptibly passed into a frame of mind (or never passed out of one) in which I was taking for granted that believers are on to something, i.e. I am myself a believer of sorts. But we are not concerned here with giving an actual psychological description of the process of becoming or being a believer, but with an attempt to explicate the epistemological status of faith. So – I have reasonable grounds for committing myself further to the sympathetic understanding of the thought and the responsible sharing of the life of believers. It is reasonable, in fact, to trust my convictions as far as they go and see how far they do go!

It is at this stage in the argument that the 'jump' occurs from the reasonableness of continuing experimentally to identify myself, at any rate up to a point, with a community of believers to the absolute assurance and absolute commitment of faith. I say at this stage *in the argument*, because I do not think that there is a *corresponding* decisive jump in the actual process of development of a particular believer. Where a conscious moment or incident of 'conversion' does occur, it may seem to the particular believer that this is *the* decisive moment in which he or she attains to 'real' faith, and one may also be inclined to identify, or at any rate align, such a moment with the decisive epistemological 'jump' to which I am about to refer. But I am very doubtful about the precise sense in which a moment of conversion is decisive, and in any case we need not investigate this, as it is quite clear that a particular moment of conversion (even if it is a genuine encounter with God) cannot be taken as being generally epistemologically decisive (cf. the possibility, already referred to, of an isolated assured individual being deluded and of an individual deciding that an isolated experience of his own of assurance is an instance of self-delusion). Moreover, it is also clear that very many assured and committed believers do not have any awareness of a moment or incident of conversion. We are therefore concerned with the logical difference there is between the reasonable pursuance of a tentative and experimental policy of investigation by association with some community of believers and the absolute assurance of faith wherein one is convinced that the believers are, in some real sense, 'on to' truth (indeed the Truth!), and one is further committed to an obligation both to follow up *and propagate* that truth.

The point at issue, then, is the passing over from being a believer 'of a sort' (by association) to being one who *knows*, or the passing over from an approach which is permeated by the awareness of the possibility that the whole thing might be untrue not merely in detail but in principle (although this is not likely) to the knowledge that the reasonable possibility that there is a fundamental mistake ('it remains possible that God does not exist and that Jesus gives us no decisive clues about him' – or the like) is not an open possibility at all.

The new and decisive position is that it is undoubtedly the case that the God to whom this tradition bears witness does exist, and that God is rightly, if inadequately, pointed to by that tradition. Consequently faith is not only a possibility, *but* a necessity. That is to say now I get to the position where my absolute commitment to God and to continuing life in the believing community is 'both epistemologically reasonable and morally compelling' (see p.203 above).

That position is reached because there is a joining together of the reasonable type of experimental commitment (at each stage 'up to a point'), which I have just been outlining, with the discovery that one is in the position of faith, which I have spent the earlier part of the essay seeking to describe. That is to say, there is superimposed upon, mingled with, arisen out of or imperceptibly added to my inclination to entertain sympathetic-ally the assertions of and tendencies to belief, the awareness that I too stand (or at least cannot deny that I have stood) before the God in whom believers believe. In following my convictions as far as they go, I have been taken far beyond them, taken to what is at least equivalent to, if it is not the same as, a glimpse of 'the one who is invisible'. Therefore I can no longer be hypothetical and I cannot deny God, although I cannot 'prove' God. More-over, I know I must not deny God because I do not need to 'prove' God. God has established himself in my knowledge – in, that is to say, my faith.

And when my faith, in intensity of awareness or conviction or control of feelings and the like, fluctuates, and I wonder once again if I do know God, or rather if it is true that God knows me, and I ask the question whether I am really drifting on a sea of subjectivity, temporarily supported, but in no way anchored, by a precarious raft of 'self-authenticating' experiences which cannot safely be distinguished from self-delusions, then I turn once again to the matrix of the community of believers out of whom and among whom my faith first grew. In their tradition, whether it be in 'church' form or in 'Bible' form, in their continuing life, whether it be in the sacraments and in formal worship or in their fellowship and their taking for granted of the Christian pattern of understanding and life, I find sufficient reasonable evidence for holding that my own conclusions and my own faith are not in fact 'mine' in the perilously undermining sense of being confined to me, subjective to me. I am thus not merely 'tided over' psychological wanings of my own faith, but I am constantly sustained and built up in this faith by the life of the community and its authorities.

But there remains a final and decisive sense in which however much my faith depends causally for its inception on the faithful community and is sustained in its fitfulness and developed out of some of its imperfections by that same community and its life, none the less the absolute assurance and absolute authority of that faith rests for me on the 'glimpsed' or 'sensed' awareness of God who is and can be the only immediate and final authority for any theological faith or truth.

I could not be absolutely assured that the tradition of church and Bible encountered in the life of the communities of believers was really in touch with, stemmed from and pointed to objective and transcendent truth (indeed I could have no assurance that there was any such 'thing'), unless I had myself been touched by the self-authentication of the supreme personal self who is the Truth. Such authentication is necessary to be assured that faith is related to knowledge and truth, not merely to opinion, attitudes and belief. But it is not sufficient. I need to be able to recognize that this faith of mine is no faith of my own, but rather the shared faith of the people of God, if I am clearly to be justified to my reflective self and at least plausible to others in my statement that I am not after all engulfed in the abyss of subjectivity. But again – and so the pendulum of argument and exposition concerning faith swings to and fro – the only unquestionable ground where the whole matter can come to any sort of rest is the assurance of faith. Here is the only certainty that one is grounded in truth and not merely searching in a flux of 'maybe's' (although one is certainly also searching in such a flux – 'living with questions', as the previous writings contained in this book seek to show).

In order to meet the demands of unbelievers for the justification of our faith or even (and quite as frequently in present practice, I suspect) to bolster up our own confidence shaken by the church's loss of prestige and our own inability to make ourselves meaningful in the cause of Christianity in one situation after another, it is quite useless to attempt to reinstate the mediate authorities (in particular church and Bible) into the position of looking like final authorities which accidents of history have allowed them to enjoy. This is to retreat from faith and therefore to retreat from God who is directly encountered only in faith. It is to retreat also from the world which is where God is to be encountered, for it is God's world and the scene of God's operations, into an increasingly limited and private field of religion inhabited by church-conditioned and biblically brain-washed persons who can continue to persuade *themselves* that they speak objectively and with authority because they speak to no one but themselves. But this is not the picture of the New Testament people of God, nor of the sub-apostolic age, nor of the time of an Irenaeus or an Athanasius. They wrestled in the confidence of their faith with the idiom and spirit of their time. They were not conformed to this idiom or spirit. They did much to transform them. But their understanding and expression of their faith was immensely influenced and shaped by this faithful and obedient confrontation.

Authoritativeness does not arise out of the authoritarian repetition of past solutions to the 'problem of communication'. Rather, we who have entered (as we believe, by the calling and grace of God) into the heritage and tradition of faith have to have the courage of that faith to submit all the 'deposits' of the tradition to the double test of the most searching scrutiny and questioning by the faithful and of the most intensive exposure to the demands and pressures of the present time. We are sure, in faith, that God is and that *God* is faithful. We do not therefore have to establish for ourselves or for anyone else the basic truthfulness that lies behind and in the tradition which has come down to us. (As has been argued above, this, in any case, cannot be done.) What we must long for and strive for is that the being and relevance and application of the truth of God may be opened up for us, and for those all around us, in whatever form we and they can lay hold on and make sense (of course, partial and not final sense) of today. Thus may we be successors of those who in the past were men and women of faith and preachers of the gospel. But we shall not be their successors by saying what they said in the terms they said it. If we confine ourselves to this, neither we who speak (and suppose we are speaking the word of God) nor those who, unbelievers, indifferent, frustrated, ought to be given a chance of hearing the word of God will come anywhere near to apprehending what the faith is really about.

The authority of faith will once more become plain to us and renew its impact in the world when we cease to look for or hanker after an old authoritarianism, but are prepared in the confidence of faith to submit ourselves, our understanding of all the tradition that has come down to us, our conviction of our commission from God and the apprehension that we at present have of the gospel that is offered to us to the questionings and searchings that arise in us and are put to us by the idiom and spirit and need of our age. Then God will give to his obedient servants such authoritativeness as is necessary to persuade others to faith. It is certain that no one, however 'heavily' authorized, can by the weight of his or her own authority establish another person in the faith of God. It is also certain to the eye of faith that God uses those who faithfully respond to him to be the occasioning of the waking of faith in others. And when this faith is occasioned, then they also see, as we do, the authority of faith. And, if we require it, there will be a little further reasonable evidence that we see what we see and do not imagine it. And we shall be thankful, because we need the auxiliary aid and comfort of reason. But we shall not forget that the demand of God is absolute and this absoluteness no unaided reason can justify.

But in order that these last paragraphs should not trail off into rhetoric without the rigour of an attempt at practical and specific application, it is necessary finally to make the attempt (promised earlier) to 'sketch out the lines along which the basic authoritativeness of faith . . . is to be related to, and up to a point transferred to, the vast complex of propositions in the forms of theological statements, ecclesiastical instructions, pastoral advice and so on', which constitute the 'deposit' of the tradition of faith referred to above. In other words, this is to consider a little more clearly the question of the 'mediate' authorities and to seek to reflect systematically on the investigations and questionings instanced in previous papers in this book.

Faith, as we have had occasion several times to point out, arises in the context of and in connection with the believing community. Men and women believe in God, humanly speaking, because men and women believe in God. But in fact, belief in God is not arrived at, experienced as, expressed as or sustained by belief *in God* – at any rate for the vast majority of believers for the most part of the time. I have been arguing that in the end (i.e. as the ultimate logical and authoritatively justifying basis) God must and can only establish himself, and that the heart of faith lies in this encounter with God. But although God is not himself an object, and this fact, when we come to ultimates, has consistently and continuously to be reckoned with, it is equally clear that the knowledge of God is evolved in us and recognizable by us through the medium of the ordinary 'object-like' world. Were this not so, we could not talk or think about God at all, for we can only deal in talking and thinking with concepts, and these have to be built up from the 'objects' which we perceive and experience in the world. Thus the context of faith is as necessary for the possibility of the existence of faith as the heart of faith is necessary for the assurance that faith is related to an objective reality. Both are necessary, neither is sufficient alone. The context is chronologically and causally prior. The heart is logically prior or ultimate. Now it is out of the context of faith that 'the vast complex of propositions in the forms of theological statements, ecclesiastical instructions, pastoral advice and so on' arise. Indeed, they, together with the pattern of living and particular characteristic activities of the believing community, constitute this context.

It is a context which has a long history of development behind it, and which consists at any given time of a great deal of material of very different types and of very different degrees of fixity and fluidity. There are certain elements which in the course of the history of the development of the believing community have emerged with a defined fixity. These are the elements in the whole context of belief which the believing community itself has come to regard as authoritative for its believing. They have therefore become the authorities of the believing community. It will not, I think, be a misleading summary for our present purposes, of the views which are current in the actually existing community of Christian believers today on the subject of authorities, if we say that the authorities are the Bible and the church. The Bible is defined by a sufficiently agreed canon (although there is, of course, dispute about the status of the Apocrypha). The definition of the 'fixity' of the church is, as is notorious, greatly disputed. Unless you first define the '*fideles*' there is no '*consensus fidelium*' on this. But there would seem to be a sufficiently general agreement to be discerned from practice that the ordered Christian community, whatever is held to be its proper form of ordering, does have authority and means of making that authority heard and brought to bear. Moreover, it is undeniable as a matter of history that the authoritativeness of the fixedly defined church experienced through its properly constituted authorities has, for a very great part of Christian history to date, been taken for granted as an integral and necessary part of the Christian context of faith. We are justified, then, in speaking of church and Bible as the authorities of the Christian community. (In order that it should not appear that I suppose that these generalizations are any more than rough and ready, and for the purposes of the argument, I may perhaps be allowed to say of a body like the Quakers that it seems to me that they represent and uphold a tradition which has borne a perfectly proper witness to the questionable status of the commonly received authorities by consistently and yet improperly underrating their importance.)

The Bible is, of course, the 'scriptures', i.e. *the* authoritative writings of the believing community, so that with it we have finally reached the point of facing up to the connection between the authority of faith and sets of propositions. We are also faced with the same problem with regard to the church, as the authority of the church is likewise naturally expressed through and attached to propositions. In some church traditions, there are more 'in the highest degree' authoritative propositions than in others. The commonly received creeds would be held to be authoritative propositions by a wide range of Christian communities; the Roman church has a carefully worked out grading of authoritative propositions; confessions have some authoritative standing in some traditions and so on. There is also the whole question of authoritative pronouncements from time to time on the application of the Christian faith to particular situations as they arise. These will range from authoritative rulings by 'competent' authorities on some matter of morals or canon law or liturgical ordering and the like, through 'pronouncements' by church 'authorities' on matters of great public interest and importance, to the particularly directed guidance or instruction of the pastor and the preacher. All this and much else which could be added to the 'pattern' (!) simply draws attention to the bewildering complexity of the problem of authority. But if there is bewildering complexity, how can there be authority at all? A mentally bemused man wandering in a fog would be bemused to the point of insanity if he set himself up as an authoritative guide to strangers.

Presumably the way to stop running into such a 'fog' would normally be said to be that one should be clear about one's *primary* authorities. Naturally there are in practice very different levels of authoritativeness, and the Christian community, or individual Christians within that community, will be faced with the same or similar practical problems about coming to decisions in particular circumstances as face any group with particular responsibilities for taking particular decisions. For example, if a particularly difficult medical case arises it is the responsibility of the local 'expert' (the general practitioner) to refer it to appropriate specialists, and when the case arrives in a big hospital then the appropriate 'authorities' in the field in question who are available are, or ought to be, assembled, and they have to take the most responsible and considered decision they can. You get together the best 'authorities' or experts in and interpreters of authoritative knowledge and 'know-how' that you can. They have to make the most responsible decision or pronouncement they can. And you go on from there. Clearly 'the church' or any church organization also has to proceed in this sort of way. The present resources of understanding and training available to the community have to be called in to use, and the persons having such resources have to make use of the tradition and deposit of the community in coming to their conclusions, taking their actions, issuing their advice or instructions. In practice there is surely much in common here between responsible members of the Christian community coming to decisions in Christian matters and, say, responsible persons of the medical profession in medical matters.

No doubt there is a parallel in procedure. But is there not a distinctive difference in the type of authoritativeness of their respective primary authorities? And ought there not to be a distinctive difference in the type of authoritativeness of their respective pronouncements or instructions? A responsible medical group will, of course, rely very heavily on the 'authorities' relevant to its concerns. But its obligation to be bound by these authorities is a purely pragmatic and prudential one. Advances in medicine are made by revising the authorities, and there are certainly no 'absolute' authorities at all. Moreover, the decision they come to is not guaranteed to be 'right', and certainly would not be held to have any unquestionable right of absolute acceptance by another competent group. If such a group came to a different decision on a question of treatment, this would not necessarily discredit the authority of medical science and medical men. It would simply underline the sort of authority it is. But is not any church group *bound* by its primary authorities, and are there not at any rate some situations in which the voice of the church is somehow or other supposed to be heard saying 'Thus saith the Lord . . .'?

Preachers, for example, do not suppose (if they are sane) that there is a straightforward equivalence or identity between what they have to say and a 'word of God'. But they know they stand in a tradition, have, indeed, been commissioned ('authorized') in a tradition of authoritative pronouncers of words which have been used as means by which men and women have heard what they have believed to be 'what God has to say' to them. They are very likely to feel that they cannot be the sort of authoritative preachers which it seems to them their like in the Christian tradition have been, unless they can appeal to some primary authority behind what they are trying to say. They seek something on which they can fall back if challenged and say, 'What I was trying to put over was "this",' and 'this' will have to be able to be referred to something like 'the Bible says . . .', or '*Roma locuta, causa finita*', or 'it says in the creed . . .'. What possible use or authority can there be in an utterance like, 'If we are able to trust the majority of critics, and on balance we *probably* can, then it is quite possible Jesus said . . . although it is more than likely that we can have little more than a guess at the original context of the saying and the original meaning is therefore obscure'? The full impact of this last point is not at all mitigated if one supposes that the justifiable degree of the hypothetical mood is much less than the 'typical' ('caricatured'?) sentence I have just made up. For the fact of the matter clearly is that if hypothesis is introduced *at all* into the *primary* authorities, then there is *never* any justification for *absolute* authority to be attached to any of the propositions either contained in, or based by watertight logic upon, those contained in the primary authorities.

This fact is perceived with exemplary clarity by both fundamentalist and Roman Catholic theologians, and it should surely be recognized by all of us. But the aim of this essay is to seek to show why it is that this position should in no way surprise us and that our way of facing up to this situation cannot and must not be that of the fundamentalist or Roman Catholic or some other position which attempts to produce the same results by asserting that either the church or the Bible or some balanced complex of church and Bible is, *in the last resort*, an absolute authority. The historical primary authorities are in fact mediate and mediating authorities, and there is and can be no other absolute authority than God. We are left, therefore, even in the realm of scripture and in the realm of church dogmatic, credal and moral statements (however we declare these are arrived at or wherever we find them) with our 'if's' and 'maybe's'. It is worse than useless, because one deplores the consequences or apparent consequences of this, *therefore* to assert that the position cannot be so, and we must 'believe in' the church or 'believe in' the Bible or 'believe in' the Holy Ghost's having miraculously conserved some *consensus fidelium* of a Vincentian sort which is none the less existent for being empirically quite undiscernible. It is worse than useless because it is faithless. And God can have little use for a church which refuses to trust him and him alone (what of justification by faith?), while the world will have no use for a church which claims boldly to be commissioned by the One whose kingdom is supreme, and yet which cannot dare to face manifest facts.

The solution lies, surely, in facing the situation in the faith we have been given. We know that the whole tradition and life of the people of God is not built or based on a lie, for we also have faith in their God. Indeed, we must not talk of 'we' and 'they', for it is we who now are the people of God (and shall we learn any better than the old Israel that this calling is to serve the world and not to lord it over the world as wielders of superior authority and owners of a superior guaranteed place with God?). We therefore know that we are entitled to take with full seriousness all the deposit and tradition of the life of the believing community as it comes down to us, all the propositions and pronouncements and practices. This seriousness will entail that we shall pay particular attention to, indeed regard undoubtedly as authorities to be carefully considered and consulted, any 'foci or faith' which the life of the people of God has produced and which clearly have nourished and guided that life. The Bible and the ordering and tradition of the church will, in particular, be the authorities to be consulted and considered. That is to say, we shall approach our task of now being the people of God in the world by seeing to it that we are as prepared as we can be by as thorough a knowledge as we can get of the Bible and of the tradition, and our technique will be always to go to and fro between the problems posed to our faith by the demands of our situation in the world and the enlightenment we can get for our faith from the deposit of the faithful through the ages. Because of our faith we are, so to speak, 'on the same wavelength' as other believers, and we are, therefore, able with confidence to accept what they say or at least to be predisposed to suppose that there is 'something in it'. We do not, therefore, for example have to establish for ourselves that the Bible has something to do with truth before we can make any sort of use of it. We know that our predecessors have found truth through it and in it. We therefore faithfully scrutinize, question and search to see what we in our turn shall be taught. The writers of the Bible are bearing witness in their various ways to the truth of which we also have had some glimpse. We know as they knew (by faith) that this truth is Truth indeed, and therefore we confidently interrogate their witness so that we in our turn may receive our understanding and be able to bear our witness.

But we do not make the mistake of supposing that all the 'deposit of the faithful' is in fact 'faithful deposit'. When we remember that the sole and possible ultimate basis of the truthfulness of our faith is the relationship between God and humankind, and when we recall the conditions of that relationship until 'the End' which we have discussed above, we are not surprised to find that all the manifestations of the human end of this relationship are inextricably 'mixed' material. The faithful of every age are still men and women whose redemption is not yet worked out in them to their completed restoration, and taking their 'deposit' seriously will be as likely to involve learning from it by rejecting some of the aspects of it as by positive illumination. (Surely, e.g. the Book of Esther is the sort of discreditable daydream wherein the unconverted underdog in each one of us allows the mean level of his soul to delight in a fantasy about the vicious discomfiture of his enemies?) The faithful are justified by their faith, not yet made perfect in perception or expression.

This situation still holds with regard to the faithful witness to Jesus. It may be that the orthodox christology of his person is to be taken absolutely seriously as the most adequate and correct indication we can give of his status and reality (I shall return briefly to this below), i.e. that in *his* case we have one unique example of 'the human end' of things where the situation is not 'mixed', but is a perfect unity of perfect God and perfect man under historical conditions. But this fact is discernible only by faith, and we are dependent for our evidence for the fact on the portrayals of faithful witness. (If they had not had faith they would not have bothered to witness.) We cannot deduce *a priori* what e.g. would be the range of the knowledge displayed by this unique figure, because as *he* is, *ex hypothesi*, the definitive evidence for the nature of God, we cannot argue deductively from generalizations about God which ignore him, and we cannot have any knowledge of what the *human* situation of such a person could be other than from what we know about him. For he is, again *ex hypothesi*, the only such human figure. Therefore *a priori* arguments are out, and we are dependent upon the evidence of the witnesses. But the witnesses, however faithful, are, again *ex hypothesi*, the 'ordinary' sort of faithful (for they do not have *his* personal status) and their witness is bound to be 'mixed' (as New Testament criticism – conducted very largely from among the faithful! – has made so abundantly and decisively clear that no one who did not have an immense vested interest in 'absoluteness' would any longer attempt to deny it). We cannot, therefore, have absolute confidence in the records of the Gospels as, say, a source of 'hard' historical data which will guarantee that the faithful view of Jesus is certainly true. (As a matter of fact *no* historical data can be absolutely 'hard', for being concerned with matters of fact and particularity it can only have degrees of probability. And further what [impossibly 'hard'] historical data could possibly *guarantee* the fact that 'Jesus was God'? God cannot be established or guaranteed by any historical data at all!)

But we are not therefore condemned to lack of or loss of faith. We are taking the Gospels seriously now (i.e. after we have developed into self-conscious faith) because they are clearly a central part of the deposit of faith. We are identified with, or rather in, that faith and we are right so to be identified. (Our faith has the two-fold support of 'heart' and 'context' referred to above.) We therefore know that that to which faith witnesses is not false. Faith is not based on a lie but on the truth. We accept, therefore, quite rightly what the faithful witnesses say as their witness to the underlying truth, and we confidently investigate and interrogate that witness to be taught its meaning for us. The acceptance and apprehension of this witness will take different forms among different believers and different traditions of believers, although all will be agreed in their faith that something is being said and that what is being said is related to ultimate reality, i.e. God – and that, for them, *what* they understand as being said must be able to be shown to be related to and in some way or other consistent with the witness born in the Gospels and through the life of the faithful community. Thus, for example, all will be agreed that the confession 'Jesus Christ is risen' is a faithful witness to an abiding reality. The question is not 'Is this true?' but 'What is the truth (reality) which is witnessed to here?' We know this is true because it is so clearly at the heart of the witness of the faithful and we are one with them. But we have the faithful task of growing into an understanding of what that reality is which is here witnessed to, i.e. we have to discover how it impinges on us and on those to whom we are sent by the risen Christ simply because we are among them. (Indeed, as far as unbelievers go, while as faithful 'we' are not 'of them', none the less as denizens of the twentieth century we are certainly 'of them' – we are all 'we' together.)

There will be different ways of accepting and understanding 'the resurrection', and this will involve differing judgments about the historical status of the resurrection narratives in the four Gospels and their connection with the faith in the Risen Christ. It is not possible to carry out investigations into such a matter as the resurrection without much fear and trembling and the possibility of a good deal of pain. For there can be no doubt that doubts about, say, the truth of or the relevance of 'the empty tomb' can and do 'upset' the faith of some. But ought we not to realize that faith is not only a joyful but also a painful thing? It is certainly not a complacent disposition. It is rather a gift of God which enables us to go adventuring further and further into the heart of his revelation of himself. And this is surely done by questioning, i.e. by asking questions in faith of the faithful witness which has come to us and submitting our faith to the questioning and testing of the totality of the world in which we live.

It certainly cannot seem unreasonable to one who has faith that God should raise the dead, but this does not settle the question of *what* God did and what his 'doing' was in connection with Jesus. It may be that the continuing intensity of New Testament study will show that the 'ultra-radical' critics, as some hold them to be, are historically mistaken. That is to say that the conclusions of a

Bultmann about the rarity of historically descriptive accuracy in the Gospels is not reasonable on the weighing of all the evidence and when presuppositions shared with (if not taken over from) Heidegger are less in fashion. But this is a matter for continuing historical, philosophical and theological study, and whatever position is reached (or held to have been reached by the prevailing competent opinion), it will only be (as Bultmann's position is) a reasonably probable position. If faith can be undermined to the point of disappearance by radical critics, then it cannot be restored to the point of assurance by conservative ones. Rather, the doubt of the critics is part of the dialogue of faith from which all responsible and obedient believers cull such insights as they can and which it is their duty to offer to the continuing life of the church.

I may perhaps be allowed to attempt to make the point of view which I am here advocating a little clearer by two further examples before I close. Consider the notorious and discomforting problem of the historicity of the Fourth Gospel. That Gospel has spoken powerfully to many of the glory of Christ. I would dare to say that it has so spoken in some measure to me. But if, to take an example, the famous discourses are not historical, i.e. if Jesus probably never spoke them in this form, if indeed it is more than possible that he never uttered most of the words given to him in this Gospel *at all*, what becomes of the glory? Is it simply a warm and golden glow of 'affective tone' compounded out of elements which might have been produced by the enjoyment of a Brahms' symphony on the one hand and an intellectual apprehension of moral worth on the other? I do not believe that this is the position.

'John' (and it does not ultimately matter who he is, for there is the internal evidence of his Gospel and the external evidence of that Gospel's inclusion in the new 'scriptures' of the faithful that he also is one of the faithful – cf., indeed, John 21.24) makes his presentation of the impact upon him of the faith which is in and through and in connection with Jesus. As one who is now conscious of the fact that I, too, am one with the faithful, I accept this witness without requiring beforehand some authentication or justification based on, say, evidence of historicity. As I have argued above, it is not unreasonable of me to do this. I have not, therefore, just plunged into religious sentiment. I seek to understand the bearing and meaning of this witness of John to Christ with all the resources at my disposal and, as I say, I dare to conclude that I see something of the glory which he has seen and sought to bear witness to. I am now satisfied that what I have seen is not unconnected with reality, is not a purely subjective experience, for two reasons. The first is that 'authentication of faith' which I have tried to explain throughout this essay. The faith of the faithful is not based on a lie, as I know for myself. The second is that there is built into the Gospel itself a statement of the objective reference *and* merely historical base of the witness which the Gospel is bearing in the prologue (turning on 'the Word was made *flesh*'), and it is also clear that the Jesus who is the 'original' of the Fourth Gospel portrayal and the Jesus of the Synoptic Gospels, where the objectively historical figure is, up to a point, clearer, are one and the same. The degree of detailed descriptive historicity and where it lies has to be left again to the debates of the critics and experts. But that there is 'historicness' is clear enough. It may be, for instance, that a combination of conclusions to be drawn from, say, a study of the Dead Sea Scrolls and recent work such as that on the Fourth Gospel will cause a revision of the estimate of what is narrowly historical in it. We shall then have more confidence that more of the Jesus of the Fourth Gospel portrait is 'as you would have seen and heard him if you had been there'. But this again will be a probabilification which will be psychologically helpful to some (very many?). It will never reach the point of guaranteeing to us that God is rightly to be understood as a reality who reaches out to us in the form of a man whose way of life was symbolized by the washing of the disciples' feet. *This* is something which demands our total commitment both in thankful submission to so gracious a God and also in an obedient desire to be taught in practice the inwardness and reality of such a way of life. (The life of him who is the way, the truth and the life.) Such things are not guaranteed by narratives, however historically undergirded. Our faith in God will take away from us anxiety about the historicity of the writers, and this sets us free to question this witness with all the intensity we can in order to hear what is to be said to us. And we shall know that what we hear we must also speak. For we believe that the witness is a faithful witness to the significance of Jesus which is rooted on the one hand in the Jesus of history (and quite possibly more than is now most commonly held), and on the other in the authentic relationship of the author to that same God whom we also have come to know through the witness rooted in Jesus. We speak, therefore, because we know that we are on to truth and that that truth is for all people. We shall, therefore, bear *our* witness. But we shall do so in so far as we are reasonably clear that it is not 'our' witness but *the* witness of the faithful. The detailed form that we give to and the manner in which we seek to bear that witness is, of course, as liable to error and will certainly be as 'mixed' as anything in the history of the witnessing people of God. (We may do well to fear that it will be more so.) But our task, like that of our predecessors, is to bear the witness, not to establish it. That lies with God, as does the authority. Our only authority lies in the fact that we have the confidence of faith to continue in the way in which God has set us. We must point imperfectly to that which we have seen imperfectly and see how, as Paul knew, it 'is God which giveth the increase', both in our faith and in the number of the faithful.

This procedure of initial faithful acceptance, subsequent faithful testing and questioning and eventual faithful bearing witness has to be applied not only to the scriptures, but also to all the elements in the deposit of the faithful which have aquired historical claims to be taken with particular seriousness. Among these would be such matters as a moral tradition concerning, say, divorce, liturgical tradition concerning the meaning and practice of the eucharist and dogmatic traditions and formulations such as the Chalcedonian Definition. In view of my earlier reference to christology I may make this last my final example.

The Chalcedonian Definition has been, in many quarters, 'getting a bad press'. My impression is that a good deal of it is vitiated by a failure to enter sufficiently into an understanding of the circumstances and ways of thought of those who were responsible for this Definition and who took part in the debates out of which it eventually grew. None the less, it is clear that the terms in which this definition is stated are completely foreign to us today. Even those traditions which make much of metaphysical words like 'nature', 'substance', etc., do not use them in the precise (if there was one!) sense of the Definition, and many would hold that terms of this sort cannot satisfactorily be rehabilitated today at all. Certainly, there is no agreed metaphysical language even among Christians for making a general statement of 'catholic' significance about permanent truths of the faith. Further, there are obvious difficulties about a concept like 'nature' in an age of post-Darwinian biology, to mention no other complications. Do we then 'start again' with christology? Surely this would not be a faithful procedure at all. The Chalcedonian Definition is a vitally important 'authority' in matters christological. Anyone who wishes to contribute to the church's understanding of the person of Christ today must come to terms with it. That is, he must satisfy himself that he understands what the Fathers were 'getting at' when this Definition emerged, and he must show that any understanding of the person of Christ which he urges the church to accept and make use of takes account of all that the Chalcedonian Definition took account of and safeguards all that that Definition safeguarded. He must show very weighty cause indeed for recommending the abandonment of any element in the Definition.

I do not think that we can exclude the possibility that in the long run some element or other of the Definition might drop out of our understanding of the person of Christ. This cannot be excluded, because although we are, in faith, questioning the truths of faith *not* in order to establish their truth but in order to see what is the truth which they now have to convey to us, none the less it may eventually appear under such questioning that some things that were taken as truths of faith are in fact not so. This is bound to be the position because, as we have seen, there is no absolute authority short of God. But no perceptive and would-be obedient servant of the tradition of faith will lightly reject anything which he or she perceives that tradition to have taken seriously, and will search the harder for an understanding of a truth the more seriously he or she perceives it to have been taken. None the less, if the tradition does not 'come alive', i.e. if the 'truth of faith' cannot be shown to be apprehensible as relevant truth for the living and witnessing of the church today, then its status is clearly in dispute, and it might be that it will not be revived, but will eventually fade out of serious significance. If this were to happen concerning the Chalcedonian Definition (I do not say it is happening or that *I* think it will) we may be sure that the faithful process of questioning, testing and eventual rejecting to which it had been subjected would have yielded for the continuing life of the faithful all that was essential in the original 'deposit'. What is quite certain is that any 'crystallized deposit' which is treated as a sacred formula but is never put to the test either of faith's questioning or of attempted use by the faithful is assuredly not crystallized but fossilized. It has become so much archaic nonsense, and the present life of the faithful has become impoverished by a failure to realize in present belief and action the truth out of which the formula originally grew and for which it once stood. It is a faithless mistake to suppose that the repetition and passing on of the *words* of 'truth of the faith' and the treating of them with a so-called reverential respect which forbids any coming to grips with them is 'believing' them. Faith grows out of, feeds on and is corrected by what was believed 'then'. But authoritative and lively faith is always 'now'. How could it be otherwise since it is concerned with the living God?

A false authoritarianism does not earn (or deserve) respect and belief, but ridicule and then indifference. Faithful men and women striving to live faithfully and seeking to address themselves to whatever situations God thrusts upon them with whatever understanding and message God has seen fit to give them will not be lacking in authority. For they will not be letting themselves and their authority stand in the way of God. And we cannot doubt that faith will continue and will grow until the End. For we know that God is and that God is a God who calls men and women to himself.

SOURCES

Part One   Concerning God

1. A sermon preached at Pusey House, Oxford, in Michaelmas Term 1956, in a series entitled 'God and the Universe'. In that series the sermon was entitled 'Signs of God in the Intellect of Man'.
2. A university sermon given at Leeds, March 1966.
3. One of the Bishop of Coventry's Lent Lectures in 1966, delivered in Coventry Cathedral to an audience invited by the Bishop from all the parishes in his diocese.
4. A lecture given in Canterbury Cathedral, October 1968.
5. An address given at the clergy conference of the diocese of Bath and Wells, June 1989.

Part Two   Concerning Men and Women and Concerning Jesus

1. A paper given at the First International Congress of Social Psychiatry, St John's Wood, London 1965.
2. The Lloyd Roberts lecture given in November 1988.
3. An open lecture under the auspices of the University of Lancaster, 1965.
4. A lecture given at Durham University in November 1968 as a contribution to a week entitled 'Christian Viewpoint 1968'.
5. Public lecture for the Chair of Judaeo-Christian studies at Tulane University, New Orleans, April 1988.
6. The Lily Montague Lecture delivered to the London Society of Christians and Jews, November 1988.
7. An Easter meditation given in the BBC Third Programme on Easter Day 1969.
8. Given in Durham Cathedral, Easter Day 1989.

Part Three   Concerning being a Christian

1. A sermon preached at Pusey House, Oxford, in Michaelmas Term 1964 in the series 'The Needs of the Church Today'. The title of the series was 'Dynamic Doctrine'.
2. First published in *Crucible*, July-September 1974, pp. 108–13.

3. A talk given to the Annual Conference of the Modern Churchpeople's Union at Oxford in 1966.

4. A talk given to the Christian Frontier Council in London in 1967.

5. A short paper given at the second consultation on 'Health and Healing' held at Tübingen in 1967 under the auspices of the World Council of Churches and the Lutheran World Federation.

6. A talk given to a conference of the Fellowship of St Alban and St Sergius held at Pusey House, Oxford, 1964.

Postscript   Specially written for *Living with Questions*, SCM Press 1969.